SWING TRADING

SWING TRADING

Simple Yet Powerful Techniques for Consistent Success in the Markets

HARNEET SINGH KHARBANDA

JAICO PUBLISHING HOUSE

Ahmedabad Bangalore Chennai
Delhi Hyderabad Kolkata Mumbai

Published by Jaico Publishing House
A-2 Jash Chambers, 7-A Sir Phirozshah Mehta Road
Fort, Mumbai - 400 001
jaicopub@jaicobooks.com
www.jaicobooks.com

© Harneet Singh Kharbanda

SWING TRADING
ISBN 978-93-48098-84-9

First Jaico Impression: 2025

Page design and layout by Inosoft Systems, Delhi

*To my parents, my wife, and
both my lovely daughters.*

Acknowledgments

My author journey would not have been possible without the constant support and encouragement I received from Indrazith Shantharaj. I am thankful for his patient guidance at every step of book publishing.

Thanks to Shushen Sharma, founder of TradingJournal.ai, who was kind enough to onboard me as an advisor for the AI-powered trading journal startup. His valuable feedback on the trading journal has been very helpful.

I am extremely grateful to TradingView and Chartink for letting me use the charts from their wonderful platforms for this book.

Contents

III : ESSENTIAL TOOLS FOR TRADING

IV : TRADING PSYCHOLOGY

I

TRADING

"When you genuinely accept the risks, you will be at peace with any outcome."

—Mark Douglas, American stock trader

1

The Secret of Swinging Into Profitable Trading

When people get into trading, they need to factor in several aspects before zeroing down on the stock and the type of trading that would suit them best. All types of trading have their own advantages and disadvantages so whichever one a trader chooses depends on the individual's

    i.   Mindset (Do they consider trading as serious business or do they just want to try it out of frustration with their current job or business?)

ii. Risk-taking appetite (Whether they prefer low or high risk options in trading)

iii. Capital (The amount of money they have to invest)

iv. Holding period (The duration for which they can stay invested)

v. Screen time availability (The amount of time a trader can actively track stock price movement)

vi. Emotional balance with strategy

Once they decide the amount of capital they have, the first thing they need to ascertain is the duration for which they want to stay invested. Accordingly, they can decide whether they want to get into short-term investing or long-term investing.

Short-term investing involves trading stocks or other financial instruments for days to weeks, for a duration shorter than a year. Traders have the opportunity to make massive gains in small timeframes, and often have more control over their finances and less risk since they can enter and exit the market within a single day, as is the case for intraday trading.

Long-term investing is when stocks are held for more than one year at least. Long-term investors usually buy and hold the stocks for much larger periods, sometimes even over a few decades. People generally buy long-term stocks for their retirement. They do not intend to sell these stocks, irrespective of how the market reacts. This creates significant wealth as they hold the stocks for so long that the real magic of compounding comes into play.

However, not all long-term investors make money. To hold on to a stock for decades, one needs to study the fundamentals of the company carefully and have conviction in their analysis.

If you buy a stock with a degrading business and poor balance sheet, you may get stuck with it for decades before you can even recover the cost price, let alone the profits.

There have been many instances when investors bought stocks thinking that they would make a fortune if they could just hold on to the investment and the stocks ended up eroding their entire capital. To top it all, the companies also got delisted.

Long-term investors are more focused on the long-term performance of the company. So they consider fundamental analysis more important than technical analysis. They look at the business and focus on what that business is actually doing, not on how the stock is responding to the market variables. Even if the company is great and the fundamentals are really outstanding, the stock can still fall a lot depending on the overall market trend or if there are factors that may cause a decrease in value or growth of the sector in the economy.

If the long-term investor has conviction in their analysis, they do not get disturbed by stock prices falling. Instead, they rejoice at getting a chance to add more of their favourite stock at a better price. They are ready to hold it for a few years and know that if their study is correct, they will eventually make a lot of profit from it.

Long-term investing is suitable for people who do not wish to make trading their primary source of income; they want to focus on their job or business while staying invested in the stock market and benefitting from the alpha that it can generate. Alpha is a term used in finance as a measure of performance. It is the excess return of an investment relative to the return of a benchmark index. This means that long-term investors ride the winning investments as long as possible, till the time the company and the stock behaves as expected.

While these are the two basic types of investing in financial instruments, they can be further categorised based on the types of trading.

SWING TRADING

Swing trading is a method where traders try to capture short- to medium-term price moves in the market which can last for a few days to a few weeks. They do not wish to hold the stock for years or decades, but just want to capture a major chunk of a price movement.

Many traders these days have shifted to this style of trading as they feel that it gives them time to focus on other important things in their life, like their full-time job or business. Since traders do not have to exit their positions on the same day, they need not stay glued to the trading terminal all day long to keep checking the prices tick-by-tick.

Image 1.1: Capturing a major part of a swing move, either bullish (left) or bearish (right)

In image 1.1, you can see that in swing trading, traders capture a major move until the trend(the direction in which the stock is moving) lasts. This can be either a bullish (upwards) trend or a bearish (downwards) trend.

The goal of a swing trader is to buy a stock before the next swing move starts, try to sit with the move till it lasts, and then exit and move to the next trade and repeat the process.

Since swing traders do not want to hold stocks for years, they only focus on technical analysis as their main study parameter. If you want to build conviction about a trade, you can learn a few basics of fundamental analysis too.

I make 90% of my trading decisions with the help of technical analysis only. If a stock does not look good according to its charts, I will not even think of looking at its fundamentals. Most of the time, I do not need to check the fundamentals as the trade usually lasts only for a few days.

Since swing traders usually hold the trade for a few days to a few weeks, the best time frame that suits them is the daily time frame. You can follow a top-down approach where you check the monthly chart first to check the overall structure of the stock. Then, move on to the weekly chart to check the major support and resistances. A support is a zone from where the stock keeps bouncing multiple times and shows that buyers are interested in buying at that price level. On the other hand, a resistance is a zone where the sellers are active and every time the stock prices reach that level, there is a rejection in the price. Finally, move on to the daily chart. You can also look at the hourly chart if you want to fine-tune your entry.

Image 1.2 is the monthly chart of Pidilite Industries Ltd.

The uptrend is intact and the stock is trading at all-time highs. Whenever a stock is trading at all-time highs, it shows that it has a lot of strength and buyers are ready to buy it at any level.

Now let us look at the weekly chart.

Image 1.2: Monthly chart of Pidilite Industries Ltd. showing an uptrend

In image 1.3, we can see that it has broken above an important zone (horizontal highlighted area) which had been acting as a resistance earlier. This stock has come out of a rounding pattern which signifies that the bullish momentum(upwards move with momentum) has started and the bearish(downward) or sideways trend has come to an end. A sideways trend shows the horizontal price movement that occurs when the forces of supply and demand are nearly equal. This typically occurs during a period of consolidation before the price continues a prior trend or reverses into a new trend. Now that the monthly and weekly charts look fine, let us move on to the daily chart.

Image 1.3: Weekly chart of Pidilite Industries Ltd. showing an exit from the rounding pattern

In image 1.4, in the recent price action itself, there were two swing moves (marked on the chart) and the latter one continues.

You do not need to enter and exit daily, and can trade very peacefully once you start swing trading. You do not even need to see the price of your stocks multiple times in a day—a glance in the morning and once in the afternoon before the market closes is enough.

Once you learn the swing trading strategies in later chapters in this book, then you will not even need to think when to enter and when to exit. The strategy itself will help you by showing clear entry and exit signals. Your main duty then will be to just follow your strategy with discipline and patience.

Image 1.4: Daily chart of Pidilite Industries Ltd. showing two swing moves

Let us take another example to understand swing trading in a simple way. Image 1.5 is the monthly chart of Bombay Stock Exchange Ltd.

You can see that it has given a really good up move and is still bullish as the upward move is intact.

We will now check the weekly chart.

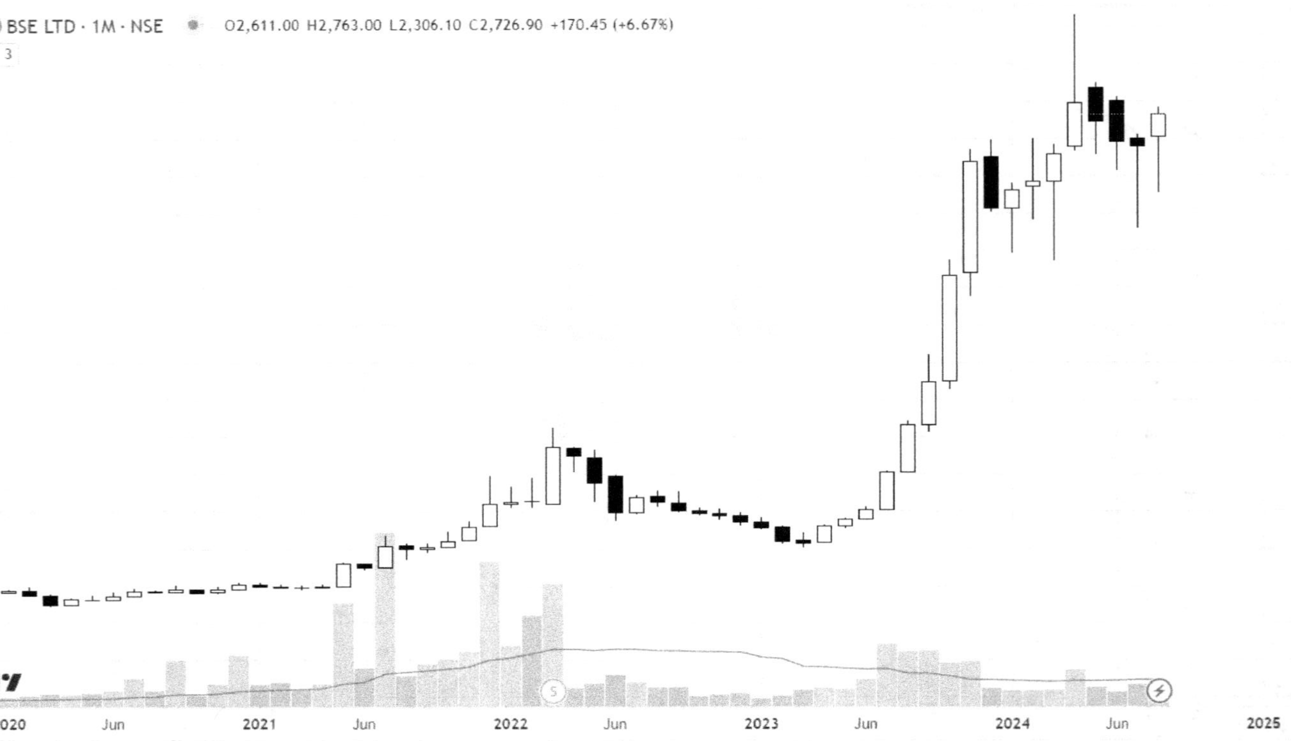

Image 1.5: Monthly chart of Bombay Stock Exchange Ltd.

In image 1.6, we can see the same thing. After a great up move, the price has now gone into a sideways trend, with no clear direction and is basically "resting" before the next move.

Just like we need to rest before we can run again, stocks do the same. You just need to know how to differentiate if the stock is resting or is injured (trend has changed), which you will learn in the section on strategies.

For now, let us head on to the daily chart.

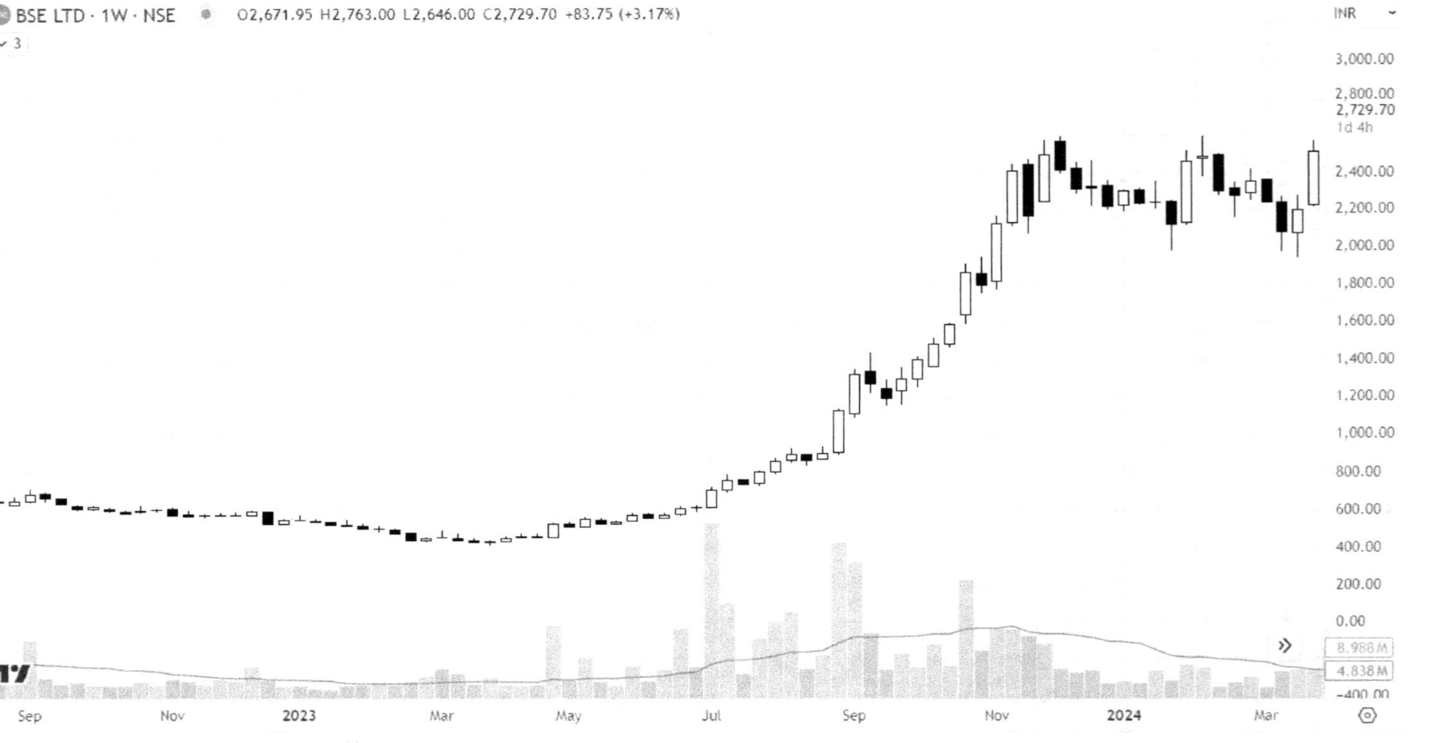

Image 1.6: Weekly chart of Bombay Stock Exchange Ltd. showing the price resting before the next move

In image 1.7, the price gave a great swing move in the daily time frame and gave multibagger (multifold) returns. Swing trading can sometimes turn into multibaggers too. Till the time the trend is intact, ride it.

Before trading into a stock, you do not know till when the trend will last—if you will be thrown out in one day or if the trend will continue for the next few weeks. You just need to follow the plan and capture a major chunk of the price move.

Remember, **when we are winning, we need to win big and when we are losing; we need to cut our losses as quickly as possible.** This is the entire concept of risk management in one line. That's it! Anything more complex is just a derivative of this one line.

Advantages of swing trading

i. *Swing traders can make more money by trading less:* They do not need to trade day in day out and can save their brokerage cost too, as most brokers charge for intraday trades only.

ii. *Less screen time is required:* Swing traders need to spend very less time to monitor their stocks and it allows them to focus on more important elements of their life like their primary job, business, relationships or their health.

iii. *They can use only technical analysis:* Their strategies could be really simple and focused only on the charts. They do not need to read a lot about the companies, annual reports or balance sheets.

iv. *Free capital:* Since they keep rotating their capital (exiting a stock and entering into another one) their capital is freed up and they can use it for their next trade. This is something which a long-term investor cannot do as they have to hold stocks for years and decades.

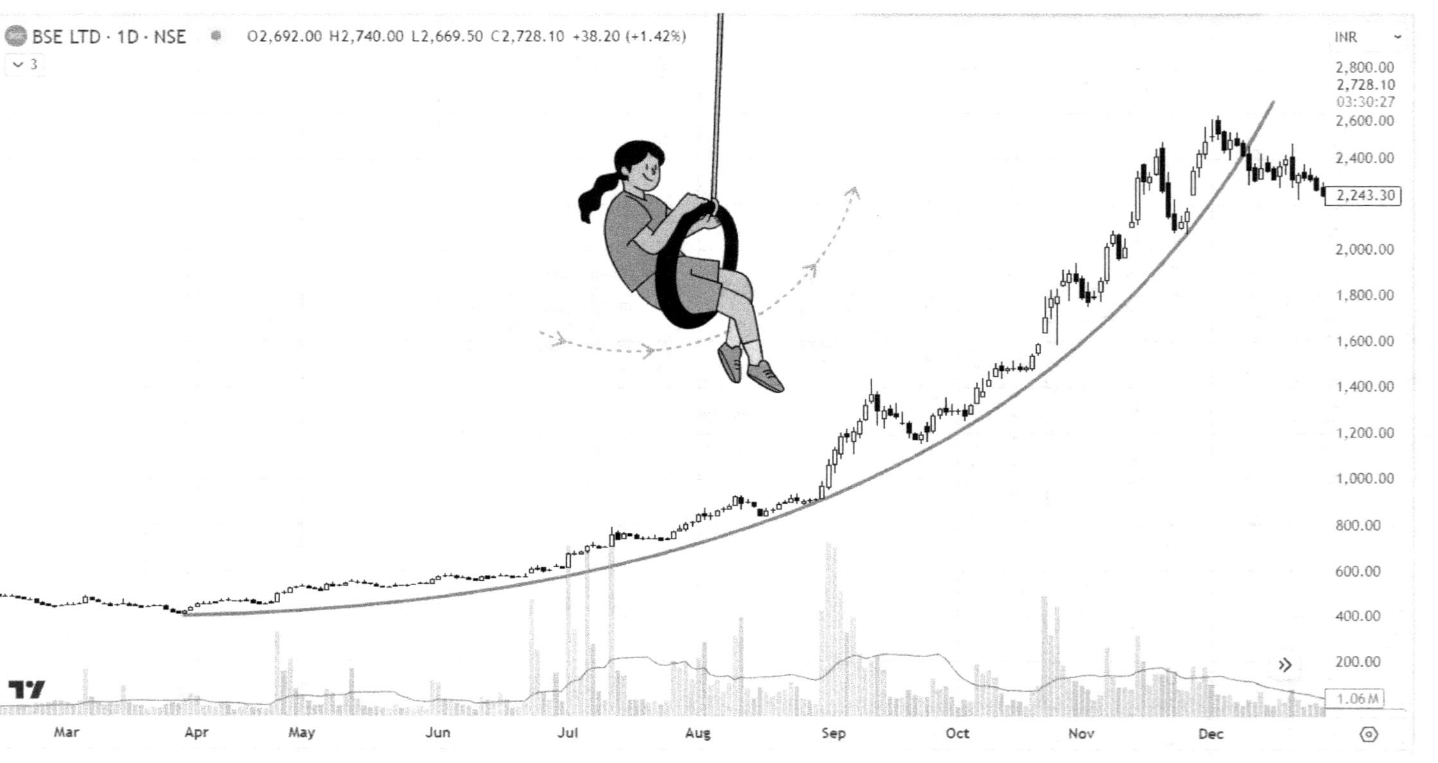

Image 1.7: Daily chart of Bombay Stock Exchange Ltd.

Disadvantages of swing trading

i. *Swing traders need to carry their positions overnight and over the weekends*: This is one of the biggest risks as it can result in some gap movements which are not under their control. Even if they have a stop-loss in mind, they would lose more than that as an overnight gap in unavoidable. A day trader can avoid this risk, as they always exit their positions on the same day itself.

ii. *Swing traders may move during the bigger price moves*: They get out of the move once they have captured a big chunk of it, unlike other types of investors. The stock price can still continue its uptrend and they may regret that they could have made much more profit if they would have just held on to the same stock instead of jumping off to the next one.

As discussed earlier, there are different types of trading based on the duration for which you want to hold on to the stock. They are explained below.

DAY TRADING

Unlike swing trading, where our positions can remain open for a few days to a few weeks, day trading is a style of trading where traders cover (close) their positions on the same day. Day traders or intraday traders never carry their positions to the next day. They are not in it for a big chunk of the move, they just want to capture a small part of the move on the same day itself (mostly in a few minutes or hours) and take the profits home before the markets take them back from them.

When the stocks bought need to be sold on the same day or, when the stocks sold need to be bought again on the same day, this style of trading requires very rapid decision-making abilities and is not suitable for newcomers.

Most newcomers have the urge to start off by day trading and it makes sense too if we think from their perspective.

If someone tells me that I can make 1% in a day, as compared to making 1% in a month, even I would choose to make 1% in a day without a doubt! But it is not as simple as it sounds because day traders mostly depend on taking huge leverage (using borrowed money to increase the position size) for making a decent return as they do not target capturing a big move but only a small part of the move. So, it will make sense to day trade only if they are trading in more shares, that is, big positions. The issue with trading big position sizes is that although it rewards beautifully when the trades are in profit, if the trade goes in the opposite direction, the losses also get magnified because of the leverage and that messes up the trader's mindset. They usually end up in the revenge trading mode (when the trader starts taking revenge from the markets to make up for the losses incurred) and eventually lose much more in order to cover their initial losses.

There are many successful day traders too out there, but I feel that they were all successful in swing and positional trading before they entered the day trading realm.

So, there are no black or white areas when we think about any style of trading—it always depends on the personality of the trader. A person who is aggressive, a quick decision maker and can take risks may be a great day trader. A person who usually prefers calm and does not want the markets to be on his mind all day long, would prefer swing trading.

Here are some types of day trading strategies:

i. **Scalping**: A strategy that involves buying and selling an individual stock multiple times throughout the same day to make a small profit over many little trades is known as scalping.

ii. **Range trading:** A strategy that involves trading a security within a specific price range so as to buy at the low end (support) of the range and sell at the high end (resistance).

iii. **Momentum trading**: A strategy that involves buying and selling assets according to the recent strength of price trends to take advantage of an expected price change and close the position when the trend starts to lose its strength.

Based on the goal of the trader, they can choose the kind of trading strategy they want to use to maximise profits.

Advantages of intraday trading

i. *Less capital is required as you get a margin for intraday trading.* You can buy or sell, basically you can play on both sides. This is one of the major reasons people prefer intraday trading as markets are not always trending. In fact, when the markets crash, the stocks and indices usually drop drastically. As they say, "Markets climb up via stairs and but take the elevator on the way down." If a trader has a knack for identifying quick falls and crashes, they can make a good profit in a short amount of time.

ii. *Day trading can be less risky if done with proper discipline.* You can always fix your stop-loss in the system and decide exactly how much you are okay with losing in a trade before taking the trade. You cannot do that in swing trading as you will always be at the risk of a gap up or gap downs due to overnight events or otherwise.

iii. *An intraday trader has to just focus on the market one day at a time.* They are least affected by what happens in the macro world. They just need to trade the stock once it is open and all the gap ups or gap downs have already been accounted for. A swing trader may lose money as soon as the market opens after a big event, but a day trader can always look at the markets from a fresh point of view and start fresh every day.

Disadvantages of day trading

i. *Leverage is a double-edged sword.* Traders look at leverage only from the profit's point of view and start calculating the total profit that they can make if their trade goes into profit with leverage. But they usually forget that if the trade turns out to be a losing one, then the loss also gets magnified. Sometimes, getting a big loss in just one trade messes up with the trader's mindset and they end up revenge-trading just to recover their loss on the same day. Traders end up stuck in this vicious circle—the losses keep getting bigger and once the market closes, they realise their blunder.

ii. *Day traders may lose in options buying* as they have limited time to close their positions. They may be right about the direction of the move too, but if the move does not happen in the desired time, they still lose because of theta decay/time value. (Theta decay is the gradual loss of value in options over time.)

iii. *Day traders may end up overtrading* as they keep sitting in front of the screen. If they make a profit in the first few trades, they try to maximise profits on that day and often end up giving back that profit and end up losing a part of their capital too. If they make a loss in the first few trades, they try to recover the loss by overtrading and usually end up magnifying their loss because of overtrading. They usually regret their decision of overtrading in both these scenarios.

iv. *Day traders have the urge to quickly book profits.* This limits them from making bigger returns.

v. *The number of decisions that need to be taken in a day and the speed at which they need to be taken* is one of the major problems with day trading which no one talks about. Since a trader takes so many quick decisions, day trading takes a toll on the health and mindset of an individual. They usually end up really exhausted by the end of the day if they do not trade with a proper plan. They usually feel frustrated or agitated by the end of the day and it is not a sustainable way of living. It may work for a couple of years, but if a person has to go through so many emotions every single day, it is definitely not a healthy way to live.

POSITIONAL TRADING

A positional trader holds the stocks for a few weeks to a few months, sometimes even lasting more than a year and then they try to capture all the moves till the peak.

Since they want to hold the stock for a longer period, positional traders use technical analysis or fundamental analysis and they often club both to follow a "techno-funda" approach which combines the best of both worlds. They basically time their entry and exit based on technical levels and indicators and decide which stock to enter based on its financials. This ensures that the stock they want to hold for a longer period is worth holding on to as it passes their basic fundamental criteria. Since positional traders want to hold on to the stock for a longer period, they tend to ignore the short-term moves and volatility. They are not affected by the day-to-day fluctuations in the market. They happily hold on to their stocks till the trend is intact and the financials have not changed drastically. A very big advantage that positional traders enjoy is that they really do not need to invest a lot of time once they buy a stock. Yes, they may have to study before buying a stock, but once they are in, they do not need to micromanage their stocks daily. Most successful positional traders check their stocks on a weekly basis. It makes sense to not check their stocks regularly as they have conviction in their analysis and are ready to hold the stock for its entire up move, which generally lasts a few months. They do not try to enter a stock near the lows, neither do they plan to sell their stocks at the top. In fact, they may exit the stocks a bit later when the stocks lose some part of the gains while retracing from the top as they try to exit a stock when the trend reversal is confirmed, and the fundamentals also confirm the same.

The advantages and disadvantages of positional trading are somewhat similar to swing trading. Swing trades which do not hit their trailing stop-loss, can continue to move with the trend and a swing trade can convert into a positional trade. We do not need to exit a position just because it has moved up a lot. In fact, the trend continuation gives us a chance to stay put with the stock we already hold in our portfolio. Having said that, let us discuss the advantages and disadvantages of positional trading now.

Advantages of positional trading

i. *There is no need to constantly monitor positions.* Since positional trades are taken according to larger time frames and we basically try to capture a major part of the price move, we need very less active screen time to monitor the stocks. We can take a trade on a weekly time frame and check the prices only near the entire week's closing, not in between. The risk is bigger in these cases, but the rewards are also much higher and totally worth the patience.

ii. *Low transaction costs.* Positional traders trade the least among all types of traders, so they enjoy the least amount of transaction and other costs. This is a big advantage as it has been observed time and again that other types of traders mess up their returns because of the huge amount in charges that they end up paying.

I know a lot of traders who pay way more as charges compared to their profit so they are in loss. Whenever I meet someone who does this, I try to nudge them to shift to a higher time frame so that they can trade peacefully and end up paying less charges too. A lot of these traders who listen to me eventually call me up a few months later to thank me and tell me that their trading has improved a lot just because of this simple shift in perspective. Many have also said that it was the first time in their trading career that their portfolio was in profit for a quarter at least.

iii. *Allows time to focus on other things.* Positional traders do not need to sit in front of the trading terminal for a long time, they can use their free time for other important things. Many positional traders are people who have full time jobs or businesses and still end up making much more returns as compared to full time traders. A major reason for this is that they do not end up overtrading as they do not constantly monitor the stock and are not tempted to trade all the time out of compulsion.

Disadvantages of positional trading

i. *Bigger stop-losses.* When we do get profits in positional trading, we get rewarded handsomely. It is not a major problem as we need to have the appetite for risk to take a big loss. So this is a part of the process and is unavoidable. Stop-loss is the cost of making these transactions.

If we keep our stop-losses very tight, we choke the trade by not letting it take its time to perform. There may be times when you enter a stock and then exit it too soon, only to see it moving up like a rocket escaping gravity later! That happens because we do not have the patience to just let the stock do its thing. But yes, this is a major disadvantage according to most people with whom I discuss positional trading.

ii.   *Fewer opportunities*. When we take positional trades, we look at higher time frames and do not really get enough trades on a regular basis. This happens a lot when the market is stuck in a sideways zone and there is no clear trend in the market. Small time frame traders may still get some opportunities as they can trade the smaller moves, but positional trades may not get any new trade for days, weeks or even months! This can be really challenging for people who feel that they need to do something all the time.

Now that you know about the various types of trading and their advantages and disadvantages, let us discuss the most suitable style of trading for you.

1. Intraday trading

Intraday trading is like driving a sports car. It is okay to drive a sports car only if you know how to drive a normal car first!

If you are someone who already has a few years of experience as a swing or positional trader; are well aware of the technical aspects; and already have a well-researched and backtested strategy that works on higher time frames, and are confident that the same strategy would work on lower time frames, too, you can start trading intraday with a smaller position size. Increase the position size only when you are confident and the results also show the same for you.

If you cannot convert Rs.10,000 to Rs. 20,000, do not try to convert Rs.1,00,000 to Rs.2,00,000. If you are not making money with a smaller capital, do not think that everything will be fine once you have more capital in hand.

Many traders complain about not being able to make high returns or trade to their full potential as their capital is very low. But having less capital in the initial phase of trading is a blessing, it is the time when we test our strategies and get to know how we respond to the losses and profits.

We all have to pay a tuition fee to the market once we start trading, so it is better to pay a smaller amount rather than bringing a huge capital to the table and end up giving it all as tuition fees. *"Screen time is a friend for an intraday trader and an enemy for a positional trader."*

2. Swing trading

This would be the most suitable style of trading for someone who is just starting out in the markets and wants to try to turn stock market trading into a second source of income besides their main job or business.

Intraday trading would not suit someone who is just starting out as it requires a lot of quick decision-making and expertise. Positional trading or long-term investing would not suit newcomers as they require a lot of patience and an understanding of fundamental concepts, which may take some time to learn if someone is a new entrant in the markets.

As discussed earlier, swing trading does not require much screen time—just a few minutes of scanning in the evening when the markets are closed and one or two hours on the weekends is enough. Swing trading is a peaceful style of trading compared to day trading so it can be managed easily along with your primary occupation, which may be your job or business. Once you have scanned stocks and taken positions in them, you do not need to spend much time on the markets. Following the end of the day stop-losses, a quick glance in the morning and a quick glance in the afternoon when the markets are about to close is enough to keep track of your positions.

Another point to note here is that since in swing trading a trader does not need to give much time to the markets and is not sitting in front of the screen for the entire day, they become less prone to overtrading. You know how you can get stuck in the vicious circle of overtrading and that happens mainly because of the excess time that you keep sitting in front of the screens in the case of day trading. Another thing which favours swing traders is that they save a lot of money as they incur lower commissions, brokerages, etc. compared to intraday traders who pay the most amount of these charges as compared to any other style of traders.

3. Long-term investing

This style of investing will suit those who are interested in capitalising stock market gains; who want to be a part of the equity markets, benefit from it but do not want to stay too involved in the day-to-day or even short-term activities of the market; and are basically trying to buy stocks as an investment which could possibly beat the fixed deposit and inflation returns over a long time horizon. A long-term investor would be more than happy if they could manage to beat fixed deposit and investment returns while focusing on their core job or business. Not everyone has the capital to invest in real estate, so the stock market is a great place to park your money in a systematic investment plan (SIP) over the long term and build a good corpus over a few years or decades.

Unlike swing traders, long-term investors just want to grow their wealth over the long term and are not looking to create a side income from the markets.

Cherry picking stocks according to their fundamentals could be a challenging task and therefore, investors can choose to invest in exchange traded funds (ETFs), mutual funds, bonds, etc. These are less risky alternatives as these instruments diversify the investments into different stocks and the chances of these securities going to zero in the future are almost nil as compared to individual stocks.

Even if someone is a swing trader or a scalper, please try to
make a portfolio of long-term stocks as well.
It is really important and will take care of your future.
Trading takes care of the cash flow,
investing creates wealth.

2

Candlesticks in Trading: Every Candle has a Story

The Japanese introduced candlesticks in the 17th century to trade rice. According to Steve Nison, candlestick charting was first practised around 1850. Candlesticks make it easy to know about the overall sentiments of buyers and sellers in the market visually. We can see what exactly the buyers and sellers are doing on the charts in the form of candlesticks. Most traders across the world, including stock traders, forex and crypto traders, use candlestick charts. How the candle opened, where it opened, how high it went, how low it went and eventually how it closed shows the collective sentiment of the buyers and sellers in the market. For example, if the price opened near the day high, but closed near the low of the day, it shows that the sellers were strong enough that day and managed to close near the lows. Let us discuss the most famous and widely used candlesticks. They are classified according to the length of their body, the length of the shadows, and whether the shadows are present or not.

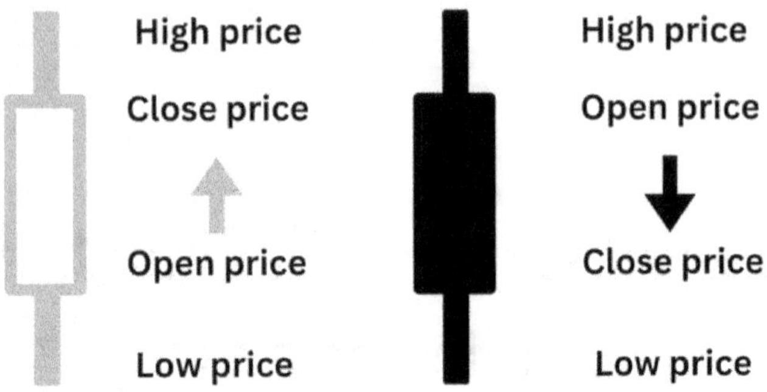

Image 2.1: Bullish candle (left), bearish candle (right)

How the candle opens and how it closes defines if the candle will be bullish or bearish. If the price closes above the open price, then it forms a bullish candle and if the price closes below the open price, then it forms a bearish candle. In image 2.1, you can see what bullish and bearish candles look like on a chart. The colour of the candles may vary on different charting software and platforms. Bullish candles are usually green or white and bearish ones are usually red or black.The lines above or below the main candle are known as the high and low range and are called shadows. These are also known as wicks or tails.

If the length of a candle is big, it shows the strength of that particular trade which can be buyers or sellers, depending on how the price closes.

Bullish or bearish candles which do not have any upper or lower shadows are called Marubozu. This type of candle shows the price at which the buyers or the sellers are in full control (depending on the type of candle, bullish or bearish) as it does not have any shadow or wick and the price closes at exactly the high or low of the day respectively.

Candlesticks which have small bodies are called spinning tops.

When the bodies are not present the candlesticks are called doji. They signify indecision.

Candlesticks are studied as patterns which may comprise two, three, four or even five candles, but the most commonly studied ones are two candlestick patterns. Even a single trade says a lot about market sentiment when we study where the candlestick has formed and how it has formed on the chart. If the candlesticks are formed near a support or a resistance, then the prior trend tells us a lot about the market. For example, if a bullish candlestick is formed near a support level, then it can indicate a reversal in the price. Many traders believe that candlestick charts are enough to know all the information of the market, which can include the news, macrostructure and microstructure as whatever action happens in the market is ultimately reflected in the price and volume on a chart.

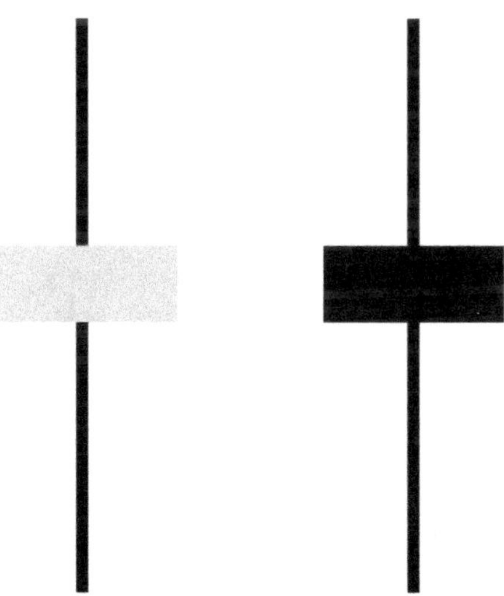

Image 2.2: Bullish spinning top candlestick (left) and bearish spinning top candlestick (right)

SPINNING TOPS

Spinning tops are the types of candlesticks which have long upper and lower shadows and a small body (image 2.2). The body could be white/green or red/black so the close could be bullish or bearish. However, since the bulls and bears kept fighting but ended up closing in a narrow range (which shows that neither of them could win the battle with conviction), it also indicates that there is no clear direction in which the next move may occur.

But, if a spinning top comes after a big bullish candle, it indicates that the trend may change to bearish. Similarly, if a spinning top candle comes after a big bearish candle, it indicates that the trend may change now and we may see some bullish action from here.

DOJI CANDLESTICKS

A doji is basically an indecision candle which indicates a tug-of-war situation where neither the bulls nor the bears could dominate and ended up closing at the same level. There is almost no difference between the open and the close values. Ideally when a doji candle is formed, it is better to wait for the next candle for a sense of further direction.

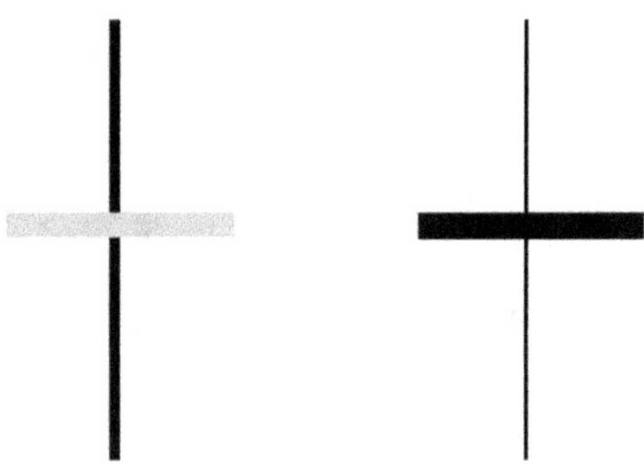

Image 2.3: Doji candlesticks

There are three types of doji candlesticks that have been discussed below—long-legged doji, dragonfly doji and gravestone doji.

i. Long-legged doji

Long-legged doji indicates a big fight between the buyers and sellers as the price moved up and down to a great extent over a particular time period. Despite so much variation, both the parties gave up and closed near the same level as when it opened. Both the upper and lower shadows are almost of the same length in this type of doji.

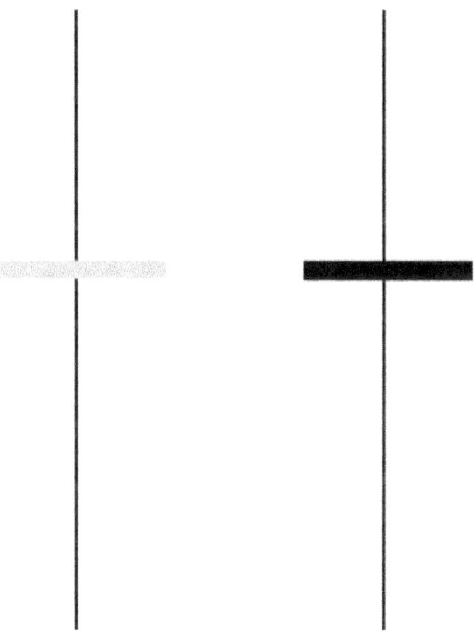

Image 2.4: Long legged doji candlesticks

Let us now study two more types of dojis—Dragonfly doji and grave stone doji.

ii. Dragonfly doji

This type of candlestick forms when there are a lot of sellers who push the price lower, but eventually, the buyers manage to close the price at the high of the day (or the time frame you are looking at). This gives it a "T" shape. This candlestick has much more significance if it is formed near a support level, after a long downtrend, or after a series of bearish candles. You also need to wait for confirmation, which you will get once the following candle breaks the high of the dragonfly doji and manages to close above it too.

Many traders make the mistake of not waiting for the proper confirmation candle and are ready to jump on the trade as soon as they see only one candlestick. For confirmation, they need to wait for the next candle to break the high of the dragonfly candle or below the gravestone candle. They do this because they may not know that they need to wait for the confirmation candle. Secondly, they feel that they may miss an entry in the stock if they do not catch it at the exact bottom.

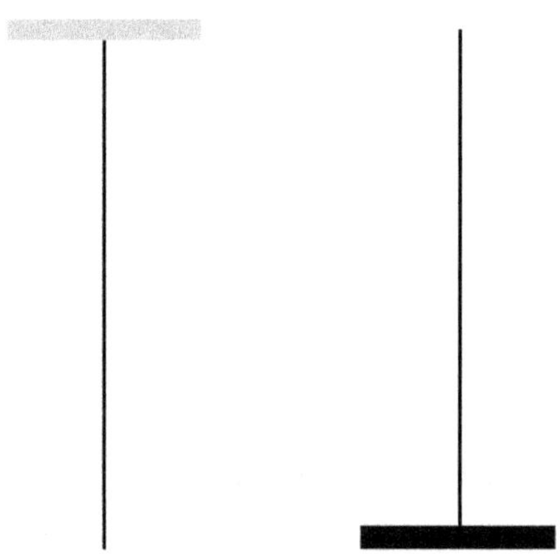

Image 2.5: Dragonfly doji (left) and gravestone doji (right).

iii. Gravestone doji

Gravestone doji is usually a bearish reversal candlestick type as it indicates that a bullish trend is going to end and a bearish trend can start from here on. It has much more significance if it forms after an uptrend or near a resistance level as these are the zones where the sellers are active and can start selling again, or the traders who had bought can start booking their profits here, near the resistance level. It is always better to wait for a confirmation in this scenario too. In a gravestone doji, the open low and close are at the same level and it has a long upper shadow. This indicates the presence of buyers and their efforts to move the price upwards but the sellers dominated the market and managed to close the price at the lowest point of that time frame. Due to this, it looks like an inverted "T".

Hammer candlestick and hanging man candlestick

In a hammer candlestick, there is a long lower shadow, and the close is almost near the top. The long lower shadow indicates the

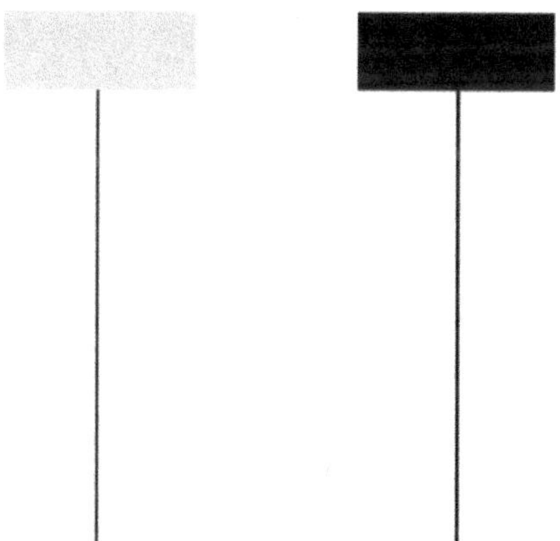

Image 2.6: Hammer candlestick (left) and hanging man candlesticks (right)

presence of a lot of sellers. The close near the top indicates that the buyers managed to close the battle on a strong note. Like other candlesticks, this also needs a confirmation. This candlestick is usually an indication of a bullish reversal pattern, especially when it forms after a long downtrend or near a support level. Another point to note here is that if the bullish confirmation comes along with higher volumes, that is an icing on the cake. The confirmation can be a gap up open (price opens with a gap above the previous candle's close) the following day (if you are looking at a daily chart) or if the next few candles are healthy, long bullish candles. Hanging man is a type of candlestick which looks similar to the hammer candle (it also has a lower shadow), but the close of the candle is below the open price, so it is a bearish close. In the case of hanging man candlestick, we need confirmation as gap down (price opens with a gap below the close of the previous candle) or long bearish candles. Hanging man would have much more importance if it forms after a long uptrend or near a resistance level as these are the levels where the sellers are active or the previous buyers look to book their positions.

Inverted Hammer and Shooting Star

The significant point in a shooting star candlestick is again near the resistance level or after an up move because this is also a bearish reversal pattern (the upward move ends and the downward move starts). It is usually found near the tops. It opens with a gap up and buyers manage to push the price further up, but the sellers dominate and manage to close the price almost near the bottom. It looks like a shooting star, hence the name. The upper shadow or "tail" of the shooting star should be twice as long as the body of the candle. The lengthier the upper shadow, the more powerful the bears are in the market. Like most candlestick patterns, a confirmation of a following bearish candle or a gap down is required. Inverted

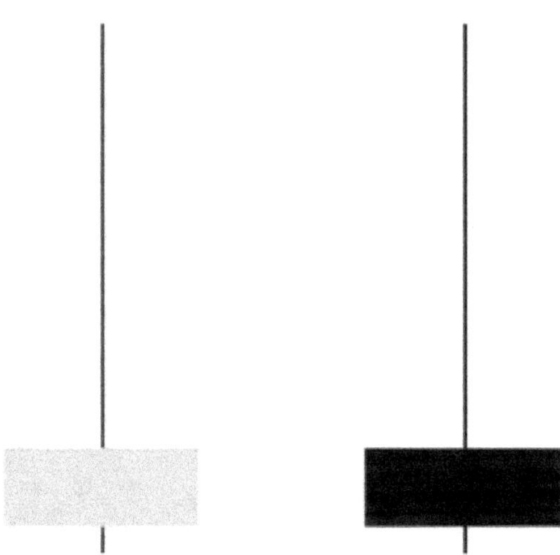

Image 2.7: Inverted hammer candlestick pattern (left) and shooting star candlestick pattern (right)

hammer looks almost same as a shooting star. The only difference is that it has a positive close and works wonderfully when it is formed near the support level or after a downtrend as it is mostly used in finding bullish reversals. The long upper shadow of the inverted hammer indicates the presence of a lot of buyers who try to push the prices up after a long downtrend. It shows that the buyers have started showing interest and now all that we need is a confirmation of the trend reversal when the following candles start moving up on the chart and the high of the inverted hammer is taken out. Once again, I would like to remind you, always wait for confirmation.

As it is said, "it is always better to be late for a good party than to be too early for a bad one."After a long downtrend, when an inverted hammer forms, it gives us a great entry point as we enter at a much better price compared to buying something after the breakout, where most of the move has already happened. It would be even better if the inverted hammer forms near a previous support and can act as a double bottom. The risk to reward ratio in this case is really favourable. The risk is really low as the stop-loss in this case is right below the support level, whereas the upside potential could be much higher.

Now let's look at candlestick pairs. There are a lot of candlestick pairs, but the following are the most common ones and are widely used by traders all over the world to trade the markets effectively.

Bullish and bearish engulfing candlesticks

Bullish engulfing candlesticks pattern is great for predicting the bottoms and bullish reversals. The bearish candle's body is completely engulfed by the bullish candle, which means that the entire range of sellers is covered by buyers. It shows that the buyers have taken out all the sellers and are showing a lot of relative

Image 2.8: Bullish engulfing candlestick

strength. This pattern is usually followed by a trend reversal from bearish to bullish which means that traders can buy at this level.

When this pattern forms near a support or after a long downtrend, it shows that the buyers are in control and they are ready to take the price up from here (again once the confirmation candle comes). Bullish and bearish engulfing patterns are one of my favourites and they help me know about the long-term trend reversals too, as you can see in a few chart examples later. But first, let us look at the bearish engulfing candle too (image 2.8).

As the name suggests, the bearish engulfing pattern (the upward trend can now reverse and a downward trend can follow) is completely opposite of the bullish engulfing pattern. This is used to identify the bearish reversal patterns and when this pattern is formed near the all-time highs or near a resistance, it indicates that the uptrend is about to end and a new downtrend may follow. A bearish engulfing pattern on higher time frames was found before all the major crashes in stock market history. This pattern suggests that the entire range of buyers has been taken out by the sellers and once the confirmation comes, the trend can reverse. These types of patterns usually result in quick falls and crashes. When a bearish candle engulfs a bullish candle, it essentially tells us that the buyers tried to gain momentum by opening above the range of the previous day high, but the sellers managed to push the price down and cover the entire range of buyers of the previous candle. When this happens on the monthly chart, it shows that the entire month's buyers have been taken out by the sellers and the sellers are in control now. Once the confirmation comes, they will start hammering the price down.

Image 2.9: Bearish engulfing candlestick

Let us look at a few examples of bearish engulfing patterns which resulted in long-term tops (from where the price reversed and the same level was not taken out by the buyers for a long time) being formed and the price saw a drastic drop.

In image 2.10, Nifty fell quite a bit from the highs and we can see the years 2008, 2011, 2015 and 2020 marked. All these falls were a result of a bearish engulfing pattern formed at the top.

In the 2008 global financial crisis crash, the Lehman Brothers went bankrupt in September 2008, but the bearish engulfing candlestick had formed in January 2008 itself. The same year, Nifty fell from the highs of 6350 to almost 2250 levels. In 2011, Nifty finally reclaimed the highs of 2008. Then we saw another bearish engulfing pattern and Nifty fell from almost 6200 levels to 4500 zone. After this there was decent upward movement in the following years and Nifty scaled new highs of 9100 levels. Once

Image 2.10: Monthly chart of Nifty showing bearish engulfing pattern

again there was a bearish engulfing candlestick pattern that resulted in a fall towards the lows of 6800. Nifty moved up for the next five years before finally crashing quickly in 2020, from the highs of 12400 to 7500 levels. All this happened in three months itself. Similar to the previous instances, this happened once there was a bearish engulfing pattern at the top. Scan your favourite stocks at this point and notice if you can find bearish engulfing patterns at the top in the weekly or monthly charts before any major fall in those stocks. I am sure you will find many and would be surprised that a simple chart pattern warned you about the consequences that followed.

Let us look at some charts of a few stocks which displayed a similar pattern.

In image 2.11, a bearish engulfing pattern appeared on the chart of Reliance Communications Ltd. at the highs of 2008 and the rest is as they say, history. We can even see a shooting star pattern in 2009 and another bearish engulfing in 2009.

Image 2.11: Monthly chart of Reliance Communications Ltd. showing a bearish engulfing pattern

In image 2.12, a huge bearish engulfing candle appeared right at the top of 2008 in the monthly chart of DLF Ltd., followed by a sharp fall which took the stock price from the highs of around 1200 levels to 130 levels! This is the time when the housing bubble of the US burst and the effect was seen all over the world's markets. That is the power of bearish engulfing pattern on higher time frame charts. It can literally destroy the wealth of investors.

Another thing to notice in this chart is that even though the price rose from below 200 levels to almost 1000 level, it is still below the highs of the year 2008. Someone who had invested in 2008 would still be sitting in loss. It is difficult to witness such a big loss and to keep waiting for the stock to recover before you can finally see a profit. It is demotivating and the investor usually loses patience and ends up exiting the stock almost near the bottom when they cannot take it anymore. That is why it is better to exit if there is a clear exit signal like the one we saw here, that is, the bearish engulfing pattern on a monthly chart.

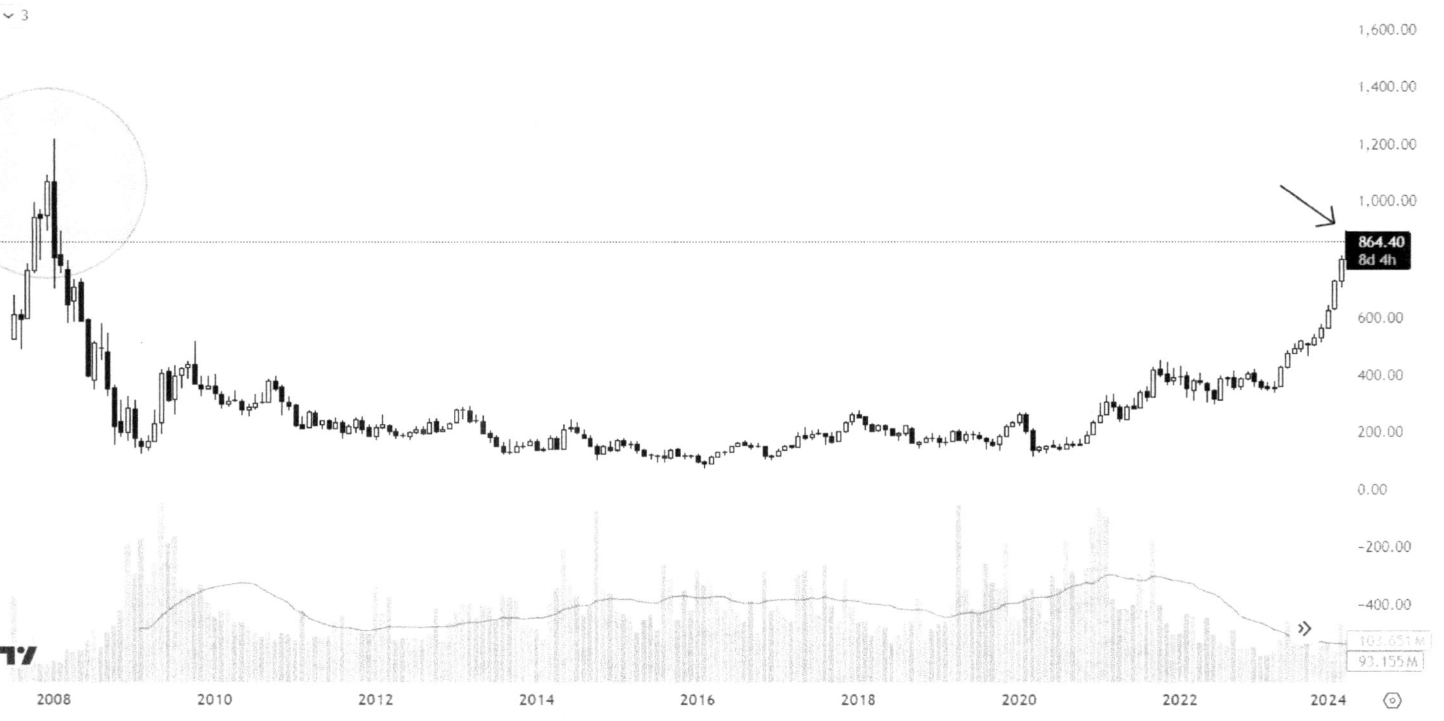

Image 2.12: Monthly chart of DLF Ltd. showing a bearish engulfing candlestick pattern

Next on the list is Kotak Mahindra Bank.

In image 2.13, the stock of Kotak Mahindra Bank Ltd. had a great run from the year 2003 to 2008. Then a big bearish engulfing candle appeared and the price of this stock fell from the highs of 360 levels to almost 60 levels. It took another six years to get back to the 360 levels after the crash.

Image 2.14 shows a bearish engulfing candle in the year 2008 and then again in 2018 on the chart of Reliance Capital. It fell from the highs of almost 2500 levels to 250 levels in 2008. Again, in 2018, it fell from 780 levels after the bearish engulfing candlestick pattern formed. Notice that the price has now been trading in double digits for the past few years. It is never a good idea to keep on holding a stock once it has formed a bearish engulfing pattern in the monthly or weekly charts. When a higher time frame chart witnesses such bearish patterns, chances are that the stock would not touch its life highs again or can take a very long time to do so, if it ever does. There is no point in holding stocks like these and waiting to see your buying price again. You may lose years of valuable time waiting for it. It is always better to exit when you see this signal and invest your money in any other stock which shows strength. If there is no opportunity in the markets, it would be a wise decision to just do nothing! Some of the best traders of the world sit on cash when the situation demands it. They do not have the urge to trade every day, every week or even every month.

As Mark Minervini, one of America's most successful stock traders, says, there is a "hard penny" environment and an "easy penny" environment. A hard penny environment is one in which there is no clear trend and the markets are choppy. An easy penny environment is one in which there are clear trends and it is easy to ride the trends and making money is relatively easy. We just need to wait for the easy penny phase and go all in when that happens, and sit on the side lines during the hard penny phase. New traders usually keep trading in the hard penny phase and get chopped out

Image 2.13: Monthly chart of Kotak Mahindra Bank Ltd. showing a bearish engulfing candlestick pattern

and end up taking multiple stop-losses. They lose their hard-earned capital and even lose the motivation to trade again when times are better and the seas are calmer again.

I would like to reinforce the fact that any pattern would have even more significance if it forms in the higher time frames such as monthly or weekly time frames. It basically tells us that the "battle" was fought for a complete week or month and the winners of the battle, bulls or bears, have shown strength for a longer period and can continue the trend for the next couple of weeks or months. These chart patterns or any patterns in fact, work on lower time frames too, like the 5–15 min charts, but such small time frames have a lot of choppiness and randomness and it is advisable for the traders to stick to higher time frames for the first few years of their career and shift to lower time frames only once they have mastered trading the higher time frames. If you are do not earn profits in higher time frames, shifting to lower time frames would not be a good idea as it requires even quicker decision making and risk management.

Bullish and Bearish Harami patterns

'Harami' means pregnant in Japanese. This pattern looks like a pregnant woman who has a baby in front of her. In a bullish harami pattern, the bearish candle has a small bullish candle inside its range. The bullish candle should be inside the complete range of the previous candle for it to be valid. Similarly, in a bearish harami pattern, the bearish candle should be inside the range of the previous bullish candle. It should not be above or below the previous candle, but should be completely inside its body. The bullish harami candle is an important pattern in finding the bottoms as they indicate that a downtrend can end and an uptrend can start. The opposite is true for bearish harami pattern. These patterns also help us to identify possible reversals in price.

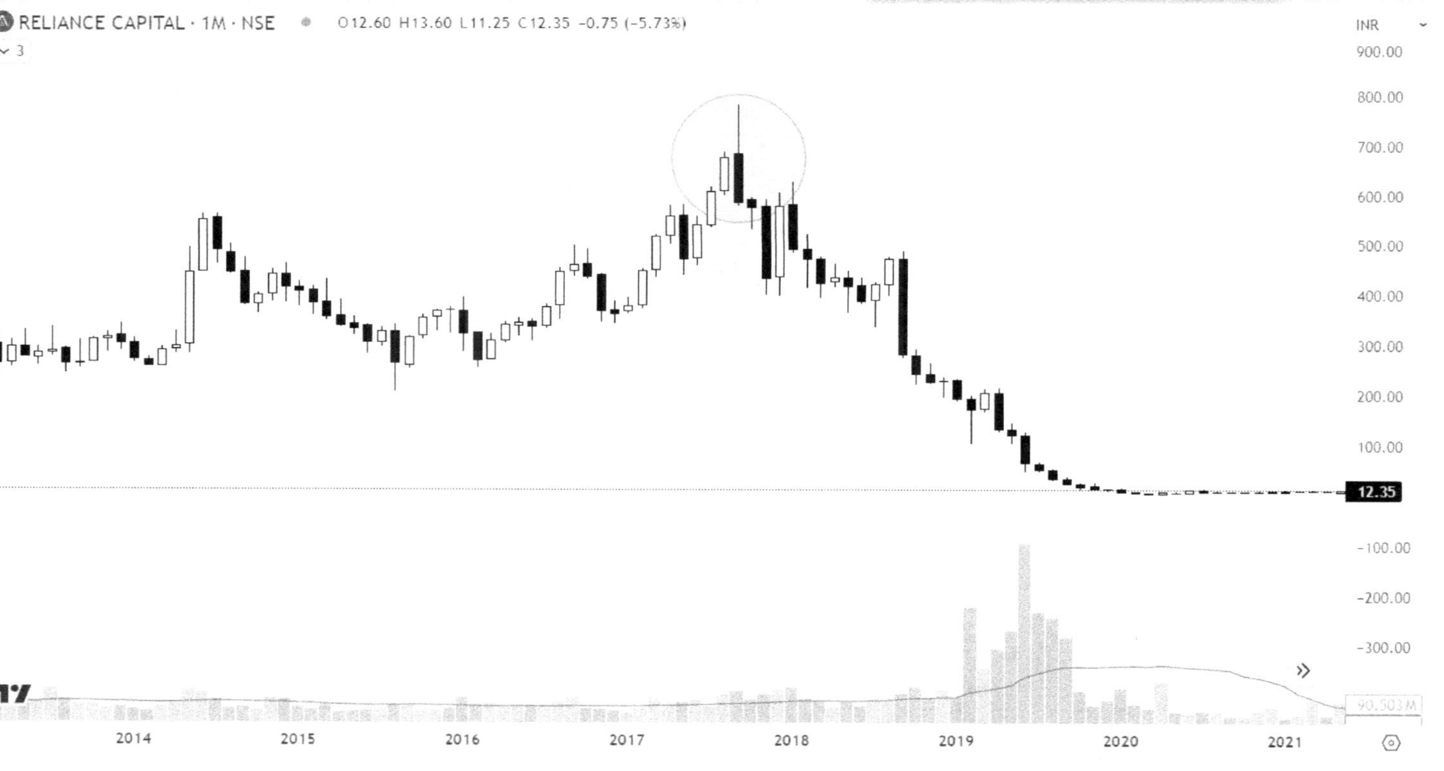

Image 2.14: Bearish engulfing candlestick patterns on the monthly chart of Reliance Capital.

The bearish engulfing pattern works best when it appears at the top, after an uptrend. Here too, we need to wait for the confirmation candle after the bearish engulfing pattern forms. The confirmation candle should break the low of the harami candle for it to be a valid confirmation signal. Inversely, the bullish harami pattern is used to find the bottom or a possible bullish reversal pattern after a downtrend or if it is formed near a long-term support or at double bottom, etc.The confirmation candle will come once the high of the harami candle is broken by the following candle. This indicates a buying opportunity.

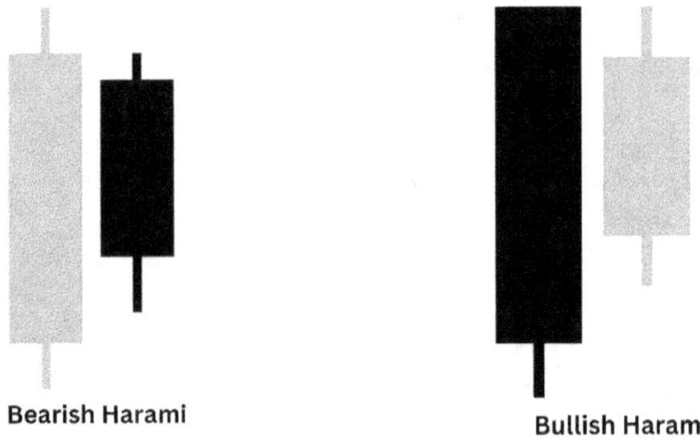

Image 2.15: Bearish harami candlestick pattern (left) and bullish harami candlestick pattern (right)

"Amateurs think about how much money they can make. Professionals think about how much money they could lose."

—Jack Schwager, author, fund manager and industry expert in futures and hedge funds

3

Price Action Trading: When the Price Finally Takes Action

Price action is the movement of a stock or any other security over a period of time. It forms the basis of technical analysis—all indicators that are calculated are derived from price action.

All chart patterns are a derivative of basic price action and that is the reason we should give a lot of importance to price action—it is basically the foundation on which technical analysis stands.

When traders look at chart patterns or use their favourite indicators to analyse if they should buy or sell a stock, they try to understand price movements. They just use a derivative of price (indicators and chart patterns) instead of directly using price. When we use candlesticks, we try to analyse the price with the mode of checking the open, high, low and close of that particular time frame of the stock to make it easy to study it. Price action is also used to analyse trends, breakouts, and reversals.

Candlestick patterns such as bullish engulfing, bearish engulfing, bullish and bearish harami, three white soldiers or three black crows, are all basically price action in visual format.

Most swing and short-term traders use price action as they want to identify trends in the near future. Fundamental analysis may or may not use price action, but it is a must for swing traders.

A trader should know the time frame they need to use to properly benefit from price action. A chart may be in a downtrend in higher time frame charts like the monthly or weekly charts, but can be in an uptrend in the short time frame charts like the 15 minute or hourly charts. So, one needs to be clear about the purpose of using price action and use it wisely to make sound decisions.

Price action helps traders to plot their entry and exits according to the historical movement of the stock's price. They can mark their entry levels and execute the trade if the stock moves accordingly.

Please note that price action, or any other kind of analysis can never assure us of future outcomes. Remember, we are not trying to predict anything, we are just trying to have a plan of execution *if* the price starts behaving as we expected, based on our study.

A very simple way to know if the stock is in uptrend or downtrend is through Dow Theory, developed by Charles H. Dow. It is a simple way of knowing the overall trend of the market or a stock.

A bull trend is identified if the price is making "higher highs, higher lows" which means that the new high is above the previous high and even the new low formed above the previous low (image 3.1).

Image 3.1: Price movement showing a bull trend

Similarly, the opposite is true for a bearish trend (downtrend) where the new low appears below the previous low and the new high forms below the previous high. It follows as a pattern of lower highs, lower lows, as shown in image 3.2.

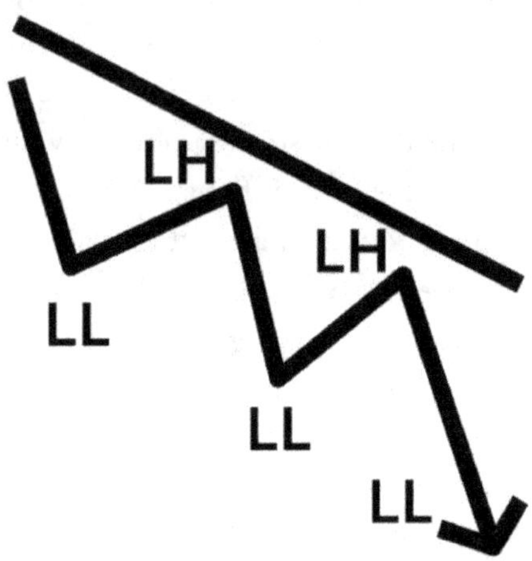

Image 3.2: Price movement showing a bearish trend

A sideways move is when the highs and lows of price are moving in a sideways zone and are trapped in a range (image 3.3). Momentum traders usually need uptrend or downtrend to make money and the sideways move should be avoided as it may lead to many false breakouts and breakdowns.

However, range-bound traders who prefer to trade short swings can trade the sideways markets too as they are not trading to hold the stocks for the entire trend and just want to buy near the supports and exit near the resistances or vice versa.

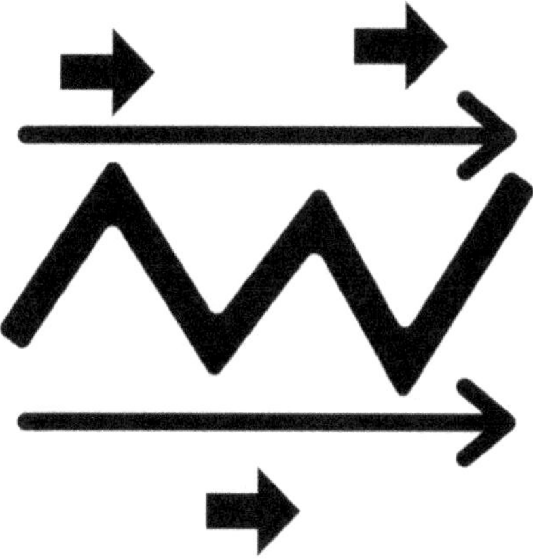

Image 3.3: Price movement showing a sideways trend

Let us first learn about the stages of a market.

The stages of a market were made famous by Stan Weinstein, the author of *Secrets of Profiting in Bull and Bear Markets.* The cycle of a stock is divided into four phases and once we understand this concept, it will be very easy to analyse which stage a stock is currently placed in and what should be the appropriate action thereafter.

If followed properly, this study will make trading really easy. Most of the time, traders get stuck in a loss because they usually buy a stock at the wrong stage. Moreover, when the stock looks ready for a fresh upward move according to the stages, traders do not enter, as they feel that the stock has already moved up a lot. These issues will not affect trading once you learn all about the stages of the stock.

There are many traders, who just trade according to just the price action and stages of the market. They do not look at any other data or use even a single indicator and rely just on the stages.

The various stages of a stock are as follows:

1. **Stage one or basing stage**: This stage usually comes after a downtrend when the stock finally makes a base and is essentially getting ready for its next move. The price moves in a tight sideways range and the volumes are also low during this stage. This indicates that the sellers are losing momentum and, in fact, the buyers have started accumulating the stock. A 30-period moving average can be used to confirm the trend. The moving averages also start getting flat at this stage, as there is a lack of momentum.

Long-term investors usually start buying the stock in parts during this stage, as they anticipate an up move as soon as the stock transits into the next stage. Investors get a good price when they enter in this stage, but you never know how long this stage can last, which can lead to their capital being blocked in a particular stock for many days, weeks or even months.

Image 3.4 shows the basing stage on the weekly chart of BSE Ltd. The stock price is moving in a sideways trend (as highlighted with a rectangle box). The 30-period moving average is also flat and hovering around the current price.

The volume has also dried up. The price kept moving inside the same range for a long time and it gave long-term investors a good chance to accumulate the stock.

As we can see in image 3.4, this stage came after a downtrend— the price was below the 30-period moving average before it entered the basing stage. The price was getting rejected (it fell down every time it touched the moving average) from the moving average. Eventually, the moving average became more or less flat, another characteristic of the stage 1 or the basing stage.

Image 3.4: Weekly chart of BSE Ltd showing the basing stage

2. **Stage two, when price breaks out of basing stage**: In the second stage the price breaks out of the basing stage or stage one. The volume of trades also starts picking up, confirming the interest of buyers and even more traders and investors.

The price starts to move above the 30-period moving average, and the moving average moves upwards, showing a positive trend. This is basically the time when investors start to enjoy the fruits of investments they made in stage one.

Momentum traders may enter at this stage, seeing the breakout levels and the rise in the volumes. They would ride the trend for as long as stage two is intact.

In the same stock's chart, we can see that it entered stage two as soon as it broke out of the range of stage one.

The price started moving above the 30-period moving average. The moving average also accelerated upwards and the volumes picked up quite well. These are all the characteristics that we need to identify that the stock is in stage two.

Once the stock entered stage two (image 3.5), it caught a lot of momentum and the price went up more than 300% over one year itself. This is the stage in which momentum traders will get maximum benefit and even the investors will see good returns as they would have entered at an even better price when the stock was in stage one.

Momentum traders will not do well if they enter a stock when it is in stage one as there are a lot of choppy moves and the stop-loss will get hit on multiple occasions during that time. For the same reason, it would be best to enter the stock and ride it when it is in stage 2 for swing traders as they need to ride with the trend and not against it.

It is rightly said that the trend is our friend, until it ends, which we will discuss in the following stage.

Image 3.5: Weekly chart of BSE Ltd showing stage two

3. Stage three, when the uptrend or stage 2 finally slows down

The price starts moving sideways once again and it shows that the momentum is on its way to cool off. The volume of trade starts to go down again as the investors start taking profits. The prices may still be higher but the volumes start to decline and it shows the lack of interest of the bulls (buyers). The 30-period moving average also turns flat once again, and it lacks a clear direction.

During this time, it is always better to wait for another breakout above this range if someone wants to buy. As in many cases, this stage gives birth to stage four, which is a downward stage where the price starts to decline rapidly, indicating an end of the uptrend.

Let us check this stage in image 3.6 for better understanding.

Image 3.6 is the daily chart for HCL Technologies Ltd. The stock was in stage two where the price was rising and was trading above the 30-moving average along with higher volumes. Thereafter, it went into sideways zone and the moving average also started to move into sideways zone or stage three (highlighted rectangle box). The price too started hovering around it. There was also a dip in volumes which shows the lack of interest from the buyers as discussed earlier.

If someone holds a stock which went into stage 3, they need to be really vigilant as this is usually the time to book profits. There is no point in holding the stock and then watching the profits vanish into thin air.

4. Declining stage, the last stage (stage four)

When the sideways zone or a distribution stage is over, followed by a clear downtrend, it is the last stage(stage four).

Stage three breaks down and the price also starts trading below the 30-period moving average. The volumes start increasing which shows the traders increasing selling as they exit the stock and book profits. The reason for this could be anything like negative news,

Image 3.6: Daily chart of HCL Technologies Ltd. showing stage three

overall negative sentiments of the markets, poor earnings of that stock, etc.

As technical traders, do not worry too much about the actual reason for the decline, focus on your study and act accordingly. There is no point in holding a stock in this stage. In fact, this is the ideal stage to short sell (sell first and then close the position by buying it later) a stock if possible.

In image 3.7 showing the daily chart of HCL Technologies Ltd., stage 3 broke down into the declining stage (stage four). The price moved below the 30-period moving average and the volumes started to rise again, indicating that the traders and investors are selling the stock. As this is the last stage, it is possible that once the downtrend is over, the price will again start to move in a sideways zone and make a base (basing pattern). It can, at some point of time, again move into stage one and the cycle may repeat.

All stocks and markets go through cycles. Stick to them only until the trend lasts. You will not get extra marks for holding it till the end of all the stages and then later think that you could have booked it at a much better price when it was showing a transition from stage three to stage four.

A trader can make an informed decision just by looking at the stages, without any fancy indicators. It is always wiser to stay with the trend, enter the stock when the trend is emerging, then hold on to it till the trend is intact, and exit as soon as the trend bends as we can see in the transition of stage three into stage four.

Now, understanding support and resistance is really important as they are basically used by everyone because they are the supply and demand zones.

The price of any commodity may move up or down because of the underlying demand or supply. Prices rise up when the demand is greater than the supply, prices will fall if the supply is greater than the demand, and prices will move inside a range if the demand

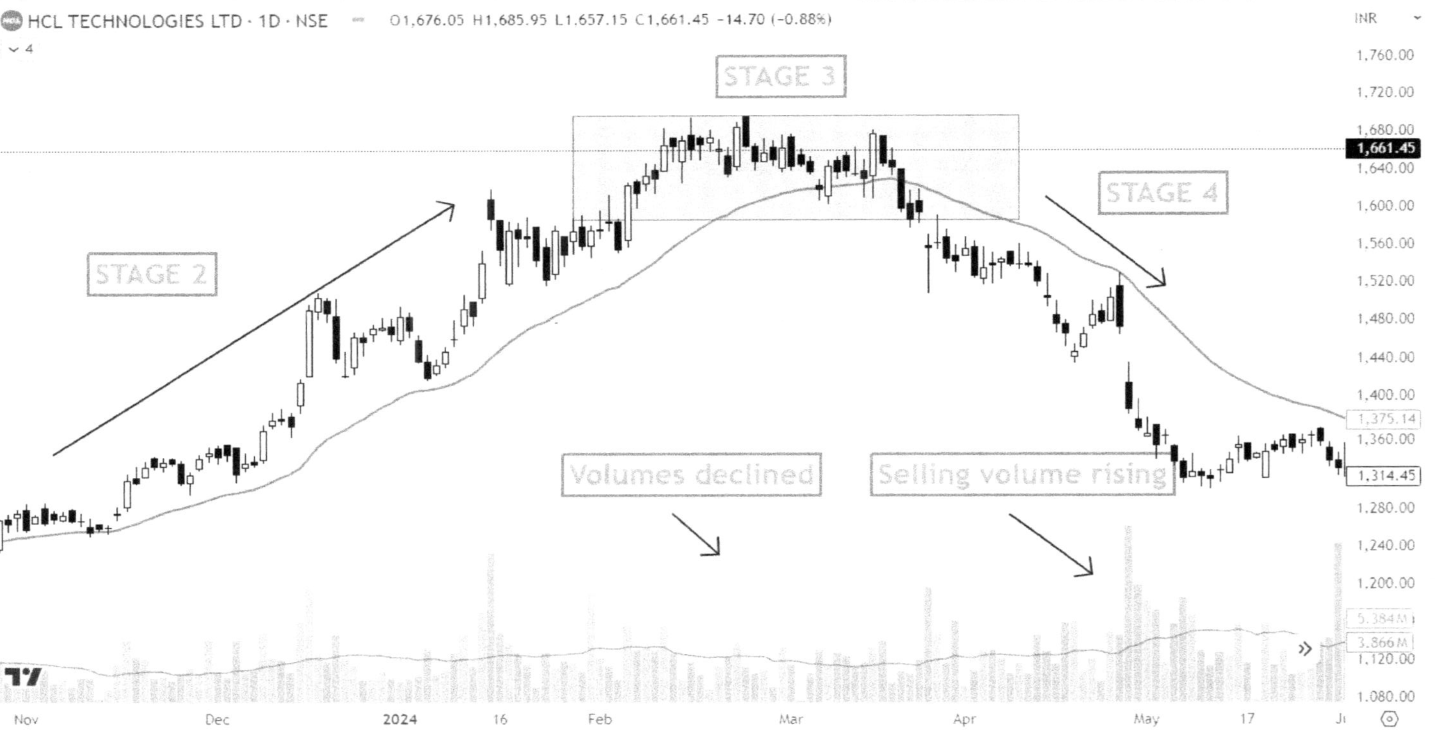

Image 3.7: Declining stage on the daily chart of HCL Technologies Ltd.

and supply have reached a state of equilibrium and a further move is awaited.

Look at a level where the buyers have shown interest earlier. This zone will be more and more important depending on the number of times the buyers have managed to move the price up, proving that they really like the price when it reaches that level and they feel that it is a bargain to buy it over there. This forms the support zone on the chart.

The demand zone or support zone is a great place to enter, as the risk is really small here and the reward is much better. Again, we cannot be sure if the prices will bounce off this zone in the future, but the probability is high, looking at the historical price action.

Technical charts help us to visually see the demand and supply zones with the help of supports and resistances. It becomes really easy to analyse our risk to reward ratio with the help of price action.

Here is an example of the support or demand zone plotted on the chart of DLF (image 3.8).

Resistance, on the other hand is the zone where the suppliers have shown interest multiple times. The supply is greater as compared to the demand, which results in the price moving down after reaching this zone. This is a level where traders can book their profits or initiate a short position. The risk to reward over here is really good for taking a short position as the sellers believe that this is the highest zone up to which the price can reach, and they start exiting the position or new sellers enter at this zone which results in the fall of prices.

Whenever we mark the support or resistance level, please note that it can be a *zone* and it is not necessary that it has to be perfect to the fraction. Some traders get worried if the price does not exactly land at a previous point where the support or demand is to be marked. This is why it is said that "technical analysis is an art, not a science."

Image 3.8: Daily chart of DLF showing support zone

Let us look at an example of the resistance zone in image 3.9.

In image 3.9, you can see an example of "price has memory." The same level acted as a resistance again in 2011 where suppliers were prominent in 2008 as well.

Now that we know what is support and resistance, let us understand the "polarity principle." It means that the zone which was acting as a support, will start acting as a resistance and similarly, the resistance zone will start acting as a support. Basically, the polars will change.

This happens as the sellers who were already active in a zone, once defeated, become buyers, and when the price reaches that level the next time, they will not allow the price to go below that level.

Image 3.9: Monthly chart of Nifty showing the resistance zone

Image 3.10 shows what the pattern looks like on a chart.

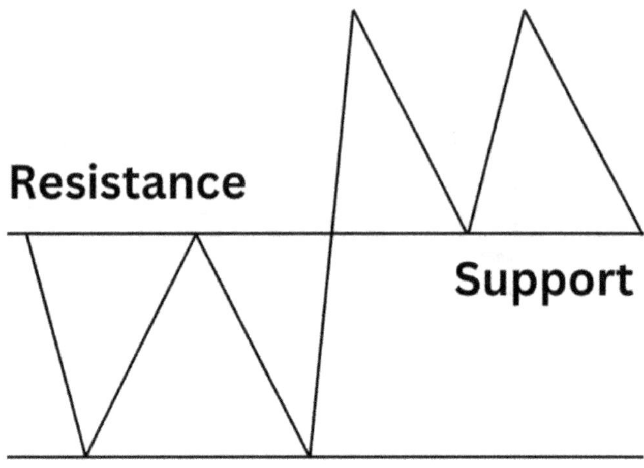

Image 3.10: Graphical representation of polarity principle

There are many cases where the support converts into a resistance and vice versa.

Let us see some examples.

Image 3.11 shows the monthly chart of Reliance. This is an extreme example of the polarity principle where the same zone which had acted as a resistance at the highs of 2008 (arrow on the left) acted as a support at 2020's covid fall (arrow on the right).

From 2008 to 2018, Reliance could not break this resistance, but once it did, it went up to 1400 levels. In the fall caused by covid, the price dropped quickly and retested the same zone of 750–780 levels (second arrow). Once it did, there was no looking back. The traders who bought at that price are sitting on good profits.

Image 3.11: Monthly chart of Reliance Industries Ltd. showing polarity principle

The next example is of Nifty monthly chart.

In image 3.12, the highs of 2008 (first arrow) acted as a resistance again in the year 2011 (second arrow). After getting rejected from the same zone, it managed to breakout above it in the year 2014 and went up to 9000 levels. Once it pulled back and fell after that, the same zone which had acted as a resistance in 2008 and 2011 (third arrow) acted as a support and showed a decent bounce from there. In fact, the covid fall was also almost at the same level, as we can see in the chart. This is exactly what we mean when we say that "price has memory."

Image 3.12: Monthly chart of Nifty depicting the polarity principle

Observe the same price action in image 3.13 on the weekly chart of Maruti Suzuki India Ltd. The resistance zone, which was active since 2018, managed to breakout in 2023. Soon after, the same zone acted as a support level (last arrow). The price moved up swiftly right after that. These kinds of moves, when the resistance becomes the support, give us a nice entry signal without the need for any other fancy indicator.

Image 3.13: Weekly chart of Maruti Suzuki India Ltd.

In image 3.14 which shows the weekly chart of Olectra Greentech Ltd, the resistance zone, which was active since 2022 (first arrow) managed to keep the price below it till the mid-2023. Once the breakout occured, the price quickly dropped back and retested the same zone twice (second and third arrow) before moving up and giving us decent returns.

Image 3.14: Weekly chart of Olectra Greentech Ltd.

Now let us check a daily chart and a recent example.

Image 3.15 is BSE Ltd.'s daily chart. Here we can see that the same zone of around 2600 price was acting as a resistance multiple times. Once the breakout happened, the same level acted as a support just after a couple of days and the price saw a sharp bounce.

Image 3.15: Daily chart of BSE Ltd.

Punjab National Bank's daily chart in image 3.16 shows a similar price action as the BSE chart in image 3.15.

The zone of 130 level acted as a resistance multiple times. When the price eventually managed to breakout above it, it retested it just after a couple of days and the same zone which acted as a resistance earlier acted as a support.

Now that we know how the support and resistances work and how beautifully the polarity principle performs, let us look at a very important aspect of trading support and resistance which almost every trader ignores.

In a hurry to enter the trade early, we miss the confirmation signal. Let us understand how this happens.

Image 3.16: Daily chart of Punjab National Bank

In image 3.17 you can see that when the price took the resistance again (second upper arrow from left) it made a bearish engulfing pattern and then fell towards the new support level. Bearish engulfing candlestick pattern works wonderfully most of the time, as we have discussed in the price action chapter of this book, too.

When the price reached the support level, a bullish harami pattern formed, from which it quickly bounced towards the resistance again. After it got rejected from the resistance level, it again went back to the resistance level after falling a bit and another bearish engulfing pattern formed. The price then fell back towards the support level where another bullish engulfing pattern formed, then the price bounced back and got rejected from the same resistance level.

Image 3.17: Daily chart of Bajaj Finserv Ltd.

Let us check another example now so that this concept is clear.

In image 3.18 on the daily chart of HDFC Bank Ltd., whenever the price reached the resistance zone, it gave a bearish signal like the bearish engulfing, shooting star, or the candles made long upper wicks/shadows, which is a sign that the sellers are dominating the market and pushing the prices down.

When it resulted in a fall in price and when it reached the support levels, we saw bullish signals like bullish engulfing and long lower wicks/shadows which indicates that the buyers are strong at that level and are pushing the prices up from a much lower level.

Another interesting thing is that when there was no bullish signal at the support levels (marked twice in chart), the prices went below the support and stayed below it for many days. New and inexperienced traders hurry to enter the stock without waiting for confirmation at this stage. They may just see that the price has reached the same level from where the price had bounced earlier, thinking "it may bounce again now, so let us enter before we miss the bus." But, it would have been a wiser decision to wait for the bullish signal as not only did the price fall below the support, causing a loss to the buyers, it even stayed below that level for many days. This would have resulted in blocking the trader's capital if they kept holding it.

One mistake which all new traders make is that they enter as soon as the price reaches a support zone and sell their position or book profits as soon as they see that the price has touched the resistance zone.

You should actually wait for a bullish confirmation signal at the support and a bearish signal at the resistance zone before taking any action. A bullish confirmation pattern could be a bullish engulfing or a bullish harami pattern and bearish pattern could be a bearish engulfing or a bearish harami pattern.

Yes, it is possible that by waiting for a confirmation signal, you may enter a bit late when buying near support, or exit a bit late

Image 3.18: Daily chart of HDFC Bank Ltd.

when exiting near the resistance as you wait a bit longer for the confirmation signal to appear, but you will be saved from the false signals and trap moves if you follow this.

"The desire for constant action, irrespective of underlying conditions, is responsible for many losses in Wall Street."

—Jesse Livermore, American stock trader considered a pioneer of day trading

4

Chart Patterns: Profitable Patterns of the Stock Market Maze

In this chapter, you will learn about the most commonly used chart patterns, and the exact psychology behind a pattern. Get to know why a chart pattern actually works so that you can use it with full conviction.

MOST COMMON CHART PATTERNS

Chart patterns are an easy way to visually see the fight between the buyers and sellers and analyse who has the higher probability of winning. We can take our trades according to the probable winner. There are hundreds of chart patterns out there, but we will discuss the most common ones which keep occurring multiple times and have a high probability of giving the desired results. These are easy to understand and can be used without any other indicator to trade effectively.

Chart patterns are divided into two broad categories—reversal patterns and continuation patterns.

i. Reversal patterns

As the name suggests, these are patterns which result in the price moving in the opposite direction of the trend. They essentially "reverse" the current trend and make it move in the opposite direction. These are helpful if you want to buy a stock which has been in a downtrend for some time or if you want to exit a stock which has been in an uptrend, or it can be sold here, or the profit can be booked.

The most commonly used reversal patterns are mentioned below.

1. *Double bottom reversal pattern*: As the name suggests, this pattern forms a double bottom, which means that the price touches a zone twice and then bounces off from that zone. In the double bottom pattern, there is a zone from which the stock price bounces off twice with a small peak in between. This pattern can occur multiple times in a downtrend, but it will be valid only if the recent resistance is also taken off, as seen in image 4.1.

If the resistance zone is not taken out, that is, the price has not broken above the resistance, the downtrend can continue and it will not be called a proper double bottom reversal pattern.

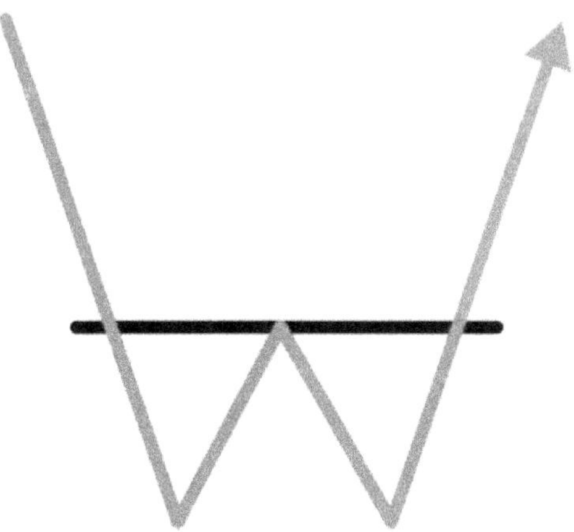

Image 4.1: Double bottom reversal pattern

So this pattern essentially goes through an initial downtrend phase, which is required if you are looking for a reversal pattern. After that, see if the price has bounced off a level, followed by a peak from where it again starts falling and takes support from the same zone till the point it had fallen earlier and from where it has taken support earlier too. Once it bounces off that zone, it should take out that high of the peak, which may act as a resistance. Once it breaks out above the resistance zone, the target price can be calculated as the depth of the pattern, or the range from the resistance to the support added on top of the resistance level.

2. *Double top pattern:* The double bottom pattern shows us a bullish reversal from the downtrend (which means that it is a pattern for buying). The opposite is called the "double top" pattern, which essentially is a bearish reversal pattern when the sellers can take advantage by selling or buyers can book out their profits.

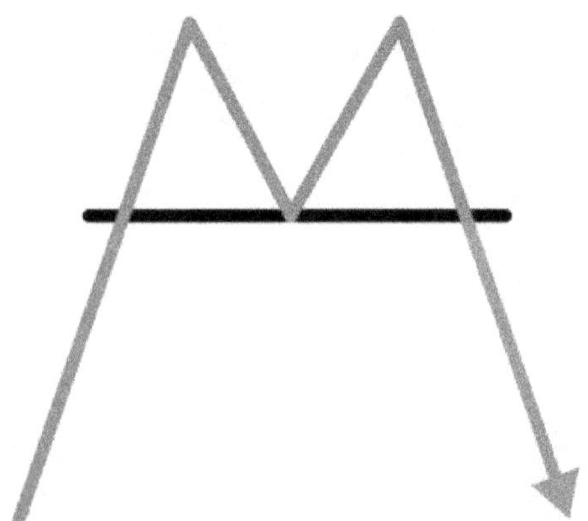

Image 4.2: Double top reversal pattern

This pattern forms when the price in an uptrend gets rejected from the zone, falls a bit before bouncing again, and then takes resistance from the same zone from where it had taken resistance earlier. Following this, the price ideally breaks that support zone and reaches toward the target price, which is the range from the support zone towards the double top resistance zone added below the support zone (image 4.2).

Falling wedge and rising wedge patterns

3. *Falling wedge pattern*: This is another bullish reversal pattern, which is broad when it starts and keeps contracting along the way, sloping downwards. Once it breaks out from resistance, it gives a bullish momentum move and a new uptrend starts, making it a great entry point for buyers.

A falling wedge should have at least two touch points at the resistance line. Ideally, three touch points are even better at the resistance line and at least two touch points at the support line.

A double bottom should ideally form after a downtrend. Similarly, falling wedges should also be formed after a downtrend, if you are looking for a bullish reversal.

The pattern starts making a cone shape, indicating that the fight between the buyers and sellers is getting stronger. The price moves up above the support line and gets ready to break out above the resistance line.

The volumes will also start increasing along the breakout time. It adds conviction that the breakout can finally occur and sustain too. A falling wedge has been shown in image 4.3.

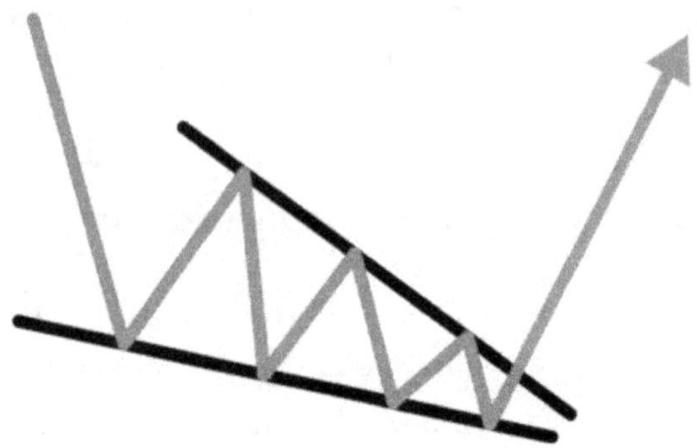

Image 4.3: Falling wedge

4. *Rising wedge pattern:* This pattern indicates the end of the uptrend and beginning of the downtrend. It is the opposite of falling wedges pattern. Here too, the range keeps getting tighter as the pattern matures, followed by a clear break down. The volume of trades generally start decreasing as the pattern rises, showing that the buyers have started to lose momentum and the volume of trades generally starts increasing as a breakdown is around the corner (image 4.4).

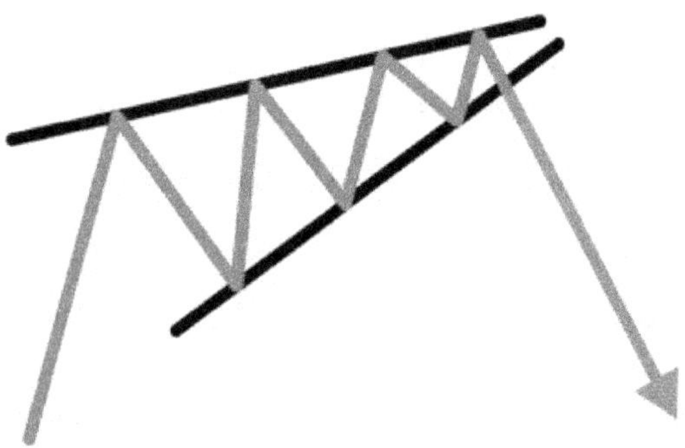

Image 4.4: Rising wedge pattern

5. *Rounding bottom pattern:* Rounding bottom, also known as the "saucer pattern" is relatively easy to identify as it is like a big cup

or a saucer. This is one of my favourite patterns because it is the simplest to use. It is another reversal pattern.

The rounding bottom pattern forms from a declining or a bearish trend, where the bearish or downward trend continues, then starts to flatten up, goes sideways and eventually the trend starts to move up (image 4.5).

The rounding bottom is basically a smoothened-out pattern and does not look like a "V" pattern, which is usually very sharp, having quick falls and quick recoveries.

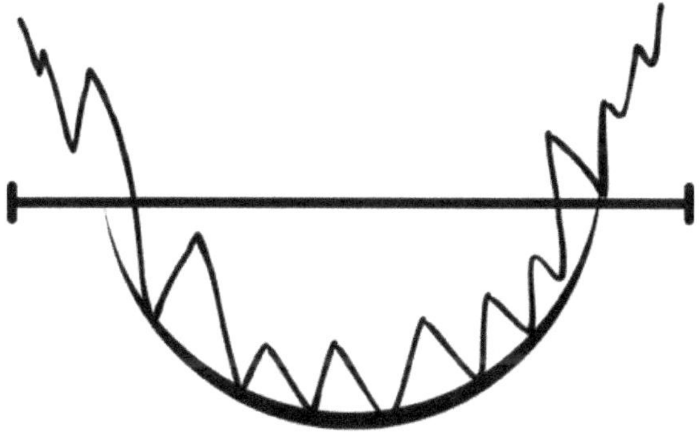

Image 4.5: Rounding bottom pattern

A rounding bottom pattern takes its time and can sometimes even last up to a few weeks, months or years before the breakout finally comes. The declining part and the recovery part or the right side of the rounding bottom should ideally take the same amount of time so that the base of the "cup" looks a little even and not too sharp. This shows that the buyers are active again and have started to take the price up.

The breakout is confirmed when the high of the rounding bottom (the zone from which the price had initially started to fall) is taken out. The target can be calculated by adding the depth of the base/cup and adding it above the resistance level.

The volumes also move identical to the patterns, that is, they are usually high during the declining phase, then the volume starts to dip along with the dip in the price and then they start to pick up along with the up move of the cup. If the volumes are highest during the breakout stage, that is the ideal scenario, as it shows that the big players are interested in the stock and are ready to take the price much higher from these levels.

Often, if the rounding bottom takes a few years to form, the corresponding move can be really big. Many times, it is observed that if the breakout comes after six to eight years, the stock moves up at least 200–300% from the breakout level, as we will see later in the chapter.

ii. Continuation patterns

Triangle patterns

Triangle patterns are further categorised into symmetrical, ascending and descending.

Symmetrical triangle: In a symmetrical triangle, usually there are at least two lower highs and two higher lows. The pattern looks like a coil as the end gets tighter showing the increasing intensity of the fight between the buyers and sellers (image 4.6). Even though it is a continuation pattern, the move can continue on either side once the breakout is confirmed.

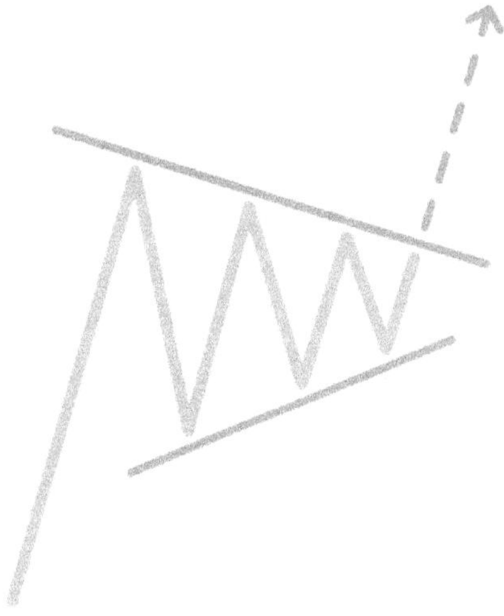

Image 4.6: Symmetrical triangle pattern

When children water the garden with a pipe, they play with it and at times squeeze the end of the pipe to push the water with force, propelling it further away than usual.

In a symmetrical triangle, the same thing happens. The end of the water pipe gets squeezed, and the result is a quick and big move, once the breakout is confirmed.

The symmetrical triangle acts as a consolidation pattern and the prior trend continues, once the breakout happens.

Like in the wedges, here too, we need at least two touch points to make a trendline. However, three points are always better. The second high should be lower than the first one and the resistance line should slope down. Similarly, the second low should be higher than the first one and the support should slope upwards, forming a contraction.

The volume of trade generally starts to fade as the pattern continues and once the breakout occurs, the volumes again start to gather momentum and validate a breakout.

The longer the price stays inside the triangle, the bigger and quicker the breakout will eventually be. We can only identify the direction towards which the breakout will occur after it has happened. We cannot guess the direction while the price is still inside the triangle, as it can break out in either direction.

The price can retest the support or resistance line once the breakout has happened before eventually continuing its move in the same direction. This can be called a breakout retest and it can happen in any pattern.

The target of this pattern is measured by adding the widest part of the triangle above the breakout point.

Ascending triangle pattern: Ascending triangles are bullish continuation patterns—they occur after an uptrend and the uptrend continues after the breakout from this pattern. However, the uptrend cannot continue indefinitely, so patterns like the ascending triangles form. They show more accumulation at higher levels which can result in a breakout and eventually the upward move can continue (image 4.7).

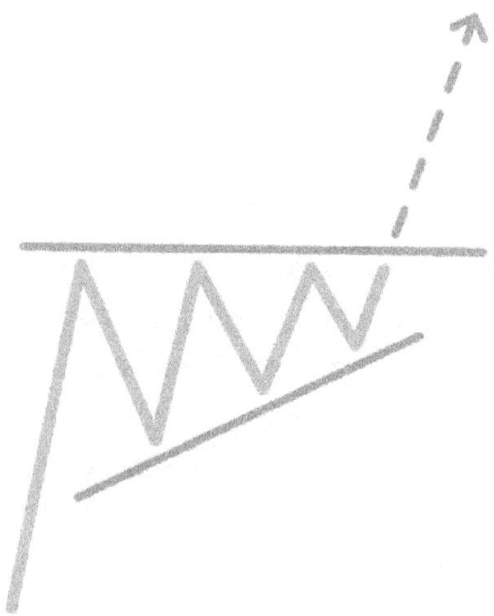

Image 4.7: Ascending triangle pattern

Accumulations are a healthy part of a trend and should be welcomed. Ascending triangles give traders and investors a chance to add to their positions or even buy new stocks when the breakout occurs.

The resistance line is almost flat and does not slope down like in the symmetrical triangle. The highs are at an equal level, but the support line slopes *upwards*, which means that the second low is above the previous low. This indicates that the buyers are strong now and are not allowing the price to move down to the same level of previous lows (the lows should be successively higher), and so on. The bears are rejecting the price from the same level and cannot push the price down. The bulls are getting stronger and are pushing the price upwards. Over time, they build momentum to finally breakout above the resistance zone where the bears will give up the fight.

The duration of the ascending channel can be anywhere from a few weeks to a few months and an average duration is around one to three months.

Here too, the volume will dip when the price moves inside the triangle and it will start to build up around the breakout level. If the breakout happens with higher volume, it is an icing on the cake.

Please note that volume of trades is a major part of the breakout in any type of pattern and it provides more conviction to the overall pattern. But if there is less volume, we will still enter the trade. Higher volume is always a plus point, but sometimes, the volumes can catch up later, after the breakout. So, we will not miss a trade just because the volume has not caught up yet. However, if the volumes are highest at the breakout level, it is the best-case scenario to enter into a trade.

The target is measured in the same way as it is measured in the symmetrical triangle, that is, measure the widest gap in the triangle's range and add it above the resistance point.

Descending triangle pattern: A descending triangle is a continuation of the downtrend. When the price is already in downtrend, it starts going sideways and the support remains flat. The highs start getting lower than the previous ones implying that sellers are getting stronger in the fight, not letting the price reach the previous level, and are hammering it down with every subsequent move (image 4.8).

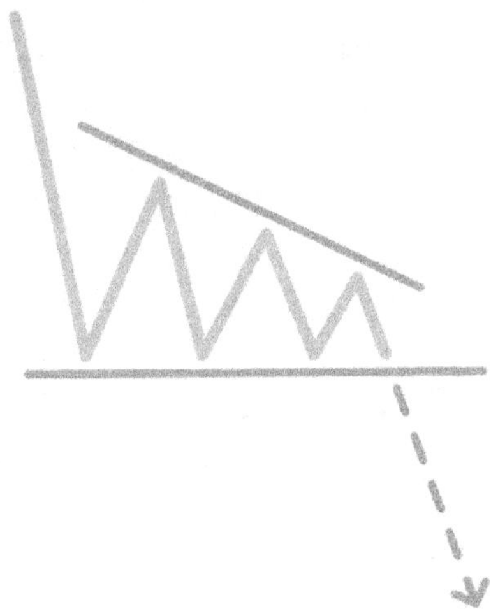

Image 4.8: Descending triangle pattern

The momentum is lacking and the bears are gaining back control, trying their best to break the support level, which they finally succeed in when the break down eventually happens. The downtrend continues and keeps pushing the price down. A descending triangle is basically the opposite of an ascending triangle pattern.

Like other resistance and support lines, we need at least two touch points, whereas three are even better. The upper resistance line is sloping down as new highs are at a lower level than the previous highs. The pattern's duration can range from a few weeks to a few months.

The volume usually decreases while the price is inside the triangle and picks up around the time of the breakdown. This gives the trader more conviction while trading in this scenario.

Once the breakdown happens, the price may retrace back up. In that case, the support which has just broken can act as a resistance, and the price can retest that level before finally falling down. This retest may or may not happen every time. It is advisable to take a position in the first breakdown itself and not wait for the retest (this is a mistake that a lot of traders make). Do not wait for a retest because often when the momentum is strong, the prices never retest. If we miss the move waiting for the retest, we may regret missing the move.

The target is calculated by adding the widest range of the triangle below the breakdown level.

Cup and handle pattern: As the name suggests, this pattern looks like a cup and handle. It gained popularity when William O'Neil spoke about it in his book, *How to Make Money in Stocks*.

Cup and handle pattern is a continuation pattern which forms after an uptrend. It consists of two parts. The first one is a big base, kind of a rounding bottom or a big cup pattern followed by another small range or a handle pattern. Once the resistance breaks after the handle is made, the uptrend continues.

Image 4.9: Cup and handle

As it is a continuation pattern, it appears after an uptrend which is ideally a few months old. The cup should be a 'U' shape or like a rounding bottom and not like a 'V' shape. If the price falls too quickly and bounces off sharply making a V pattern, that will not qualify for a cup. The round pattern shows that the consolidation of price took time and was not a knee-jerk reaction to some news. Once the right side of the cup's high touches the resistance, making it a proper U-shape pattern, another small cup appears on the right side, which looks like a handle of the cup.

The handle of the cup should ideally retrace around one-third of the total depth of the big cup. If it retraces more than that or reaches 50% of the big cup's depth, then the cup and handle pattern will not be valid.

Like other patterns, volume of shares traded is usually lowest when the formation is under process and starts to rise as it gets ready for the breakout.

The target of the cup can be calculated by adding the depth of the cup above the breakout level.

Volatility contraction pattern (VCP): This pattern indicates that the supply is constantly being absorbed over time as the price range keeps getting smaller. The range finally breaks on the upside and a trending move is expected thereafter. The pattern also indicates that there is accumulation. It generally occurs in an uptrend, as it is also a continuation pattern like the few others we studied earlier. Similar patterns, like the cup and handle pattern were used earlier too, but this is like an extended version of the same. The term volatility contraction pattern was coined by Mark Minervini.

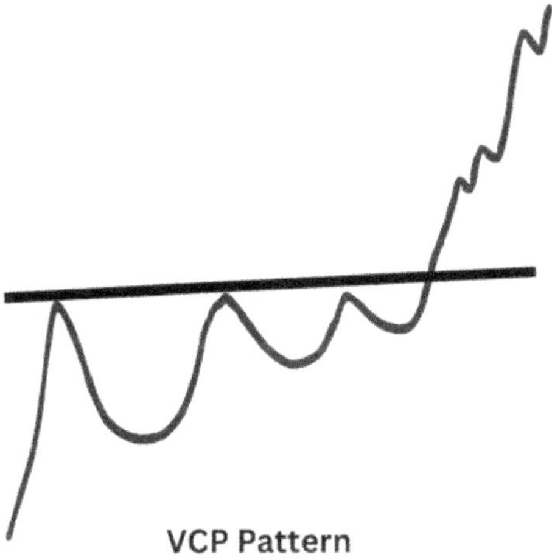

Image 4.10: Volatility contraction pattern

The main characteristic of this pattern is that the consecutive drops in price would be smaller than the previous ones, indicating the increase in buyers and sellers losing strength (image 4.10). The volumes generally dry up during declines within the base, and usually start to pick up during the up moves within the base, and are the highest when the price eventually breaks out. Higher volumes during the breakout add conviction to execute the trade. Many times, the price may fall and retest the breakout zone and bounce back again, which is perfectly fine. Mark Minervini talks about the concept of "eggs and tennis balls" here. Some retests are like tennis balls, they just fall to the breakout zone and then bounce back right up while some are like eggs which keep falling after the breakout and cannot sustain above the breakout zone.

We need to stay alert during the retest and see how the stock reacts. Usually, when the price declines, it happens with low volume and then bounces back with relatively higher volume.

Another important trait of the VCP is that the last contraction near the breakout level is really tight. It shows the final fight before the breakout getting more intense as the sellers try their best to keep the price below the desired level. If they do not succeed in it and the price finally breaks out along with higher volume, there will be an uptrending move which may last really long.

II

TRADING STRATEGY

If you can't take a small loss, sooner or later you will take the mother of all losses."

—Ed Seykota, commodities trader

5

Swing Trading Strategy: Basic Chart Patterns

Have you ever noticed that most professional traders use basic chart patterns? They just follow basic price action and do not rely on any complex indicators.

That does not mean that indicators are not useful in our trading journey. They are really useful and help us get the conviction to enter any trade. Indicators are really effective and that is why in the subsequent chapters, you will learn about a lot of indicators and how to use them to trade effectively. Every professional trader who uses clean charts may have used a lot of indicators in their initial years of trading. Suppose you are from Delhi but you plan to go to Mumbai by flight and over there you wish to hire a rental car for the next few days to visit all the happening places. Since you are not familiar with the routes, you would use maps or GPS on your phone to navigate through the city. The roads which are already there are like the price action and the indicators are like the GPS which give you an idea of where the roads are headed. A person who has been living in Mumbai since childhood may be familiar with the routes, so they may not use the GPS, but an outsider would. Similarly, professional traders are so used to the indicators that they develop an idea of where they may be and eventually start trading with just the virgin price action.

Now that does not mean that they never used GPS or they may have learned the routes of the city with frequent travels like we develop the knowledge of price action trading through regular practice and studying the charts.

Therefore, once you practise and study charts long enough, you start to develop a sense of what the price action wants to say. A chart is basically a visual representative of what the buyers and sellers are up to during a given period.

TECHNICAL INDICATORS

As the name suggests, they indicate where the trend may be headed by analysing the underlying price action. All indicators are derived from the price action itself and do not suggest anything different from the price action. They are just used as a complimenting tool. Indicators are usually plotted above the price action itself and some of the most common indicators include moving average, super trend, Bollinger bands, Ichimoku cloud, etc.

Oscillators help to confirm the trend by giving us an idea about the momentum of the stock or index, and as the name suggests, oscillate between a range. Relative strength index (RSI) and moving average convergence divergence (MACD) are some of the most widely used oscillators.

I have discussed a few trading strategies using indicators and oscillators in later chapters.

One of the common mistakes almost all amateur traders make is that they tend to learn a lot of indicators at once and then apply all of those on the chart. They think that they are being smart by using more indicators because they believe that more means better.

With technical analysis, often, *less is better*.

Study all the indicators if you want to and try them out for several weeks, months or even years, but stick to the ones which you are most comfortable using and do not mix them up. If you use multiple indicators, you may get mixed signals sometimes, where one indicator may give a signal to buy and at the same time, the second one may give a signal to exit.

Trading in itself is difficult as it involves managing your emotions and mindset and, therefore, it is best not to complicate the decision-making process.

Remember, complex strategies may be good to show off your skills and knowledge, but efficient trading is a result of a process that is simple and easy to follow.

Many traders get carried away by the technical part of trading and end up learning about all the indicators out there. They get so stuck in the analysis that they end up having 'analysis paralysis' and cannot actually trade when needed.

We enter the markets to make money, not to write a thesis on technical subjects. You do not get extra points or grades for using multiple indicators or the most complex strategies. The golden rule is, try them out and then stick to the ones *you* are comfortable with using for your lifetime. Once you find the indicator or oscillator that works perfectly for you, stick to it and do not jump to other indicators or oscillators.

I made this mistake earlier and would hop from one tool to the other in search of the best one. I was under the impression that someone out there has the holy grail of trading and knows what works best in the market. There is no concept of best, something that may work wonderfully for one trader may not work at all for the other.

In the previous chapter, we discussed various chart patterns. Now let us study them on actual charts and figure out how we can use them to trade without any indicators.

Double bottom pattern

In image 5.1, the daily chart of Intellect Design Arena, the stock was in a downtrend. It bounced off the zone of 380–390, went towards the 420 zone, from where it fell down again and then took support near the 380–390 zone. When it bounced off again, this double bottom pattern would be considered a legitimate one only if it breaks the resistance, which it did. It eventually reached the target too, which is the range from the resistance and the support added over the resistance on the upside.

Image 5.1: Daily chart of Intellect Design Arena showing a double bottom pattern

Double top pattern

The double top pattern is a bearish reversal pattern.

Image 5.2 is the daily chart of Ashok Leyland Ltd. The stock was in an uptrend before getting rejected from the 56 level. Once it did, it fell towards the 48–50 zone and bounced back up again, but got rejected once more from the 56 zone and formed a double top pattern there. Once it got rejected again from the same resistance zone, it fell and even broke the support zone of 48–50. It fell quite quickly. This is expected in this type of reversal pattern.

There are more patterns like triple top and triple bottom. There is no need to explain those in detail as they are an extension of double top and double bottom with basically one more leg to it—one more top or bottom, depending on the pattern that we look at.

Another set of reversal patterns which we had learned in the previous chapters, were falling and rising wedges. Let us see how they trade on an actual chart.

Image 5.2: Daily chart of Ashok Leyland Ltd. showing a double top pattern

Image 5.3 is Nifty's daily chart showing a prior downtrend. Then it started moving in a falling wedge pattern and started making a cone shape with the range getting smaller.

Once the breakout occurred along with confirmation, there was a quick up move, reversing the downtrend and turned into an uptrend.

Image 5.3: Daily chart of Nifty 50 Index showing a falling wedge pattern

Rising wedges

In image 5.4 on the daily chart of Nifty 50 Index there was a prior uptrend and then the rising wedge started to form. The range kept getting smaller as the fight between the buyers and sellers started to get intense. The price finally broke below the support line and the uptrend turned into a downtrend indicating that the sellers eventually won. The price near the breakdown level was 18000 and went towards a high of 18800 at the top of the resistance line, which eventually came all the way down to 16800.

This is the beauty of simple price action, which can help us immensely in finding out patterns in the charts and take trades accordingly without the need of any fancy indicators or strategies.

Now let us understand how to use the simple but really effective rounding bottom patterns using two examples.

Image 5.4: Daily chart of Nifty 50 showing a rising wedge pattern

Rounding Bottom Pattern

In image 5.5 showing the weekly chart of BSE, a rounding bottom formed and the breakout came after almost two years. The volumes also worked perfectly, that is, they were a bit high during the initial phase, then they dipped along with the price and started to pick up momentum again along with the price. High volumes were accompanied the breakout.

The base of the rounding bottom went up to 60% and that was our initial target if we add it above the resistance level. We got the move, and the move continued well beyond that level too and went all the way to a high where the price was up 150% above the breakout level and that too almost in a straight line. That is the power of this simple yet effective pattern.

Now look at another example.

Image 5.6 is the weekly chart of Pidilite Industries Ltd. This one has a similar pattern where the price started to move down and the volumes were the least near the lows as shown in the image. The volumes started to pick up as the price moved up and the breakout eventually happened. The depth of this cup was around 60% and once the breakout came, we saw a similar up side move fulfilling the target of the cup.

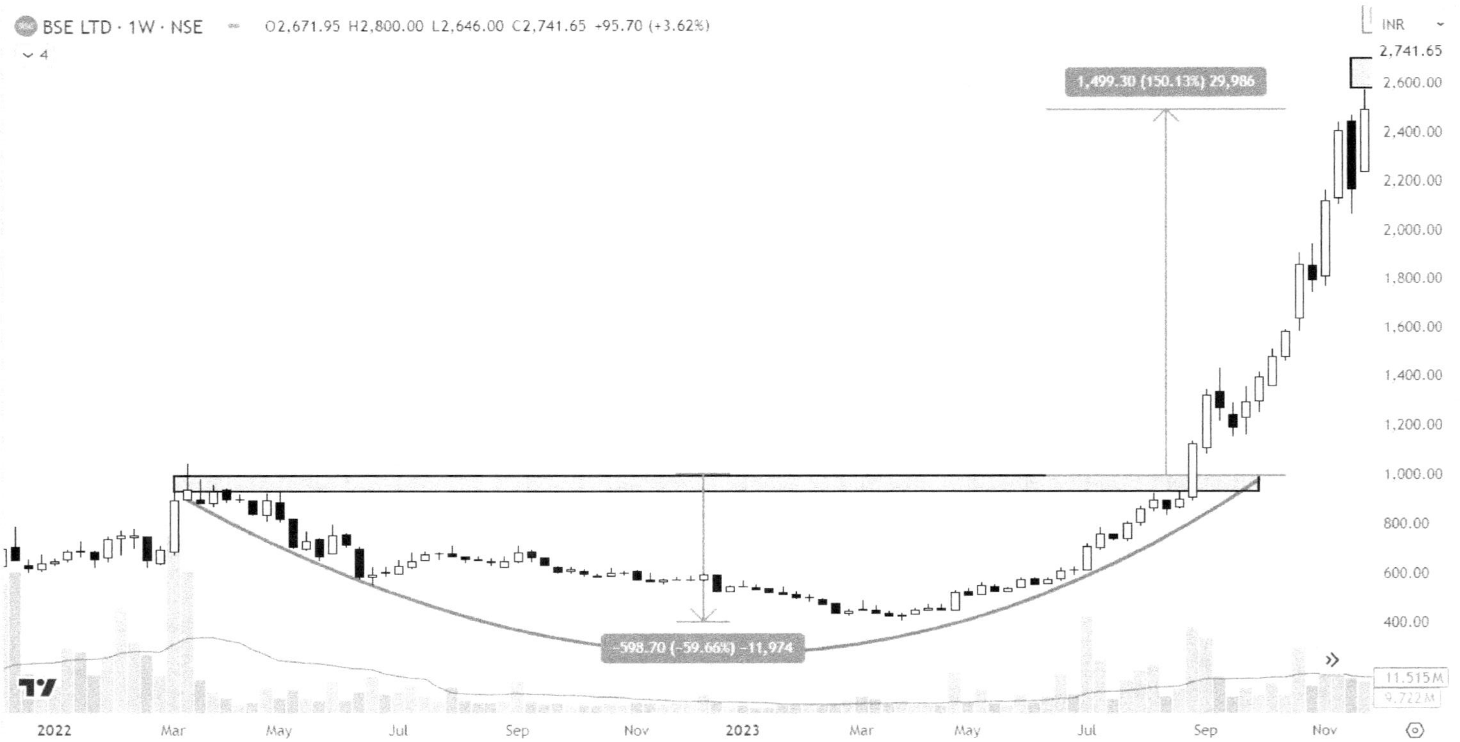

Image 5.5: Weekly chart of BSE Ltd. showing the rounding bottom pattern

Image 5.6: Weekly chart of Pidilite Industries Ltd showing a rounding bottom

Triangle pattern

One of my favourite patterns to use is the triangle pattern. Let us look at examples of symmetrical triangle patterns—one bullish and one bearish—to understand how to use them in a real-world scenario.

Symmetrical triangle pattern

Image 5.7 is the weekly chart of Relaxo Footwears Ltd. It showed a prior uptrend before the price started to consolidate inside a symmetrical triangle. The volumes of trade started to fade as the pattern continued and it finally picked up as the breakout occurred, in the desired manner. The touch points on the upper line or the resistance and the lower line or the support can also be observed. For calculating the price target, the widest part of the triangle showed a 65% gap, and the same was achieved once the breakout happened above the resistance level.

As this is a weekly chart, it will take time to achieve the target, but you can see how easy it becomes to trade and even calculate the target of these patterns. The only thing left is to actually ride the pattern with discipline and patience and not exit it without any exit signal.

Image 5.7: Weekly chart of Relaxo Footwears Ltd. showing the triangle pattern

Now let us look at image 5.8 where the symmetrical triangle broke on the downside on the daily chart of Nifty Bank. The symmetrical triangle broke on the downside, that is, the bears won this fight as the sellers were able to bring the price down and even break it below the pattern.

Observe that we got the required touch points on the resistance and support levels. The range started getting very tight—as the characteristics of a triangle demands—and the breakdown occurred with a bearish confirmation.

The widest part of the triangle had a range of almost 10% which became the target for the breakdown. It was easily achieved and that too very quickly.

Ascending Triangle Pattern

The second type of triangle pattern is the ascending triangle pattern, which is a bullish pattern where the buyers manage to break out above the triangle.

Image 5.9 is the daily chart of Interglobe Aviation Ltd. to understand how the ascending triangle pattern works.

The stock was already in an uptrend after which it started to move into the sideways zone. The resistance zone is flat, which means that the bears or sellers are not letting the price cross that zone while the bulls or buyers are getting stronger with every move and bringing the price up gradually. The pattern started to emerge as an ascending triangle.

Each consecutive low is higher than the previous one, which shows that the momentum is slowly building up, the fight is getting intense and overall, the bulls or buyers have started to show strength. Eventually they manage to break out above the resistance and the uptrend continues as the price keeps climbing up. The target of the pattern, which is the depth of the triangle added above the breakout level, is also achieved quite quickly.

Image 5.8: Daily chart of Nifty Bank Index where the symmetrical triangle broke on the downside

Image 5.9: Daily chart of Interglobe Aviation Ltd. depicting the ascending triangle pattern

Descending Triangle Pattern

The descending triangle pattern is bearish in nature. We already know its structure and characteristics. Now let us look at how it is used in image 5.10.

In image 5.10, there was a prior downtrend which turned into a descending triangle. The volume also behaved as it should have, that is, it dipped while the price was inside the triangle and started to pick up later around the breakdown level.

The consecutive highs were lower, and the chart showed the buyers losing strength and finding it difficult to keep the prices up. The range of the triangle pattern was around 32% which was achieved pretty quickly once the price broke down below the highlighted support level.

Image 5.10: Daily chart of Vodafone Idea Ltd. showing a descending triangle pattern

Cup and Handle Pattern

The cup and handle pattern formed on the weekly chart of Nifty 50 Index (image 5.11). The stock was already in an uptrend, which is required for a valid continuation pattern. Once it started to decline and formed a U-shape, it again got rejected near the previous high which acted as a resistance.

When it got rejected from the previous high (the level which acted as a resistance earlier too), it started to retrace and formed another small U-shape which acted as a handle of the cup.

Once the breakout happened, the target was also achieved, around 26% from the high to the depth of the cup, which was added to the above resistance level.

As it is a weekly chart, the pattern took its time to form and the target also took the required time. But the point to note is that the target was met perfectly before it started to decline again.

This is a comparatively easy to follow but really effective pattern and you will find it on many stocks. Check your favourite stocks again on the monthly, weekly and daily time frames and try to spot this pattern. Once you can spot it, check if the target was met or not. In most cases, you would notice that the target was also met. The higher the time frame, or the more time it took to form the cup and the deeper the depth of the cup, the bigger the eventual target would be.

Image 5.11: Weekly chart of Nifty 50 Index with a cup and handle pattern

VCP Pattern

Now let us see a few examples of the VCP pattern and see how we can actually trade it.

Image 5.12 is the daily chart of Tata Consultancy Services Ltd. The volatility is contracting within the base. The criterion for a valid VCP is that the stock should be in an uptrend before the base starts to form as shown in image 5.12. The consecutive falls are lower than the previous ones. The first fall of stock price went down to 14%, then 10%, and finally 8%. There was a clean breakout, the price moved up quite rapidly and gave the target of the depth of the base added to the breakout zone—similar to the cup and handle examples. It later fell back down and the same breakout zone acted as a support and moved back up again.

Image 5.12: Daily chart of Tata Consultancy Services Ltd. showing VCP

Image 5.13 is the daily chart of Indian Terrain Fashions Ltd. The price is beautifully contracting within the base and a still resistance is present from where the price keeps getting rejected. Every time it gets rejected, it forms a higher base showing that the strength of the buyers is increasing and they are not ready to let the price fall down towards the previous lows. The last contraction was also tight, and the breakout came with a much higher volume as compared to the last few weeks. We can see the 'tennis ball' example here as the price retested the breakout zone with declining volumes and moved back with increasing volumes.

Image 5.13: Daily chart of Indian Terrain Fashions Ltd. showing VCP

If you open the freezer again and again to check if the ice cream is ready or not, it will never get ready!!

6

Moving Averages

Moving averages are one of the most followed indicators by traders worldwide. Moving average is basically the average of the price. It is called 'moving' as it is calculated according to the fluctuating prices. It is used in other areas of study like the weather, population census, anything where we have a specific data and we need to see the underlying 'trend' in it.

Moving averages do not predict future trends—they reveal the underlying trend and that helps us make informed decisions. It becomes really easy to ride a trend with the help of moving averages. They smooth out the price and remove the noise of choppiness which may be present in the price action. Even during the covid pandemic when the data of the number of cases were plotted with a seven-day moving average to identify the overall trend, it helped us understand if the trend was rising or declining. Numbers and data may not be easy to understand for everyone, but it is really easy to see a line and notice where it is headed. That is the reason why moving averages are so widely used. A rising moving average indicates an uptrend and a downward sloping moving average indicates a downtrend.

Like most indicators, moving averages are a lagging indicator. The higher the period of the moving average will be, the greater will be the lag. A 200-moving average would be lagging compared to a 50-moving average. The former may be used to check the long-term trend of the stock or index, while the latter could be used to check the medium-term trend of the same.

Various traders and investors use different moving average periods but the most common ones are the 20, 50 and 200.

The 20-moving average is useful for trading short-term trends and is used frequently by swing traders. The 50-moving average is good for medium term and is used widely by positional traders. The 200-moving average is mostly used by investors who want to see the overall trend of the stock and they may add fundamental studies along with the technical study to conclude.

Let us see what these moving averages look like on a chart.

In image 6.1, on the daily chart of Indian Railway Financial Corporation Ltd., the 20-exponential moving average is moving much closer to the price as compared to the 50-exponential moving average and the 200-exponential moving average is further away as it is the long-term moving average.

Moving averages are also used to identify trend changes when one moving average converges with another.

When a short-term moving average crosses above a longer-term moving average, it confirms an uptrend or a bullish momentum indicating that the buyers are strong. Similarly, when a short-term moving average crosses below a longer term moving average, it indicates a bearish momentum letting us know that the sellers are strong.

Moving averages also act as *dynamic support* and *resistances.* When the price is trading above the moving average in an uptrend, it retraces back towards the moving average and usually bounces off it, giving us a significant entry point where the risk is minimum. When price is in a downtrend, trading below the downward sloping moving average, the price moves up and takes resistance from the moving average, giving us a chance to short the stock(sell first and book later) or book profits in case we hold that stock.

Image 6.1: Daily chart of Indian Railway Financial Corporation Ltd.

There are two types of moving averages, namely, the simple moving average (SMA) and exponential moving average (EMA).

Simple moving average (SMA): As the name suggests, these are simple moving averages which are derived by the basic formula of averages, that is, by adding the prices of the stock and dividing it by the number of prices in that set. It is the average of a given set of values over a given period of time. A simple moving average can be used mostly by investors who want to see an overall trend of the price and are not so concerned about the latest price fluctuations.

Exponential moving average (EMA): An exponential moving average gives more weightage to the recent price and therefore tends to move a bit closer to the price. It is the go-to choice of a lot of traders as they are more concerned with how the price has been moving in recent times instead of a few weeks or months back.

Here are a few examples where moving averages acted as dynamic support and resistances.

Image 6.2 is the daily chart of Siemens India Ltd. with 20-exponential moving average. On the left side, the price broke below the 20-EMA and then the same started to act as a resistance. When the price eventually broke above it, the same moving average started acting as a support and this is what we mean by dynamic support and resistance. The best part about moving averages acting as a dynamic support and resistance is that, as it is a mathematically calculated indicator, there cannot be any biases. A trader may apply a trend line or a support or resistance zone differently than other traders and may lack conviction because of that. But when a moving average acts as a dynamic support or resistance, it is same for everyone—there is no scope of confusion in it and a trader can have full conviction to trade it along with their position sizing and risk management.

Image 6.2: Daily chart of Siemens India Ltd. with 20-exponential moving average

Another example with 50-moving average can be seen in image 6.3.

In image 6.3, on the daily chart of Escorts Kubota Ltd. with 50-EMA, it acted as a support earlier (October and November in the year 2023), then it broke down below it. The same moving average started to act as a resistance multiple times later. The price finally managed to break above it and then the same moving average again started to act as a support.

Let us see the difference between EMA and SMA on a chart for a better understanding.

In image 6.4, the SMA is moving a bit far away from the price whereas the EMA is moving closer to the price as it gives more importance to the recent price action. Both these moving averages are used according to the strategy of the user and one type of moving average is not better than the other. If you want to take quick decisions and are into short-term trading, then the EMA would be more suitable as it does not lag like the SMA and turn quickly towards the price. But if you are into positional trading or investing, you may be better off using SMA as you are not concerned about the recent move, rather you want to know the true average of the price for that specific time period.

EMA is more responsive to the recent price changes and hence it becomes the favourite for most swing traders.

Image 6.3: Daily chart of Escorts Kubota Ltd. with 50-exponential moving average

Image 6.4: Daily chart of Indian Railway Financial Corporation Ltd. showing SMA and EMA

Pullback trading strategy

A pullback is basically a small retracement or dip in the price which is already in an uptrend. The small dip differs from a crash as a pullback is just like a 'breather' for the stock. It is taking a healthy rest before it restarts its upward journey.

Pullbacks are a healthy sign and they are a necessary part of a trend, as no trend can continue without pullbacks for a long period of time. So, pullbacks need not be feared. In fact, these could be great entry points for swing traders as they give the opportunity to trade into a stock at a place where the risk is minimum and upside is decent.

Often when a stock reports good earnings, we see a huge uptrend pretty quickly and then the price starts to retrace as the traders may book out their gains. But since the fundamentals of the company are good, the stock price may again start its upward journey and the dip or pullback towards the moving averages could be a great opportunity for new investors to enter. You would still need a confirmation at the moving averages like a bullish hammer, bullish engulfing, bullish harami, or a candle with a long shadow, etc. Confirmation like these add more conviction that the pullback was a genuine one and not a trend reversal (which would have broken below the moving average support too).

When investors enter after waiting for the confirmation, they may buy it a bit costly, but as the saying goes, *it is better to be a bit late to a good party than be very early to a bad one*. Entering a bit late and then riding the complete trend is always better than getting stuck in a bad trade and then *hoping* to get out with minimum loss. Hope is not a strategy. It never is.

When you buy a pullback, the stop-loss could be just below the moving average or just below the recent swing low, while the target could be the swing high, which could be two to three times away from the stop-loss zone.

The most commonly used moving average for pullback trading is the 20-EMA which is used mostly by swing traders followed by 50-EMA, which positional traders prefer.

Some people also use the 100-or 200-moving average as they may want to focus on the fundamentals of the company and are not interested in capturing small moves of 10–15% but want to stay in the stock for a longer period of time.

Here are a few examples where pullback strategy is applied.

Image 6.5 is the daily chart of Trent Ltd. with 50-EMA. It was already in an uptrend as the moving average rose upwards.

All the pullbacks towards the 50-EMA were great buying opportunities as they offered entry at a very low risk level.

Most of the time, when the price pulled back towards the moving average, a bullish engulfing pattern formed which acted as a confirmation signal giving more conviction to the trader to enter at that level.

You can use multiple approaches to exit the trade once you enter near the support or the pullback level. Some traders use the approach of exiting at the recent swing high level as that is the level where the sellers were present and booked profits, and it may happen again.

Some prefer to exit when they see a bearish sign, like a shooting star, bearish engulfing, bearish harami or a candle with a long upper shadow near the top of the trend because these act as bearish reversal setups when the uptrend changes into a downtrend and the sellers outpower the buyers.

I try to remain in the trade till the time the price is trading above the moving average. In fact, I add more positions if it there are more pullbacks and the stock price bounces off the moving average.

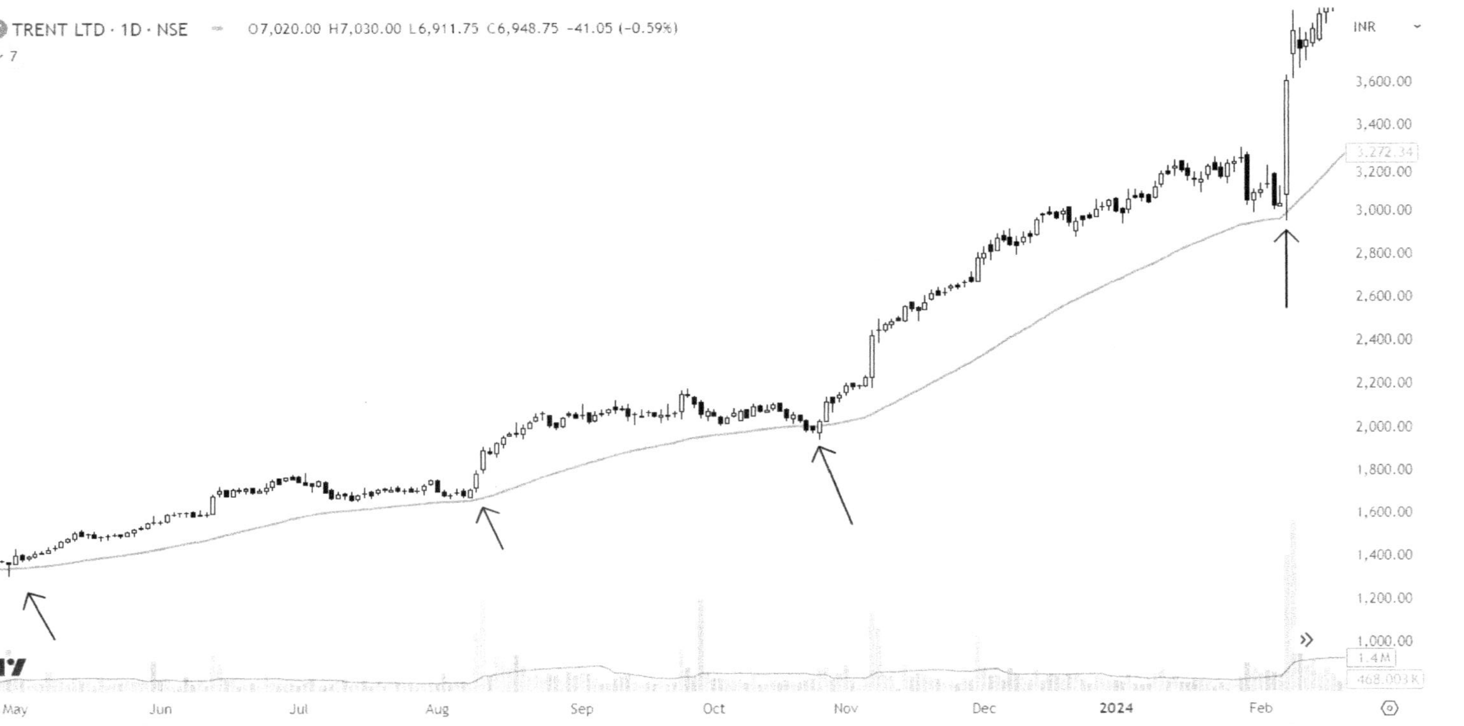

Image 6.5: Daily chart of Trent Ltd. with 50-exponential moving average

Let us study the same chart more closely and see where exactly we should enter and exit (image 6.6).

When the price pulled back and bounced off the 50-EMA for the first time, it made a bullish engulfing pattern, which indicates that the buyers are in control and even gave a confirmation right in the next candle when it traded above the high of the bullish engulfing candle. The stop-loss was just below the 50-moving average and low of the bullish engulfing candle.

Some traders may prefer to exit the trade and book profits when they notice the shooting star pattern getting confirmed at the top. The low of the shooting star also broke which indicates that the sellers are in control or they can keep holding the position and add more positions when there is another pullback with another bullish engulfing pattern at the same moving average again, which indicates that the buyers are back in control as they have engulfed the entire range of the sellers.

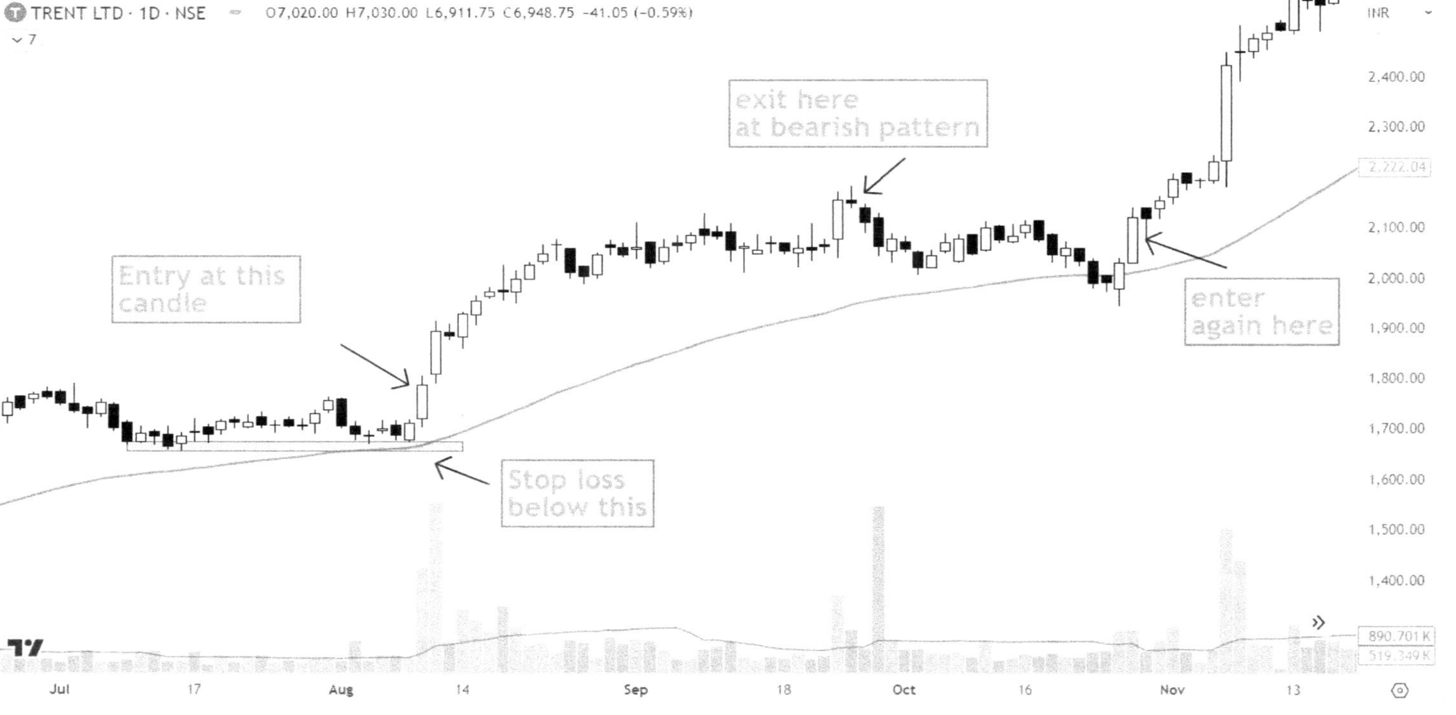

Image 6.6: Magnified version of daily chart of Trent Fashions Ltd.

Now let us look at another example using the 100-EMA.

Image 6.7 is the daily chart of Godrej Properties Ltd. with 100-EMA applied. Once the stock broke above the 100-EMA, that same moving average kept acting as a support every time the price pulled back towards it. All the pullbacks were healthy pullbacks (which are very common in uptrending stocks) and gave good entry points. As this moving average is 100-EMA, you have a bigger perspective and do not plan to book profits quickly. It is advisable to ride the move till the time the stock trades above the moving average.

A trader who uses a higher moving average like the 100-or 200-EMA ideally plans to ride it for longer. Notice that the stock has doubled since it broke above the moving average. A trader would have benefitted even more if they kept adding positions in the pullbacks as essentially, they would hold a good position size in it because of the pyramiding up every time the price retraced and bounced off the moving average as marked with arrows.

Image 6.7: Daily chart of Godrej Properties Ltd. with a 100-EMA.

Crossover strategies

A pullback strategy uses one moving average. A crossover strategy uses two or more moving averages to identify potential buy or sell signals. The moving averages are usually of different lengths and one of them crosses above or below the other one to form this strategy. The moving averages used are usually of the same type, that is, if one moving average is simple moving average, then the other one would also be a simple moving average. However, some strategies use different moving average lengths and types, too.

Crossover strategies give us a clear entry and exit signal. Any bias is not an issue as the trader does not need to draw any trend lines or plot the support and resistances. Instead, they just need to trade according to the signals given by the crossovers.

When a moving average crosses above or below the other moving average, it shows a trend change. We can take the trade accordingly. Generally, when a shorter-term moving average crosses above the longer-term moving average, it indicates a bullish signal indicating that the buyers are in control now and a trader can enter at that point. When a shorter-term moving average crosses below the longer-term moving average, a trader can book profits or if it is a futures stock, a trader can initiate a short position (selling it first and then booking later) in it as the crossover indicates that a downtrend has started.

There are a lot of variations of moving average lengths used by different traders, but the most common one is the 50-EMA and 200-EMA crossover strategy.

When 50-EMA crosses above the 200-EMA, it indicates a bullish signal(buyers are in control) and we can go long(buy) at that point. This is also known as the 'golden cross'.

Similarly, when the 50-EMA crosses below the 200-EMA, it indicates a downtrend and is a sell signal. Traders can either book their profits or initiate a short position which is also known as the 'death cross'.

Let us take a closer look at a few examples of this strategy to understand this concept better.

Image 6.8 is the daily chart of Godrej Properties Ltd. The 50-and 200-EMA (thicker line) have been plotted on it.

See how the 50-EMA crossed below the 200-EMA, giving a sell signal and demonstrated a 'death cross'. The price went from INR 1,750 all the way down to INR 1,000 at one point of time. It did not give any buy signal till the price went to INR 1,250. At that point, the sell signal got converted into buy signal. Someone who did not hold this stock got a good entry point as the 50-EMA is crossing above the longer-term moving average, that is, the 200-EMA, giving us a 'golden cross'.

The golden cross came around INR 1,300. As I write this, the price of this stock is around INR 2, 600 levels and there is no sign of bearishness so far on the chart. Anyone who bought at the golden cross would have already doubled their money on this stock.

The only thing required after entering a setup like this is to hold it with patience and discipline, which is true for any strategy, for that matter.

If you think that you may not hold stocks for a longer period initially, you can always start with a smaller time frame like 4 hours or 1 hour. Once you develop the patience to ride the trends in these time frames, then you can switch to the daily and even weekly charts. Weekly charts will give late entry and exits, but they have the power to give you multibagger (multifold) returns using this simple strategy.

This strategy could be one of the simplest to follow, yet the most effective strategy out there. Most strategies explained in this book are really easy to follow and anyone can master them quickly.

Image 6.8: Daily chart of Godrej Properties Ltd. with 50-and 200-EMA

Let us see how this strategy works on smaller time frame charts.

Image 6.9 is the 1-hour chart of United Breweries Ltd. (UBL). We can see that it gave a clear sell signal when the 50-EMA crossed below the 200-EMA, giving us a death crossover. Later it gave a buy signal too when the 50-EMA crossed above the 200-EMA and gave us a golden crossover. It is still trading comfortably in bullish territory and we need to exit only when the 50-EMA once again crosses below the 200-EMA.

Image 6.9: 1-hour chart of United Breweries Ltd. showing a death crossover and a golden crossover

Let us check this strategy on a 4-hour chart too.

Image 6.10 is the 4-hour chart of Whirlpool of India Ltd. When the first sell signal came, the stock came all the way from INR 1,700 to make a low at almost INR 1,200 zone. It gave a buy signal around INR 1,380, then reached a high at INR 1,700 again once the crossover strategy gave a buy signal when the 50 EMA crossed the 200 EMA from below, giving us a golden crossover.

It made a low near INR 1,200 again and then gave another fresh entry near INR 1,380 once again. So, you can take multiple entries and exits in the same stock.

Many of my friends trade only in index and some of them have a very small universe of stocks and prefer to trade only those. This eliminates the need to keep scanning for new stocks or to keep looking for different opportunities every other day. Instead, they have their strategy in place and focus on a very small list of stocks and just concentrate on execution.

Image 6.10: 4-hour chart of Whirlpool of India Ltd. showing multiple points of entry and exit

Like in image 6.11, if you get a good stock which is trending, you can capture great returns by using this strategy. When the golden crossover came in the Larsen and Toubro Ltd. stock, it was around INR 1,800. The stock doubled in less than two years from there. It did not give any exit signal and is still going great so far.

Image 6.11: Daily chart of Larsen and Toubro Ltd. showing a golden cross

Let us check a 15-min chart too and see how this strategy works on a smaller time frame.

In image 6.12, the 15 minute-chart of United Breweries Ltd., there are multiple entry and exit signals and the overall moves are really choppy. You can use the crossover in smaller time frame charts too, but smaller time frames usually have choppy and random moves. It would be best to stick to higher time frames if you want to get better results as a swing trader.

There are some points to keep in mind while using the crossover strategy.

Moving average crossover strategies are relatively easy to follow. As they depend on crossovers for an entry or exit signal, the signals are usually a bit delayed and you may end up giving back a part of the profits before finally exiting the positions. This may not be a big deal for a swing or positional trader but if someone has a mindset of booking quick profits, they may feel that this strategy does not fulfil their requirements.

You can get great returns with this strategy but it works best only in trending markets. If the markets are choppy or if we switch to shorter time frames, we may not get the expected results.

Though we can use this strategy in multiple time frames, this strategy may fail to work in volatile or range bounce markets.

Moving averages have an in-built quality to reduce the noise as they take the averages of the price which could be a good thing. But it can be a disadvantage too as they move slowly and tend to give late entry and exit signals.

These are a few things which we need to keep in mind before applying this strategy and see if it suits our temperament, risk appetite, mindset, etc.

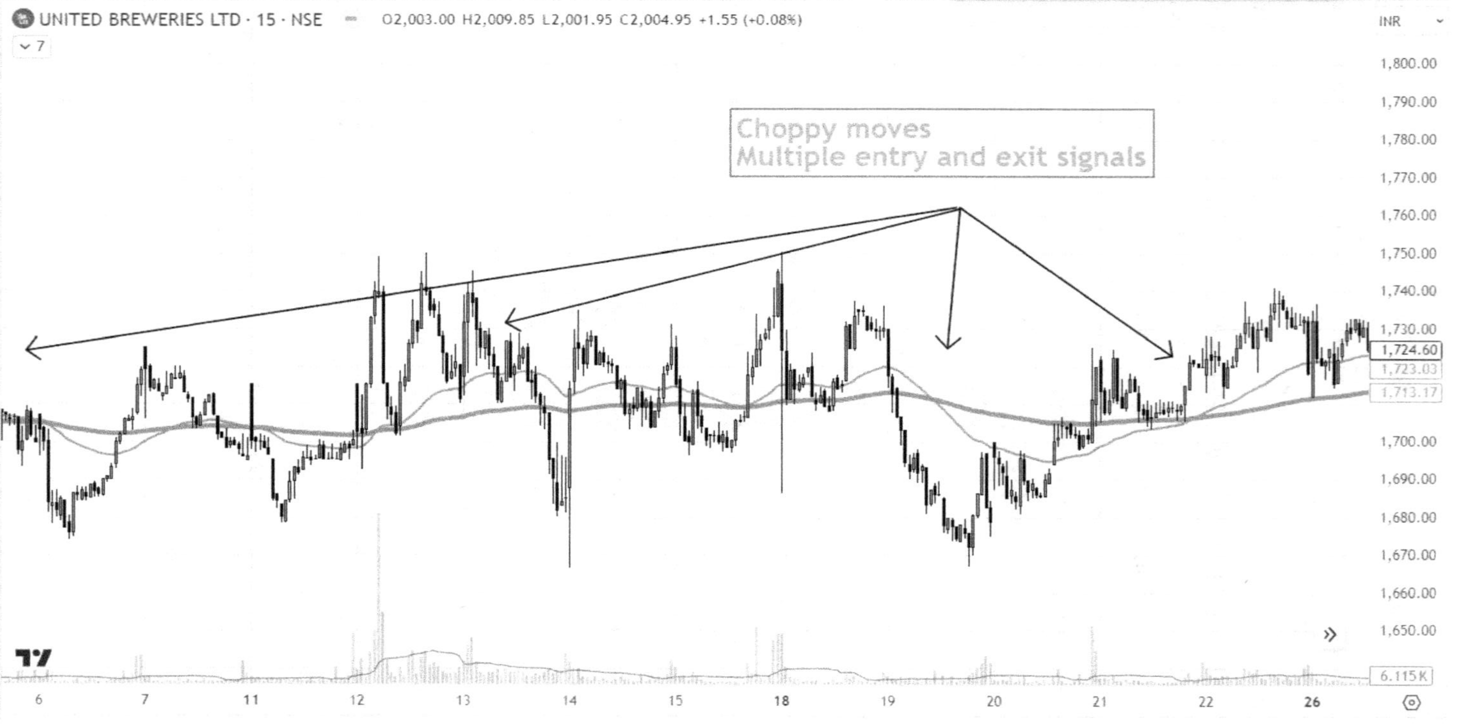

Image 6.12: 15 minute-chart of United Breweries Ltd. showing crossover strategy

Complex strategies are only good for teaching.
Money is made with simple strategies combined with discipline
and patience.

7

Heikin Ashi and Supertrend

When you trade, you want your strategy to be the most simple to follow and execute. I always say,

"We are in the markets to make money and not to write a thesis."

This is my favourite strategy and can become your favourite strategy too. Almost all my students tell me that they use this strategy so many years after they first learnt about this strategy from me. This strategy will eliminate all kinds of confusion which a new trader has—when to enter a stock, till when to ride it, and exactly when to exit. You will be amazed to see how simple to follow, yet effective this strategy is. Even if you do not follow any other strategy, but are able to focus on this single strategy, you can do wonders in swing trading. Your results will actually improve by a huge margin and the best part about this strategy is that it gives you a clear signal for entry and exit on its own. You will not need to ask anyone or confirm with others about your trades. This strategy will tell you everything in the most straightforward way.

I find it really funny when I see people plot nine to ten indicators on a chart and then struggle to find the price which gets buried underneath all the indicators. I do not blame them—even I was like that when I started learning about the markets. I thought that more is better—the more indicators I would apply to the chart, the better understanding I would have of the price action, or at least one of the indicators would fit in perfectly that would make me a profitable trader. The issue was that I always felt overwhelmed and got stuck in analysis-paralysis and could not put on a trade at all. That was when I realised the need to simplify things to achieve results. I kept on searching for better and easier ways to navigate the markets. I read a lot of books, watched videos, attended many workshops and finally stumbled upon the better candlesticks—the Heikin Ashi candle.

HEIKEN ASHI

'Heikin Ashi' means 'average bar' in Japanese. By using Heikin Ashi charts, you make it easy to follow the trend of a particular stock by smoothening out the chart as they average the price action compared to the usual choppiness of a basic candlestick chart.

Open of a Heikin Ashi candle
= (Open of previous candle + Close of previous candle)/2

So, the Heikin Ashi candle opens from the middle of the previous candle.

Close of a Heikin Ashi candle
= (Open + Low + High + Close of current candle)/4

Let us understand what different types of Heikin Ashi candle sticks look like on a chart and what they indicate.

1. Green or white candle indicates an uptrend (the colour will vary according to the charting website/platform that you use).

2. Red or black candle indicates a downtrend.

3. Hollow or green candles with no lower shadow indicate a strong uptrend. It signals traders to keep riding the trend. If it was a basic candlestick chart, it would have a lot of bearish candles in between a few gap ups or gap downs, which usually confuses a trader. But with Heikin Ashi, following the trend is much easier.

4. Small body with upper and lower shadows indicates that the trend can reverse from this point on. Just like we get a doji candle in a normal candlestick chart, this type of candle indicates indecision and the trend may change from this point on. It also signals that the strong momentum in a particular stock has been lost. It is always better to wait for confirmation on either side when this type of candle forms and then trade accordingly.

5. Filled or red candles with no higher shadows identify a strong downtrend. This indicates strong bearishness indicating that the sellers are really strong. Do not buy in this scenario and keep riding your short positions if you have any, that is, keep holding the short positions (positions in which we first sell and book later at a desired profit).

Let us understand more about Heikin Ashi candlesticks now with the help of a few charts from the Indian markets.

The normal candlesticks daily chart of Nifty is shown in image 7.1.

If we switch to Heikin Ashi candlesticks, the same chart will look like image 7.2.

Just by looking at these two charts, you can easily see the simplicity in Heikin Ashi charts. Look how beautifully the trend has been smoothened out.

"The less noise there is in the charts, the better would be our trades."

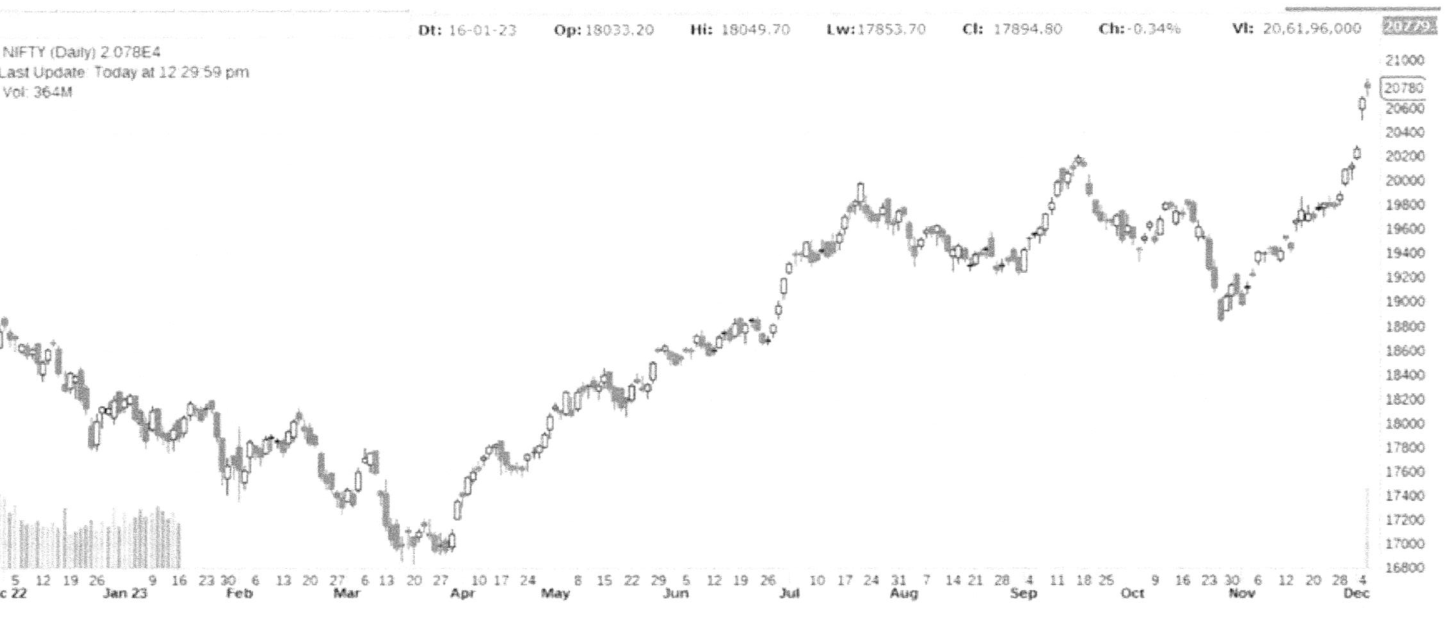

Image 7.1: Daily chart of Nifty showing normal candlesticks

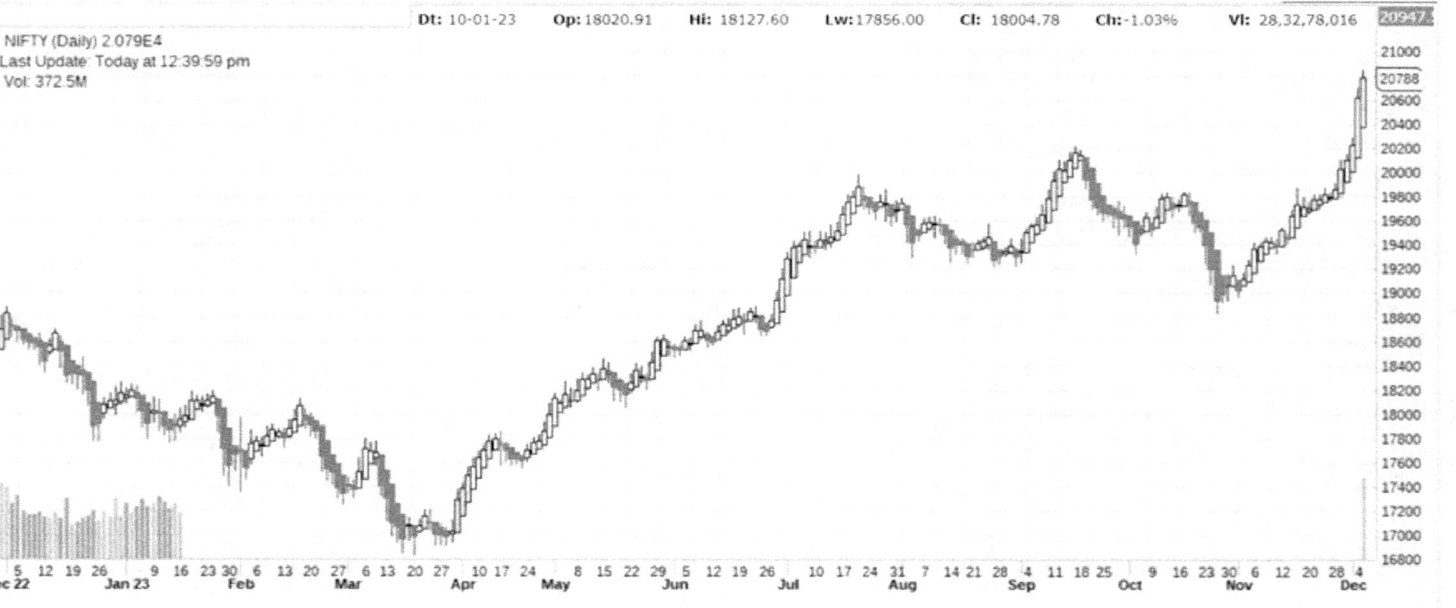

Image 7.2: Heikin Ashi candlesticks on the daily chart of Nifty

Let us check out Bank Nifty's charts using basic and Heikin Ashi candlesticks.

Now that we know what are Heikin Ashi charts, let's look at supertrend indicator.

SUPERTREND INDICATOR

It is an indicator developed by Olivier Seban which plots a line on the chart which acts as a dynamic support and resistance, similar to moving averages. You can apply this indicator on Heikin Ashi chart to get a super easy but super effective swing trading strategy.

The supertrend indicator reveals the following

1. When price is trading above the supertrend line, it indicates that the stock is trending upwards. The supertrend is green when this happens.
2. Similarly, when the price trades below the supertrend, it shows that the trend is down as the supertrend turns red(colors may vary according to the charting platform that you use, but most of the platforms use these colors).
3. When the price retraces back to the supertrend and bounces, it acts as a dynamic support and resistance as well.
4. It is a complete indicator in itself, which means that we do not need to combine it with any other indicator to trade.
5. Supertrend combines multiplier (a predefined measure that adjusts the supertrend line closely or loosely, depending on the value) and average true range (ATR) (the average high and low of the instrument over a certain period) to calculate its value.
6. When the supertrend moves from above to below the price, or vice versa, it indicates that the trend has changed.
7. The multiplier changes the sensitivity of the supertrend to the price. A higher multiplier means that the supertrend

will be less affected by the price and vice versa. It can help
in avoiding false breakouts or breakdowns, but we will get
the signal late in case of a trend change.

If we keep the multiplier to a lower setting, it will result in quick
signals to the trend changes, but we can get a lot of false breakouts
and breakdowns along the way. So, we have to manage it according
to our needs and trading style. (I prefer keeping it at '2'.)

In the normal candlestick chart (image 7.3), you can see that it
can get a bit 'noisy', that is, even in a uptrend, there may be a lot of
bearish candles and gap downs which can confuse a trader. Whereas
the Heikin Ashi candlestick chart (image 7.4) shows a smooth trend.
The absence of gaps makes the trend much better to look at and
there are fewer chances of getting confused by individual candles.
Let us look at some Heikin Ashi charts with supertrend indicator
applied to them.

Image 7.5 is the same Nifty chart that we had seen earlier using
Heikin Ashi candles. In image 7.6, we have applied supertrend
indicator with the settings of (10, 2) where '10' is ATR and '2' is
the multiplier. ATR is the average true range and it calculates the
average range of the price movement in a given time frame. So,
if we increase this number in the settings, it moves close to the
price and if we reduce the number, it moves away from the price
and gives a delayed signal.

If we reduce the multiplier in the settings, it makes the
indicator more reactive and it starts moving very close to the price.
Alternately, if we increase it, it moves away from the price and
hence it gives less false signals, but increases the chances of hitting
a bigger stop-loss as the indicator moves away from the price and
you will get delayed signals.

So after thorough back testing and playing with the settings, a
setting of (10, 2) works best for the supertrend indicator.

Image 7.3: Daily chart of Bank Nifty with basic candlesticks

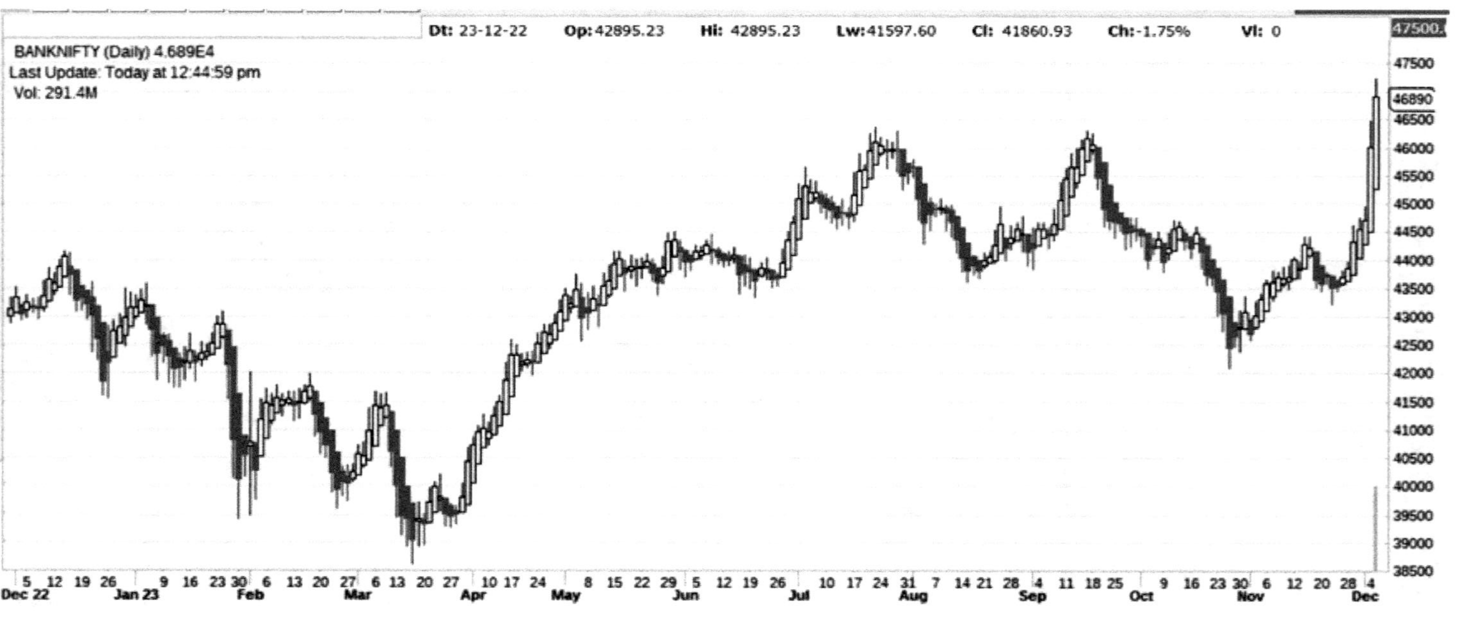

Image 7.4: Daily chart of Bank Nifty with Heikin Ashi candlesticks

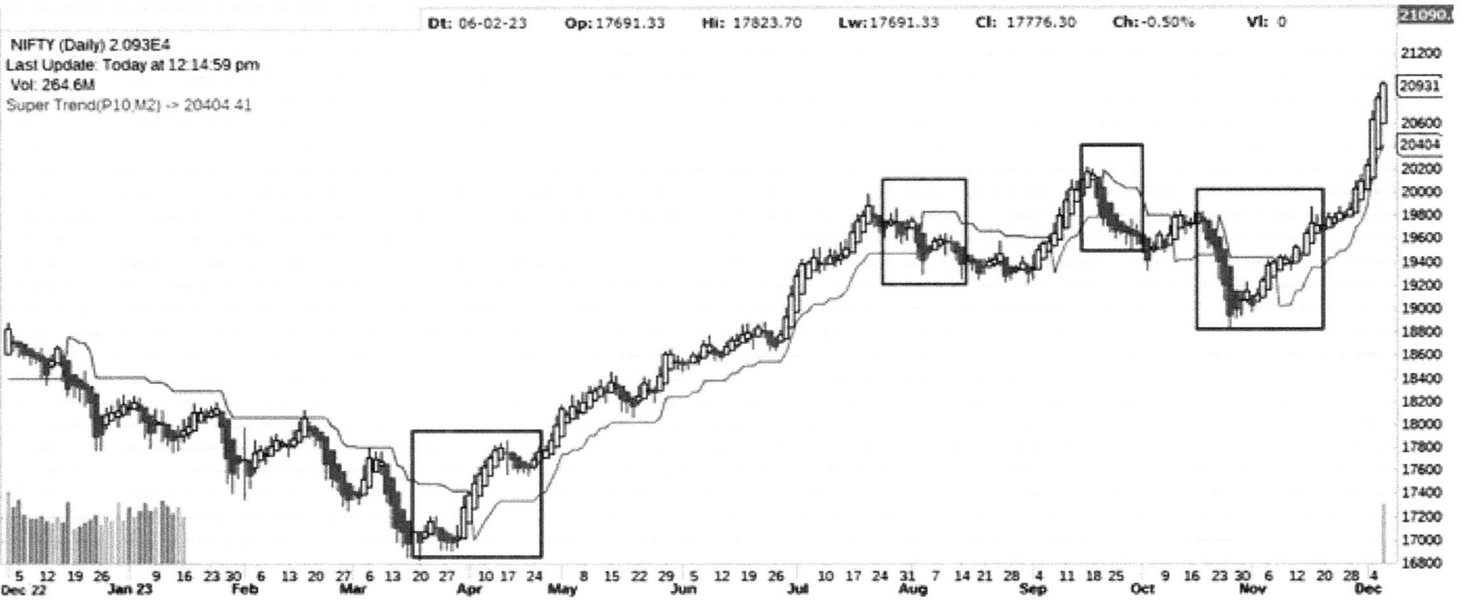

Image 7.5: Daily chart of Nifty using Heikin Ashi candles

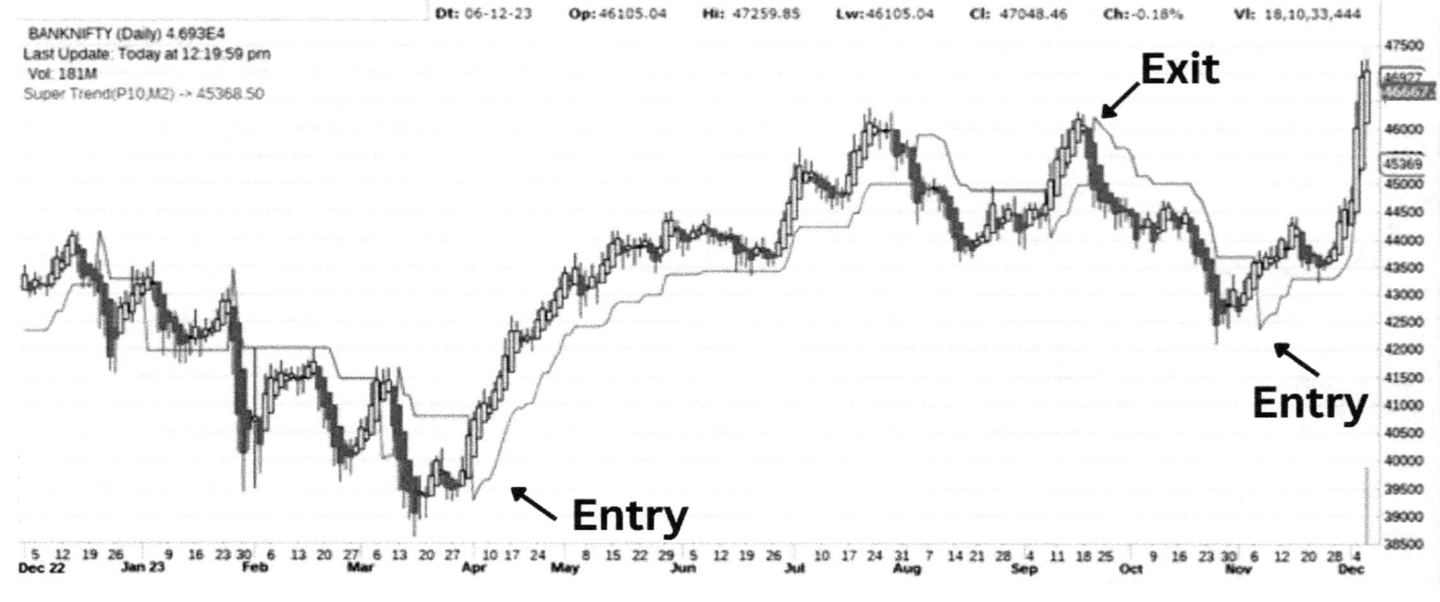

Image 7.6: Daily chart of Bank Nifty with supertrend indicator showing clear entry and exit signals

The supertrend indicator is clearly giving a buy and sell signal. It would be a buy signal when the supertrend turns green from red and goes below the price, and sell signal when the supertrend goes above the price and turns red. Image 7.6 shows the points of entry and exit on the chart.

Through the Nifty images, you could capture such big moves without any confusion. You did not have to ask anyone the most important questions

- When to Buy
- Till when to hold, and
- When to Exit

This strategy, which combines Heikin Ashi candles with Supertrend indicator, is doing that for you in the simplest way possible! It can be used on any time frame, but I prefer using it with the daily time frame. We can check the overall price structure of the chart by considering higher time frames like monthly and weekly charts and then finally switch to daily time frame for the final execution of the trades.

In image 7.7 the supertrend is giving clear entry and exit signals.

Another thing to notice in image 7.7 is the way supertrend is acting as a dynamic support and resistance.

Notice how the price moved up and touched the red supertrend during a bearish move and then fell back down again. When the price was in uptrend, it retraced downwards, bouncing off the green supertrend and bouncing up again. This way, it becomes really easy to manage the positions. Aggressive traders can add to positions when the price comes and bounces off the supertrend.

There is another important thing to keep in mind while using this swing trading strategy. You would have noticed that when the supertrend turns from bearish to bullish (buyers take control over sellers) or vice versa, it does that with an angle. Sometimes

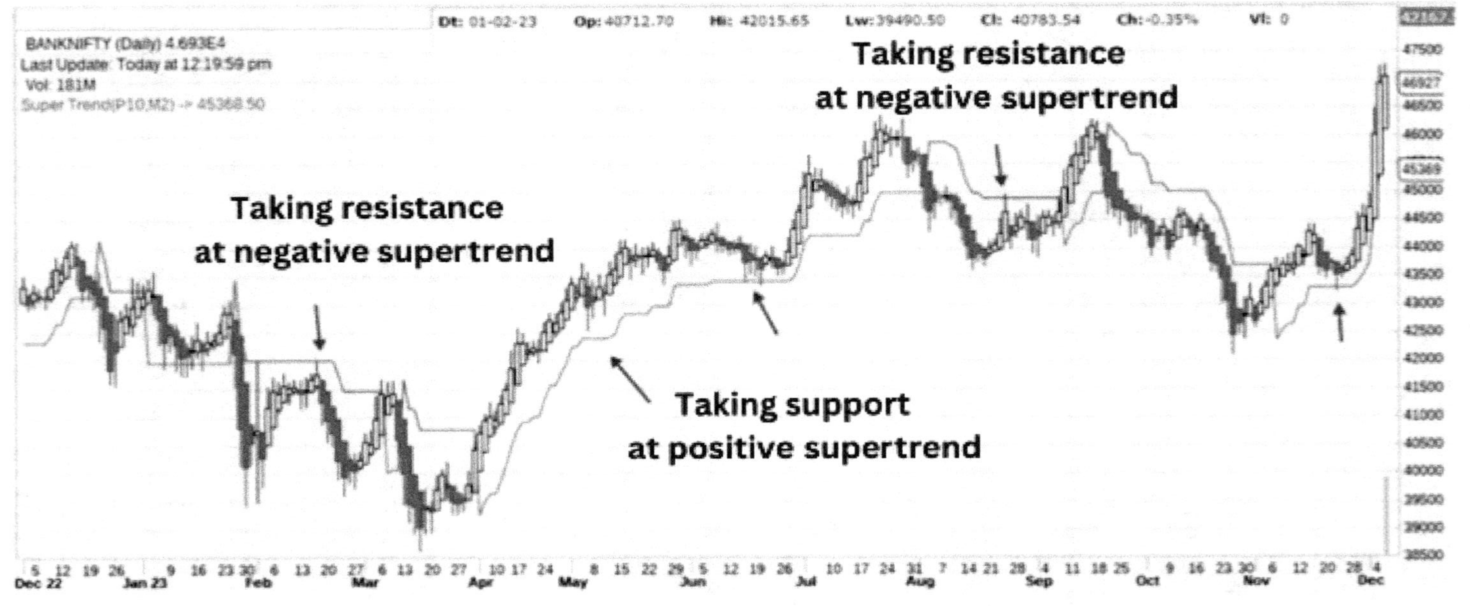

Image 7.7: Daily chart of Bank Nifty showing supertrend acting as support and resistance

the angle is flat and sometimes it is sharp, 45 degree or more. This indicates the momentum of the price. If the angle is higher, it shows higher momentum in the price and we can take the trade accordingly. If the angle is flat, it shows that the buyers or sellers (depending on the change in supertrend) are not that strong at the current moment.

Let us see the example of the change of angles on a chart.

In image 7.8 on the daily chart of Tata Motors Ltd., when the angle was flat, the price kept moving in a sideways zone as there was a lack in momentum which means that the buyers and sellers are equally strong and there is no clear trend. But once the angle eventually came, it gave a good move.

In image 7.9, the monthly chart of Nifty, you can see that this strategy works on higher time frames too. You just need to have the conviction to sit with patience.

Notice how the high angle results in good moves, indicating that the buyers are strong and flat angles lead to sideways moves which shows that the buyers and sellers are equally strong and no clear trend is present with supertrend acting as a dynamic support. All the above-mentioned aspects can be seen here in image 7.9 itself.

You may wonder if this works on smaller time frames too, and if we can use this strategy in intraday trading. Yes, you can! But, if the market is choppy, it may give false signals, and it is best to trade on the daily charts.

Image 7.8: Daily chart of Tata Motors Ltd. showing the angles of supertrend

Image 7.9: Monthly chart of Nifty

Image 7.10 is an example of Nifty's 15-minute chart with Heikin Ashi candles and supertrend indicator. As you can see, it showed moves in intraday trades as well. You can try this same strategy on smaller time frames on index charts as well as your favourite stocks to see how it holds up.

Now let us apply this strategy to some of the stocks. Image 7.11 is the daily chart of BSE Ltd. As you can see, the supertrend gave a buy signal at 450 level and continued in an uptrend. The price touched 2600 levels. It gave the exit signal once but soon after showed the entry signal again. This is also another important point to note. Whenever a stock gives an exit signal, keep it on your watchlist for any re-entry signals.

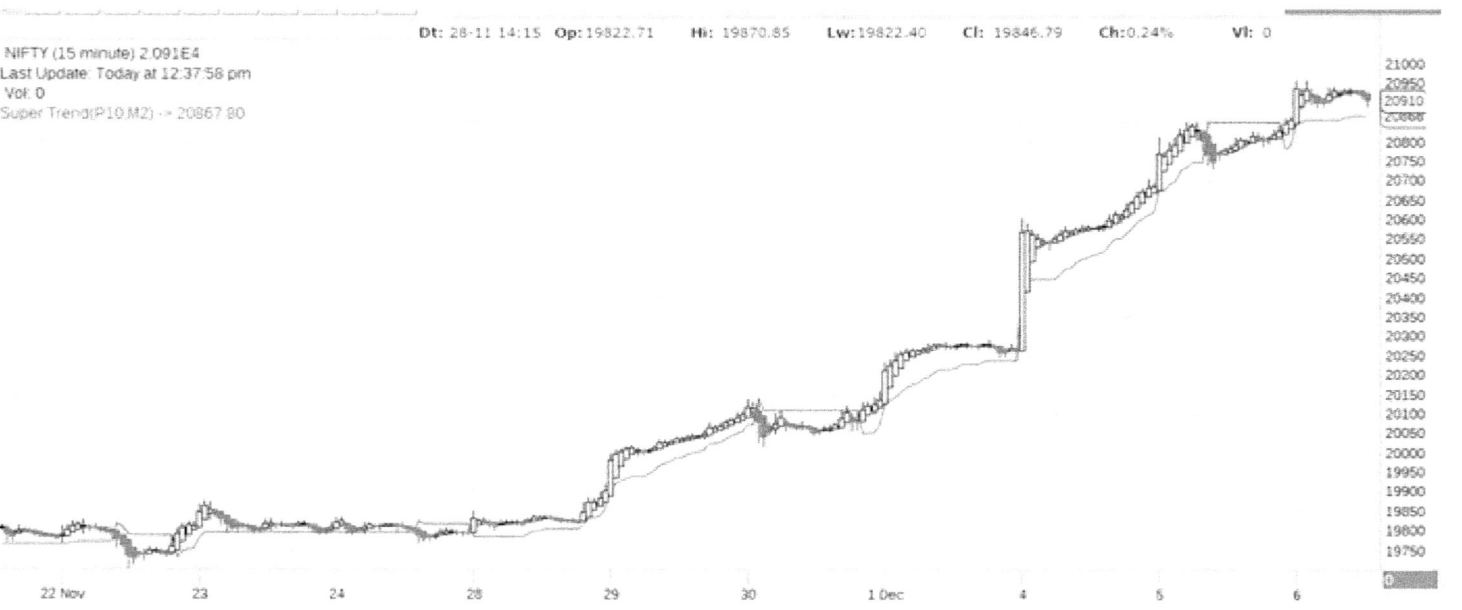

Image 7.10: 15-minute chart of Nifty with Heikin Ashi candles and supertrend indicator of Nifty

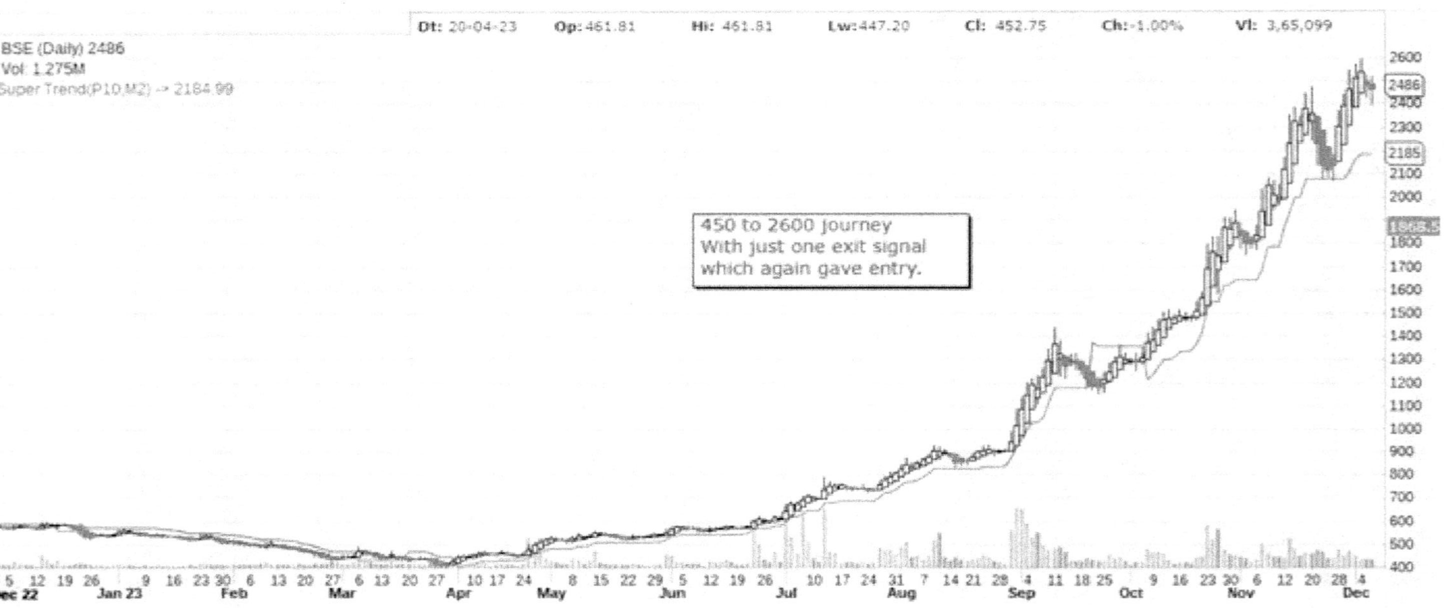

Image 7.11: Daily chart of BSE Ltd.

Image 7.12 is the daily chart of ITC Ltd. where you can observe the journey of ITC from 350 to 480 levels. It took multiple supports at the supertrend line and continued to move up. When the exit signal finally came, there was a proper angle, then it fell and did not give another re-entry for a long time. In the latest move, we can see that it is giving a fresh entry along with a proper angle which means that the buyers are now very strong (as the supertrend turned positive with a steep angle).

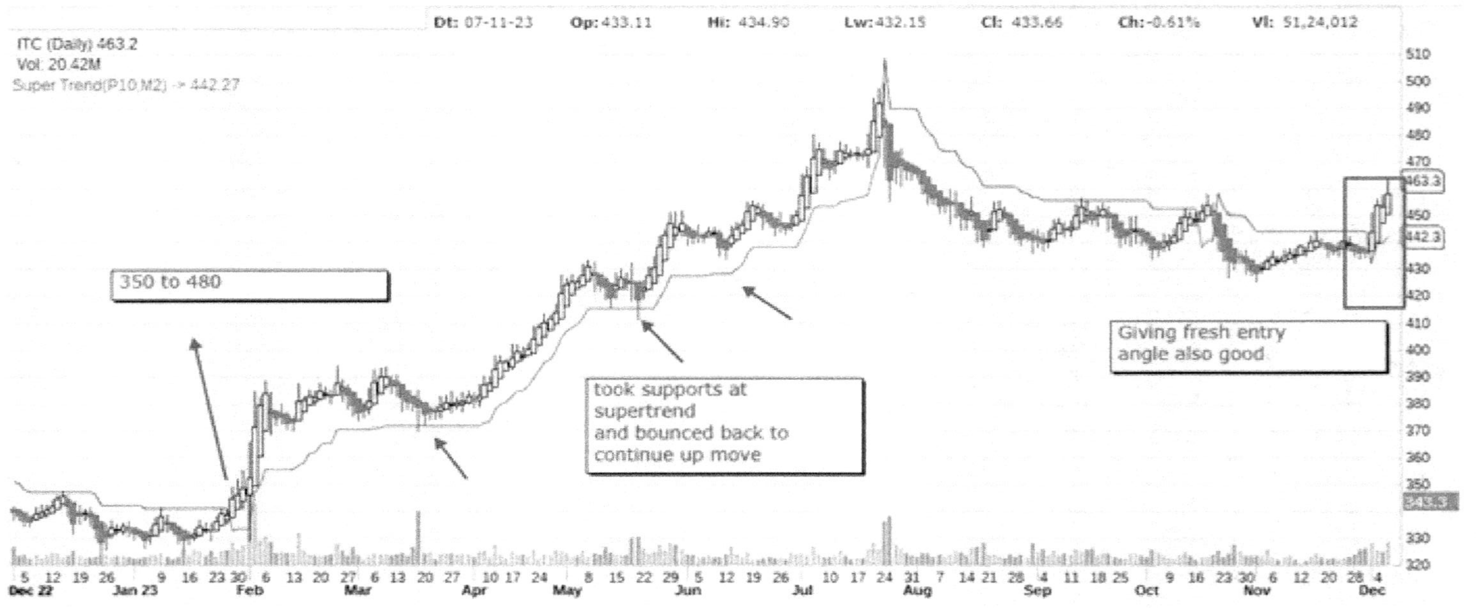

Image 7.12: Daily chart of ITC Ltd. with supertrend indicator

Image 7.13 is the daily chart of Reliance Industries Ltd. I want to draw your attention to the square boxes. Look at the way the supertrend indicator has given clear entry and exits here at a proper angle. We will not be able to buy at the bottom and sell exactly at the top, but that holds true for any kind of strategy.

Always try to ride the big swing move between an entry and exit signal; do not try to predict the exact top or bottom.

Notice how the chart clearly tells you to exit, saving your capital and time. Many traders exit a stock, then keep trying to reenter it without any proper entry signal and they keep getting chopped by the moves of the stock or indices.

This strategy is a complete trading system in itself. It will clearly tell you when to buy, hold, and exit. You do not need to 'predict' anything here—just follow your system and let this strategy tell you when to take action.

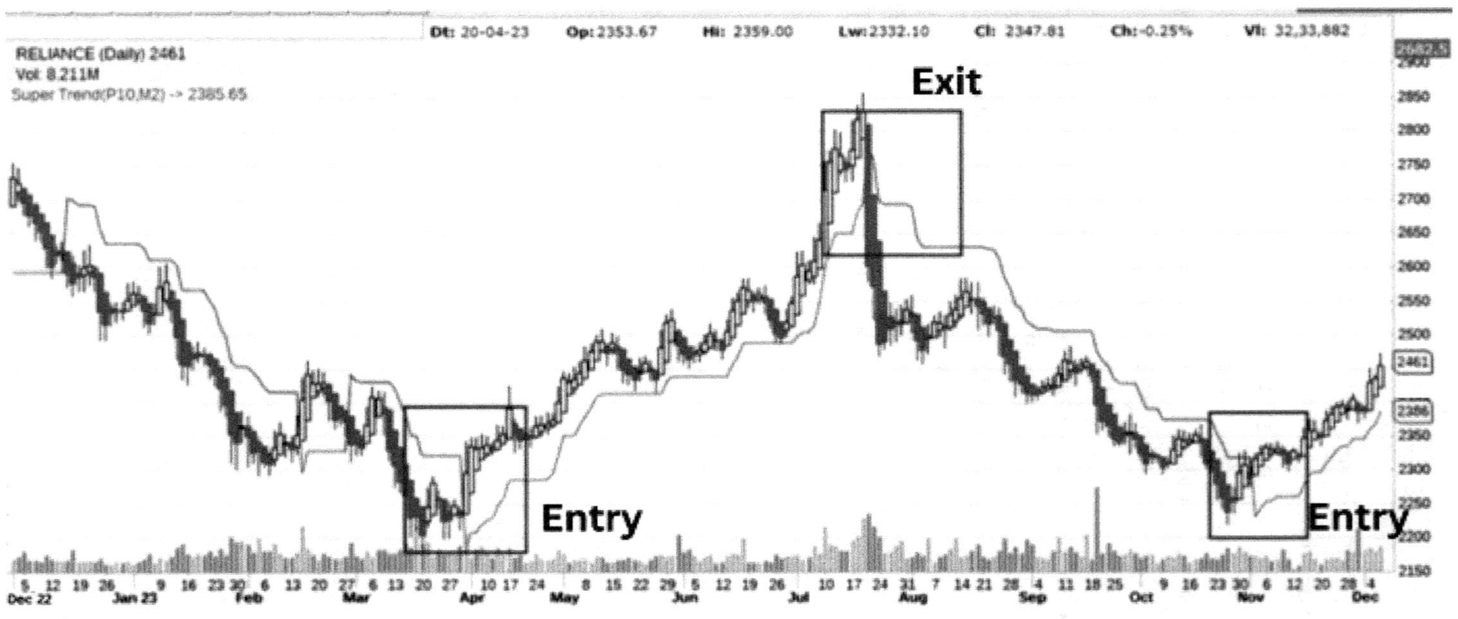

Image 7.13: Daily chart of Reliance Industries Ltd. with supertrend indicator

Image 7.14 is the daily chart for Power Finance Corporation Ltd. The price rode up from 130 to 378 levels. There were two exit signals on this journey, but both were weak exit signals (angle was not higher) which demonstrates that the sellers were not strong enough to change the trend of the stock. When the supertrend turns bearish but gives a flat signal, it is ok to keep riding the trade as most of the times it will again turn green (upward move will continue).

Image 7.15 is the daily chart of Bajaj Finance Ltd. There are clear entry and exit signals. The most important thing here is that even though we have just entered it, the angle is missing. As soon as you get a higher angle in it, in one or two days, it can give a very good opportunity for entry. This is how you should wait for your setups. Most of the time the angle will build up in one or two days itself and sometimes it can take longer time. But it is always better to wait for that higher angle because if the angle is not present, the stock may get stuck in a sideways move or even continue its downward move turning the supertrend red (bearish) indicating that the sellers are again in control.

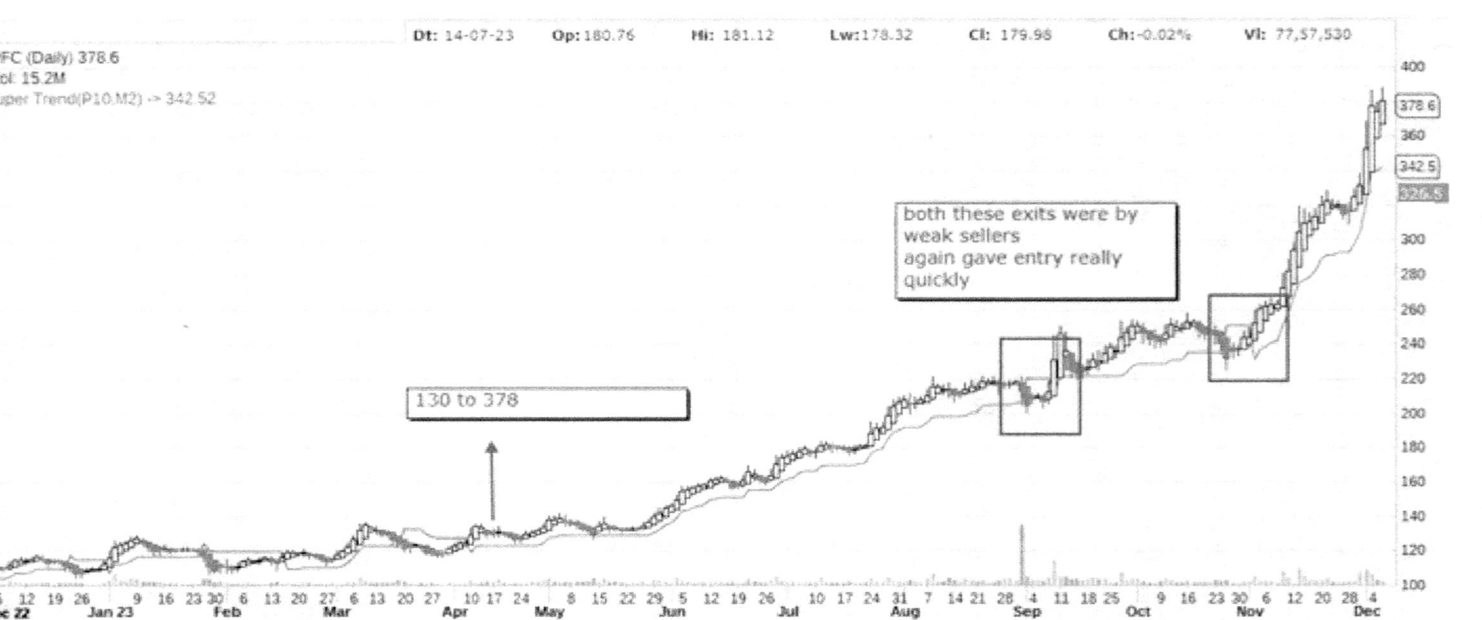

Image 7.14: Daily chart of Power Finance Corporation Ltd.

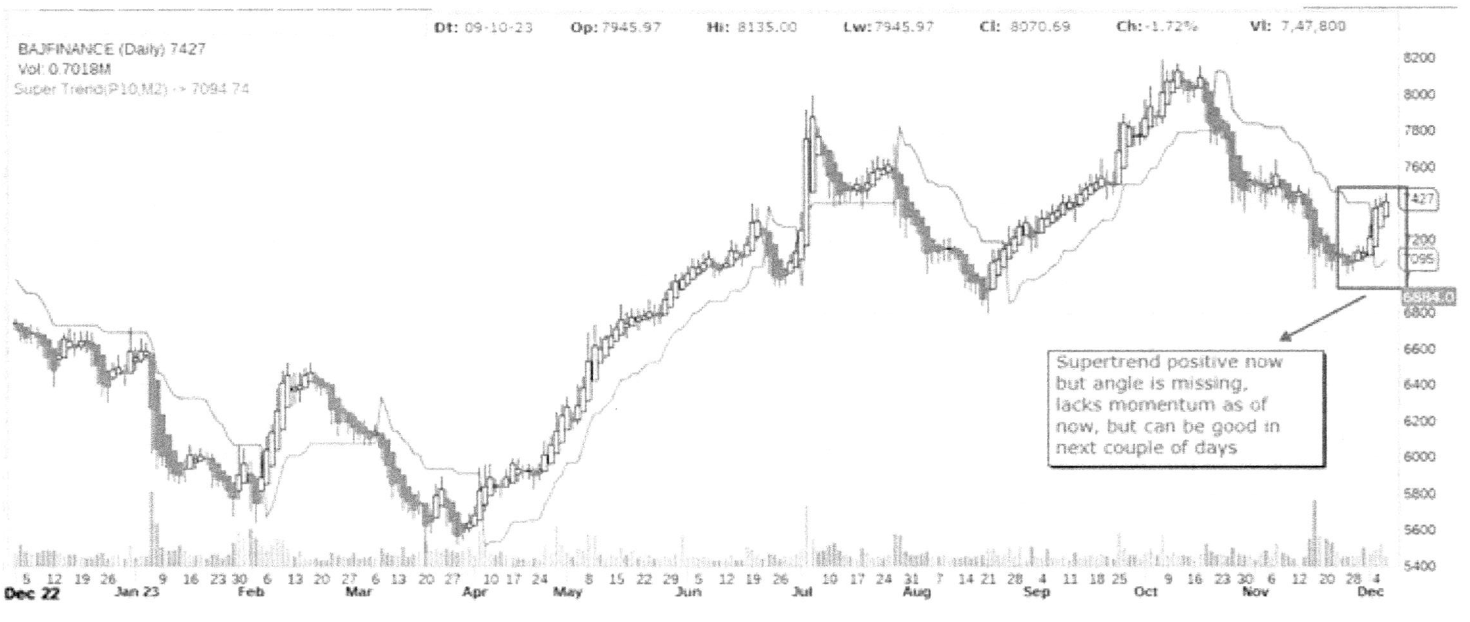

Image 7.15: Daily chart of Bajaj Finance Ltd.

In image 7.16, we can see how the stock price for Metals and Minerals Trading Corporation of India Ltd. (MMTC) rode from 33 to 80. I want to highlight here that sometimes the supertrend may turn green (bullish) which shows that buyers have entered, but the angle remains flat. At this point, wait for it to get a proper angle. Once you get it, enter at that point. Keep it on your watchlist and wait for that perfect entry signal (with higher angle).

Here it is giving a perfect entry (latest move) and you can see how quickly the angle came along with the supertrend turning bullish from bearish (red to green) showing that the buyers have entered with momentum. This is exactly what you need and it shows that the trend has changed to bullish along with proper momentum now. These kinds of signals can give you a great move, maximising our chances of bigger profits.

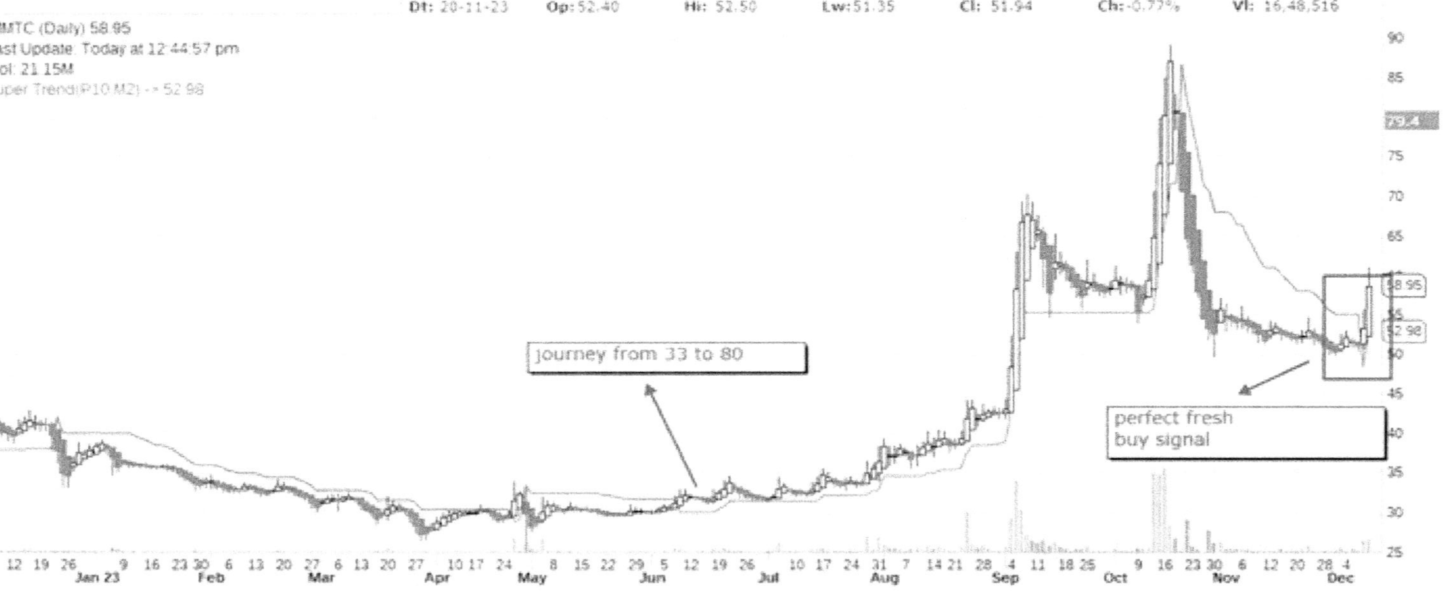

Image 7.16: Daily chart of MMTC Ltd. where it turned bearish to bullish.

Image 7.17 is the weekly chart for Delhivery. Since its Initial Public Offer (IPO) happened, there has been a lot of buzz around it. Everyone who missed getting the IPO allotment rushed to buy it as soon as it got listed in the primary exchange.

One rule I follow in such cases is to switch to the weekly chart and apply the same strategy. In most cases, I found that the newly listed stock never gives a buy signal. If some stock does, it keeps getting more momentum but most often, it bounces for a few days and then just remains in a sideways move to a bearish trend (there was no clear trend and ultimately the sellers won, moving the price down) and wastes our precious time and money.

It is always better to buy a bit late, but only with a confirmed signal. I still do not understand why people rush to buy stocks as if the market is going to close just before they buy it and it will not open for the next few years.

In the weekly chart of Delhivery (image 7.17), it never gave a buy signal when it got listed. In fact, it dropped 50% from the listing price. Anyone who bought on the listing day or later would have panicked and sold or would be averaging down with every 5–10% drop in price, and eventually gave up and exited when it cracked 50% from the top.

But if you followed this strategy, you would have just waited on the sidelines, looking for the perfect signal to enter. This way, you not only save your money but also your time. Buying something like this on impulse and then hoping to get back your cost price while cursing yourself and regretting your decision with each passing day would not be advisable. It is always better to invest in a stock which has given a proper entry signal and is in upward momentum.

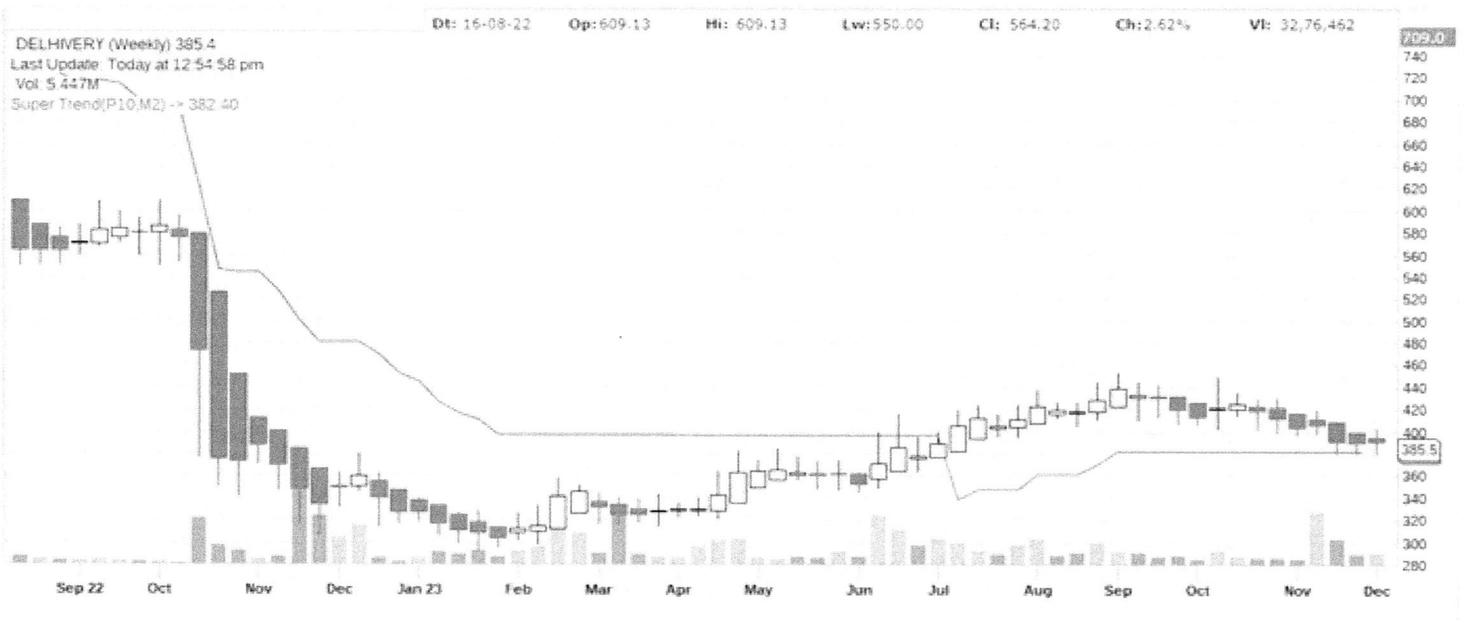

Image 7.17: Weekly chart of Delhivery

In image 7.18, we can see a similar pattern. Nykaa E-Retail Ltd. got listed with a lot of buzz and a lot of retailers had the fear of missing out when they did not get the allotment. What do people do when they fear missing out on an opportunity? You guessed it right! They jump on to buy it as soon as they get a chance.

If someone bought Nykaa at the time of listing, they would have wasted more than one year of their precious time and seen their capital get eroded by more than 50%. When someone buys a stock with high hopes and dreams amid all the hype created around it, only to see it crack more than 50% it is not a good state to be in. It crushes the dreams of the trader and even though they may have a few positions which may be profitable, the losing position will always keep bugging them on a daily basis. Whenever they open their portfolio, their focus would always be on that losing stock.

According to neurobiology, we experience a financial loss 250% more intensely than an equivalent financial gain. So, this is my humble advice to all of you—please follow the process and do not get influenced by your emotions or what is looking hot at the moment.

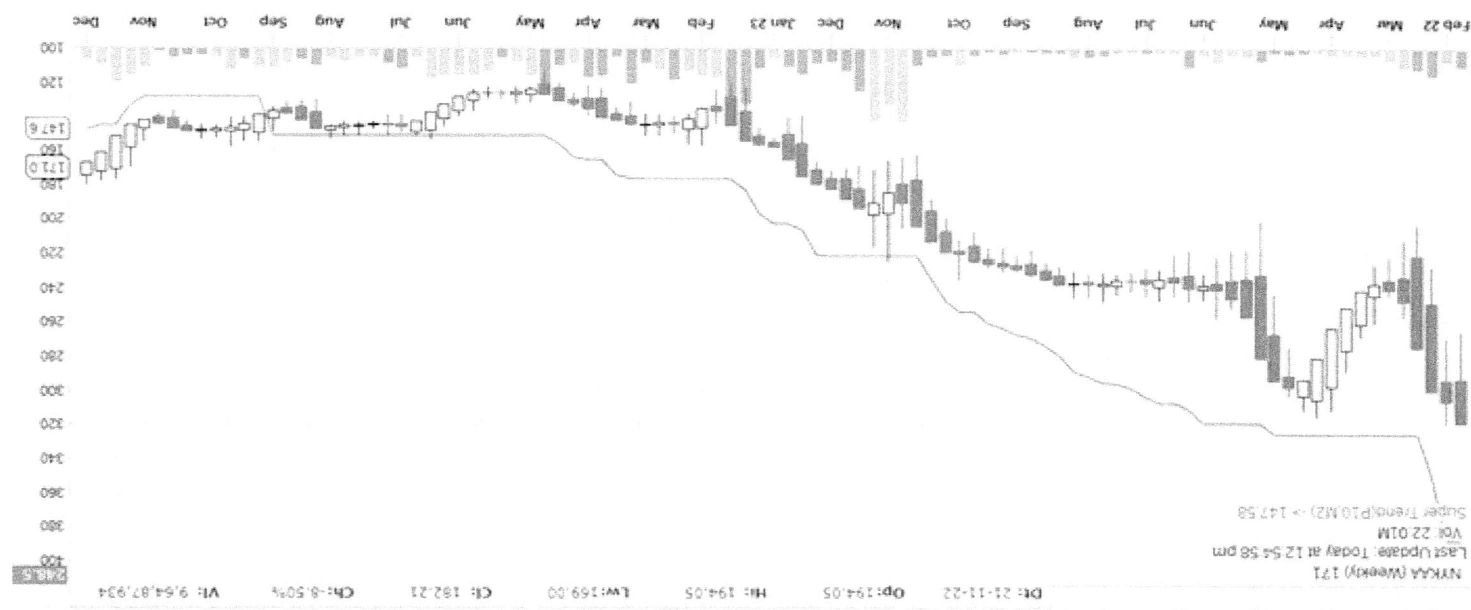

Image 7.18: Weekly chart for Nykaa E-Retail Ltd.

In image 7.19 which is Zomato Ltd.'s weekly chart, we can see the same thing. I want to show you a lot of examples of the same pattern so that it gets engraved in your minds and the next time you get excited to enter a hot and sizzling stock, you actually ask yourself if you will buy it according to a system or just because everyone else may be excited to buy it.

Perhaps you are emotionally attached to a company and you really want to be a part of its growth story. Sure, no one is stopping you, but be a part of the 'growth' story, not the entire story. Swing trading is all about staying with the trend until the end, when it bends. So, keep your favourite stocks on your watch-list and enter only when they give a proper entry signal (supertrend turning positive which shows that buyers have entered with momentum) and keep riding them till the time the supertrend is green.

In this example, we can see that the stock price gave a very nice opportunity for entry near May 2023 around the price of 55 and went on to give more than 100% returns from there without any exit signal in between. The current price of this stock is at 160 as I type this, still there is no exit signal in sight. This strategy is simple, but not easy as it will give very clear entry, hold and exit signals but it will demand your patience and discipline.

Image 7.19: Weekly chart of Zomato Ltd.

Next is the weekly chart of BSE Ltd. (image 7.20). Initially, it moved from 160 to 800 levels without any exit. When the exit eventually came, it went down for one year. It saved time and capital as it did not give any re-entry signal. Remember that you can always keep your best-performing stocks on your watch-list for future possible entries.

Once it gave another clear entry signal (green supertrend with proper angle), it went up from 500 to 2500 and the trend is still going strong as I type this chapter! Yes, I know it sounds too simple, because it is! The hard part about this strategy could be to actually ride these kinds of moves with patience and discipline. That is true for any kind of strategy. So why not follow a simple strategy and actually work on your mindset instead of searching for a new strategy every other day?

Now let us take a look at the daily chart of Ugar Sugar Works Ltd. in image 7.21. Once it gave a proper buy signal and went from 90 to 130, it gave a clear exit signal too. And once the chart shows an exit signal, just exit! Do not sit there and 'hope' for it to keep moving up for eternity. Everything moves in cycles, and nothing can keep moving up without any pullbacks or even major falls.

Here we can see that once the price movement gave an exit signal, it went back to even below the initial buy point of 90 and has not given any fresh entry signal yet, saving both our time and money.

Another thing to notice here is how the bearish supertrend kept acting as a resistance once the price was in downtrend. The price kept bouncing up but was rejected from the supertrend as it was acting as a dynamic resistance because the sellers were active at the level. This level earlier acted as a dynamic support when buyers were buying when the trend was up and supertrend was bullish.

Image 7.20: Weekly chart of BSE Ltd.

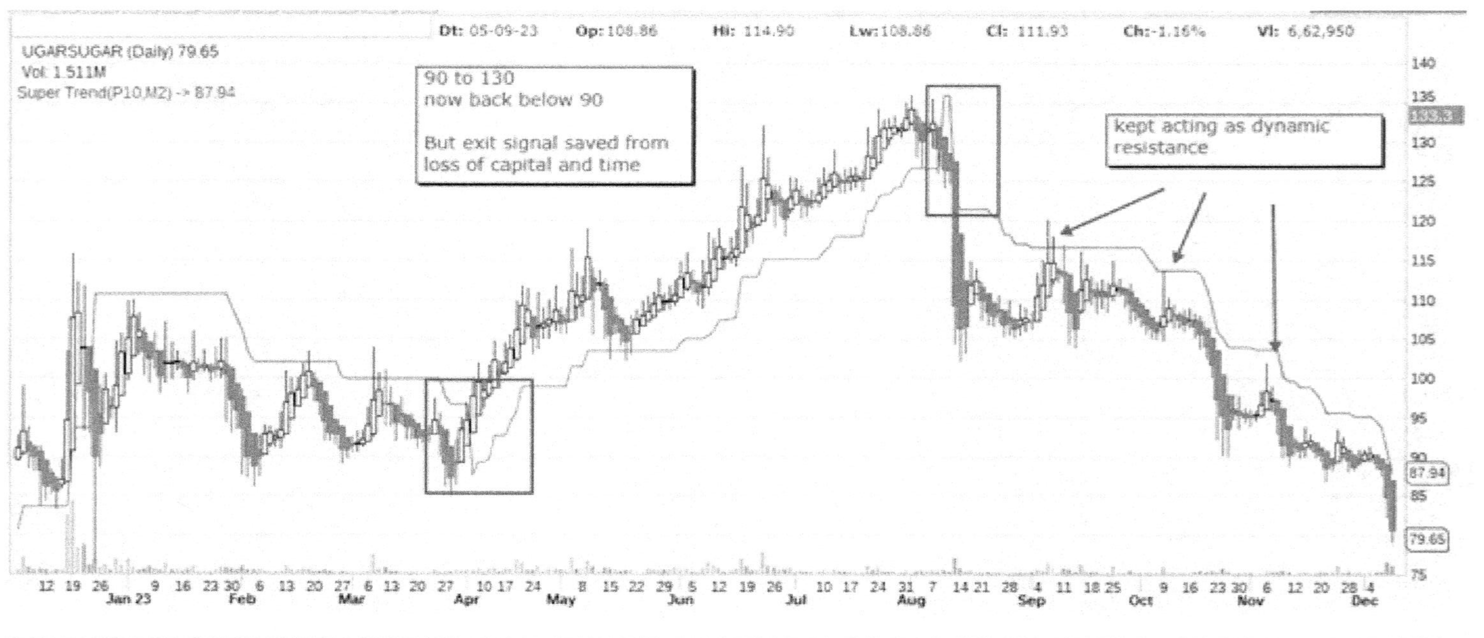

Image 7.21: Daily chart of Ugar Sugar Works Ltd. showing dynamic support and resistance

In image 7.22, on the weekly chart of Campus Activewear Ltd., we can see how the IPO played out. There was a clear buy signal after getting listed and even a clear exit signal on the chart. In these kinds of scenarios, traders who could not enter near the 400 levels when it first gave the entry signal, would jump to buy it once they see that level again when it was in downtrend. They may totally ignore the price trend and just focus on the price at which they had missed the bus earlier—they do not want to miss it again and repent later. So, they just keep buying at the same zone. But, the stock price did not give any fresh buy signal and the price is 50% below the earlier level without any bullish sign.

This one is a great example of how this strategy can make us ride multibaggers!

Image 7.22: Weekly chart of Campus Activewear Ltd. showing clear buy and exit signal

Image 7.23 is the weekly chart of Kirloskar Electric Company Ltd. Once it gave an entry signal, the supertrend kept acting as a dynamic support multiple times and whenever the price pulled back and touched it, it bounced back up and the uptrend continued. The momentum was so strong that it went up 10 times without any exit signal. I know, not all stocks will show moves like this one did, but even if one of our 50 trades gives us a move like this, that is all we need to make enough money for the next 2–3 years at least. We just need to follow our process and take one trade after the other.

Image 7.23: Weekly chart of Kirloskar Electric Company Ltd. where supertrend kept acting as dynamic support

Indian Railway Finance Corporation(IRFC) has been the favourite for many traders recently. Image 7.24 is IRFC's daily chart. See how supertrend gave a clear entry, and then it kept acting as a dynamic support. It went up from 27 to 77 levels during this time and when the supertrend gave a clear exit by turning red indicating that profits were booked. Then the same supertrend kept acting as a dynamic resistance as the price kept getting rejected from the same supertrend.

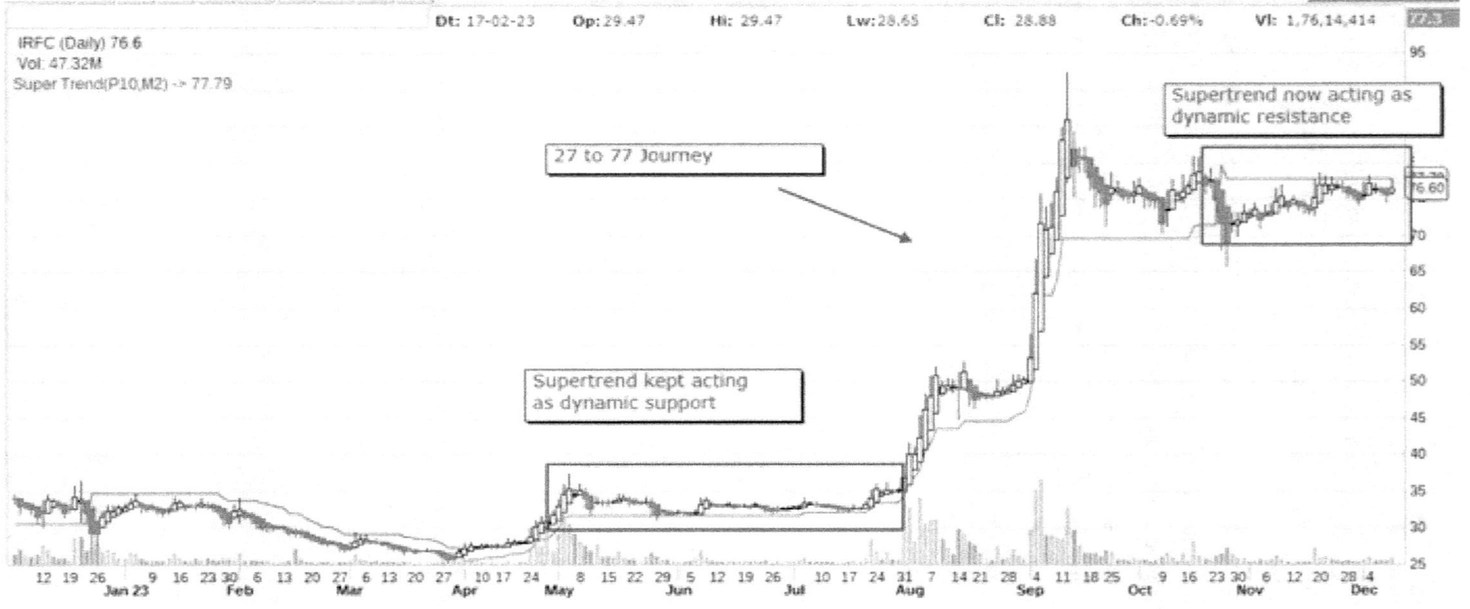

Image 7.24: Daily chart of Indian Railway Finance Corporation where supertrend gave clear entry and exit signals

Now let us look at a monthly chart for a change. Image 7.25 is the monthly chart of Axiscades Technologies Ltd. By now you would have already tested this strategy on many of your favourite stocks and realised that this strategy works on almost all time frames.

Highlighting the two big moves from this chart, it went up 300% when it gave a fresh buy signal in 2014 when the supertrend turned green and buyers entered with momentum and then went up 600% when it gave another buy signal of supertrend in 2021.

Another very important thing is that it even saved capital and time when it gave an exit signal in 2017. If you would keep holding it, you would have lost all your time, profits and even some of your capital.

Image 7.25: Monthly chart of Axiscades Technologies Ltd.

Now let us look at a chart which made many traders lose their hard-earned money. Image 7.26 is the monthly chart of Yes Bank. It showed a 300% move and eventually gave an exit signal almost near the top. When that happened, it did not give any entry signal. In fact, when it bounced from 160 to 180 levels, many people started buying it aggressively based on the news, which made it look as if everything was fine with it and it could be a turn-around story.

Many of my friends and relatives started buying it at this level and some who had it from higher levels started adding more to their losing positions. This is what happens if somebody does not have a strategy in place and just starts trading or investing based on emotions and news.

If you want to check out this same strategy in a video format, you can scan this QR code to visit the Upsurge platform.

Image 7.26: Monthly chart of Yes Bank showing a clear exit signal

"If most traders would learn to sit on their hands 50 percent of the time, they would make a lot more money."

—Bill Lipschutz, American forex trader

8

Moving Average Convergence Divergence

Moving average convergence divergence(MACD) was developed by Gerald Appel in the 1970's. It is a trend following indicator and shows a relationship between two moving averages.

An oscillator is an indicator which fluctuates above or below a centerline or moves between a range. MACD is one of the most widely-used oscillators as it is really easy to use and effective. It is calculated by subtracting the 26-period EMA from the 12-period EMA. There is also a signal line with a 9-period EMA which basically gives us the signal to enter or exit a stock. It is plotted on top of the MACD.

You get a *buy* signal when the MACD line crosses above the signal line. When the MACD line crosses below the signal line you get a *sell* signal.

There is also an MACD histogram (displayed as a graph on MACD) which plots the difference between the MACD line and the signal line. It tells us if the difference is positive or negative. Accordingly, you can identify if there is bullish momentum or bearish momentum at any given point in time. But even if you ignore it, you can just focus on the convergence and divergence part of it, as that is what you will use in your MACD strategy to know exactly when to enter and exit any stock.

Convergence means that the moving averages start moving closer to each other and 'converge' or start moving in a tight zone. Divergence means that there is a large difference between the moving averages.

While MACD can also be used with any time frame, I have noticed that it is most suitable for the daily time frame. Like other strategies, we can follow a top-down approach here too. We can start analysing the trend by checking the monthly chart first, then the weekly chart, and eventually trade on the daily chart.

Image 8.1 shows the MACD on the daily chart of ITC Ltd. You can see that MACD is plotted below the chart, as this is an oscillator.

The MACD and the signal lines are marked. When the MACD line goes below the signal line, the histogram goes below zero and enters into the negative territory which shows bearish momentum(sellers overpowering buyers). When the MACD line crosses above the signal line, it shows that the histogram has turned positive and the stock is now showing bullish momentum (buyers overpowering sellers).

Image 8.1: Daily chart of ITC Ltd. showing MACD

Image 8.2 is the weekly chart of Suzlon Energy Ltd. We can always combine any indicator with basic price action to get even better results. Every indicator is derived from the price which it follows. Price is of utmost importance and all indicators act as assistance tools to make the job of a trader easy and convenient.

In image 8.2, Suzlon Energy Ltd. had a breakout above a resistance zone after a long time. Along with that, the MACD line also crossed above the signal line, which basically indicates that bullish momentum will start soon (buyers can enter with momentum) as indicated by the MACD line.

When basic price action adds confirmation to any indicator or oscillator, it is like icing on the cake! Once that happened on the chart, the price went up around 250% before finally giving an exit signal (when the MACD line went below the signal line).

Image 8.2: Weekly chart of Suzlon Energy Ltd.

Let us see MACD on a monthly chart now so that we get an idea of MACD on various time frames.

Image 8.3 is the monthly chart of Indian Railway Construction (Ircon) International Ltd. For several years; it kept moving sideways and showed no clear trend.

MACD was also converging as there was no sign of a trend at that time. It finally gave a breakout above the sideways range. The MACD line also crossed above the signal line and we can see the results: the price moved up 300% in less than 1.5 years!

Investors generally use the 'techno-funda' approach where they study the financials of a company with all the basics of fundamental analysis like earning per share, return on capital employed, price-earnings ratio, etc. and then combine it with a technical study like this one where they would study how MACD moves on a monthly or a weekly chart. This gives them more conviction to keep holding a stock which has good fundamentals and is trending nicely according to the technical charts.

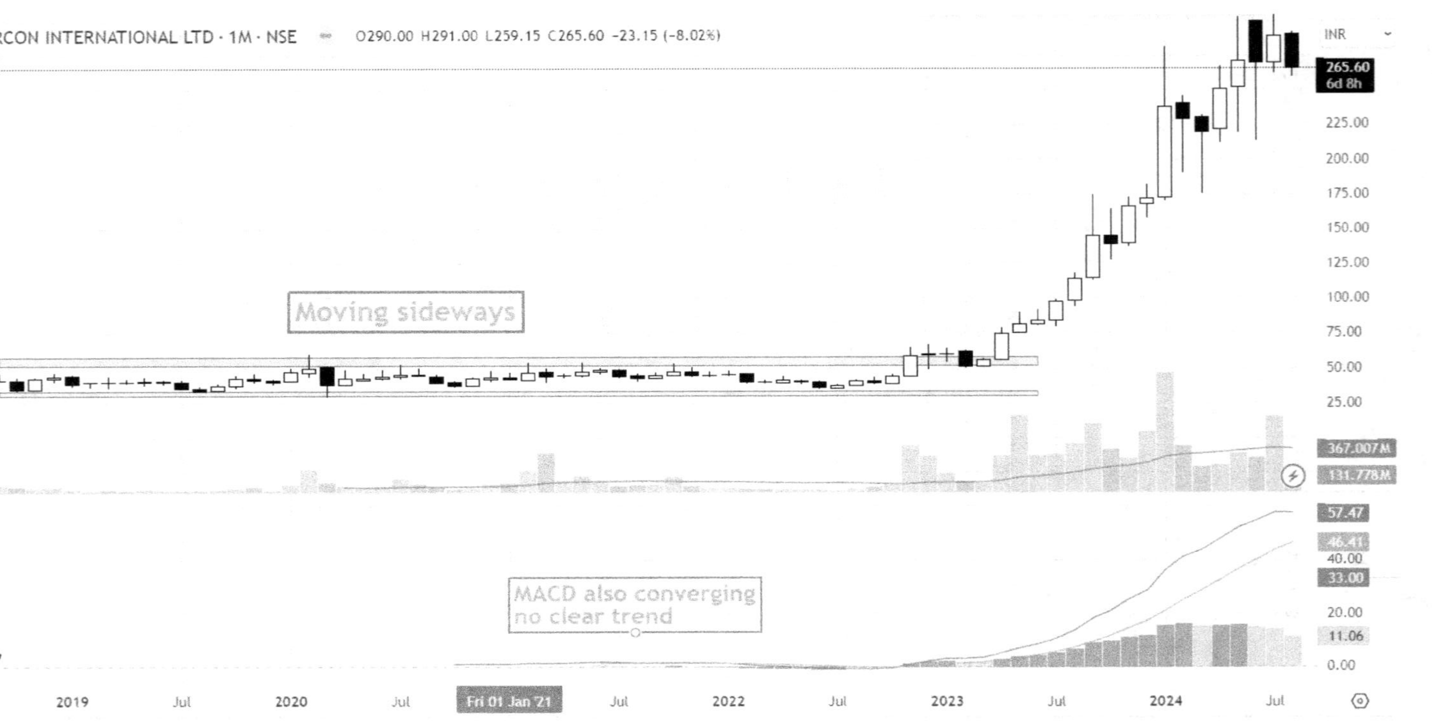

Image 8.3: Monthly chart of Indian Railway Construction (Ircon) International Ltd.

Next, let us check MACD on a 15-minute chart.

Image 8.4 is Nifty's 15-minute chart with the points marked with arrows where the MACD line crossed above or below the signal line, giving us buy and sell signals, respectively. We can see that the buy and sell signals are very clear and all a trader has to do is ride the moves with conviction till the move lasts, that is, till the time the trend does not reverse.

We can see that MACD can be used by intraday and short-term traders as well. A trend is needed for this indicator or any other indicator to work smoothly, as almost nothing works well in a sideways or choppy scenario.

Image 8.4: 15-minute chart of Nifty showing where the MACD line crossed the signal line, giving us buy and sell signals

Let's check another chart of 15-minute time frame on the chart of Apollo Tyres Ltd. in image 8.5. Notice two things. When the move was trending, there was a clear buy signal and exit signal (marked with arrows on the MACD). But when the stock started to move sideways, the MACD also converged and there was no clear signal, which shows that we need a trending move for any type of trending indicator or oscillator to work properly.

Do not go below the daily time frame as lower time frames usually have random and choppy moves. If you keep trying to capture small moves in the markets, you will develop a mindset of very short-term trading and will not be able to capture big returns. Very short-term trading also involves much more brokerage charges. Also, buying and selling multiple times will incur more transaction charges and other expenses.

Another thing which you need to keep in mind is that even if someone starts to make some returns on intraday trading, they usually exhaust themselves. Seated in front of the trading terminal for the entire day, they usually take multiple buying and selling decisions each day. That drains physical and emotional energy.

Remember, we entered the stock market to make our life better and live on our own terms, not to be a slave to our emotions and the markets.

Once you finish reading this chapter, please apply MACD on your charts and check as many stocks as possible. These could be from your watch-list, any stocks which you wish to buy but were confused where exactly to enter and when to enter, or it could be stocks from a specific sector which you like.

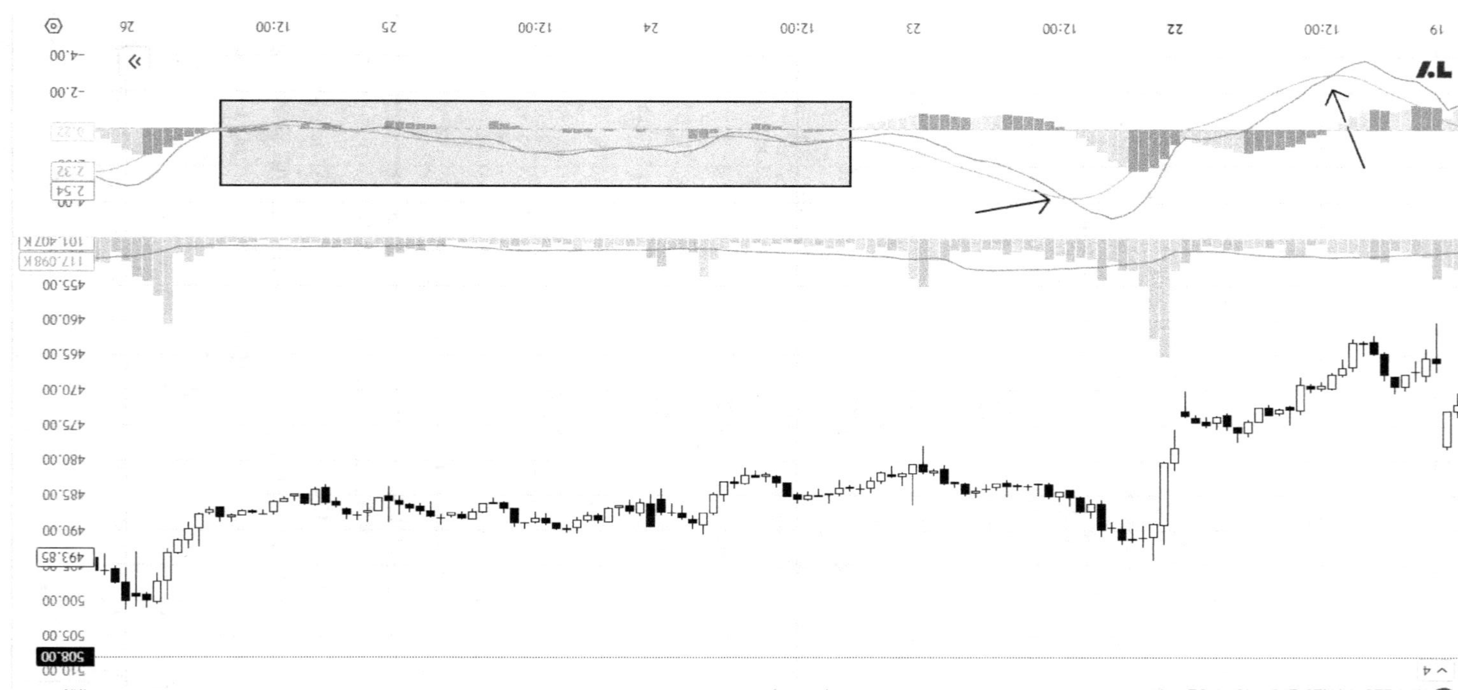

Image 8.5: 15-minute chart of Apollo Tyres Ltd. showing buy signal and exit signal

Let us check a few more charts of various time frames and see how much returns we would have got if we traded just using MACD.

Image 8.6 is Shree Cement's daily chart. I have marked the last few buy and sell points with arrows on the chart and on the MACD indicator. When the first sell signal came (first arrow), the price dropped from 27, 200 level to 24, 900 level giving us an approximately 8% move in almost one month. When the fresh buy signal came, it gave a small upward move of around 4% in a couple of days.

Following this, it gave a bearish move (fall in price) of almost 6% in 12 days. Then it gave a fresh opportunity for entry as the MACD just crossed above the signal line. Notice that the histogram shows a green graph (above the base line), which basically means that MACD's divergence is now positive. It is a bullish sign which depicts an uptrend for the stock.

Image 8.6: Daily chart of Shree Cement with the MACD indicator

Image 8.7 is the weekly chart of Hindalco Industries Ltd. The first thing you notice on this chart is that the basic price structure looks really good as it has broken above the highlighted resistance after a long time. It could not cross this resistance since April 2022. Finally, it did so after a gap of two years, in April 2024.

When it started to fall initially (first arrow) it fell from 580 levels towards the low of 309, a fall of almost 50%. The MACD remained negative all this time, and it finally gave a fresh buy signal near the 380 levels. Once the fresh buying came, it moved upward by 25% before the signal again turned bearish warning investors to exit the trade.

Coming to the recent price action, it has given a fresh breakout just a couple of weeks back and the MACD is also complimenting this move as it also crossed above the signal line giving us a fresh buy signal. Signals on weekly or monthly charts take time to emerge. It will require a lot of patience and discipline to ride moves like these, but this is where a good amount of money is made as a trader. Remember, you want to make better trades, not more trades!

Image 8.7: Weekly chart of Hindalco Industries Ltd. showing MACD

Let's check another chart where MACD is compliments the price action.

Image 8.8 is the daily chart of Birla Corporation Ltd. The stock price fell down from 1,700 levels to 1,400 levels recently when the MACD indicated a bearish signal (sellers were overpowering the buyers).

After that, it started to move to a small range and MACD also started converging. The price fell again and took a support near the same level from where it had bounced earlier, making a double bottom pattern. The MACD also crossed over, giving a fresh entry signal and compliments the bullish price action indicating that the buyers have entered again and are ready to drive up the price.

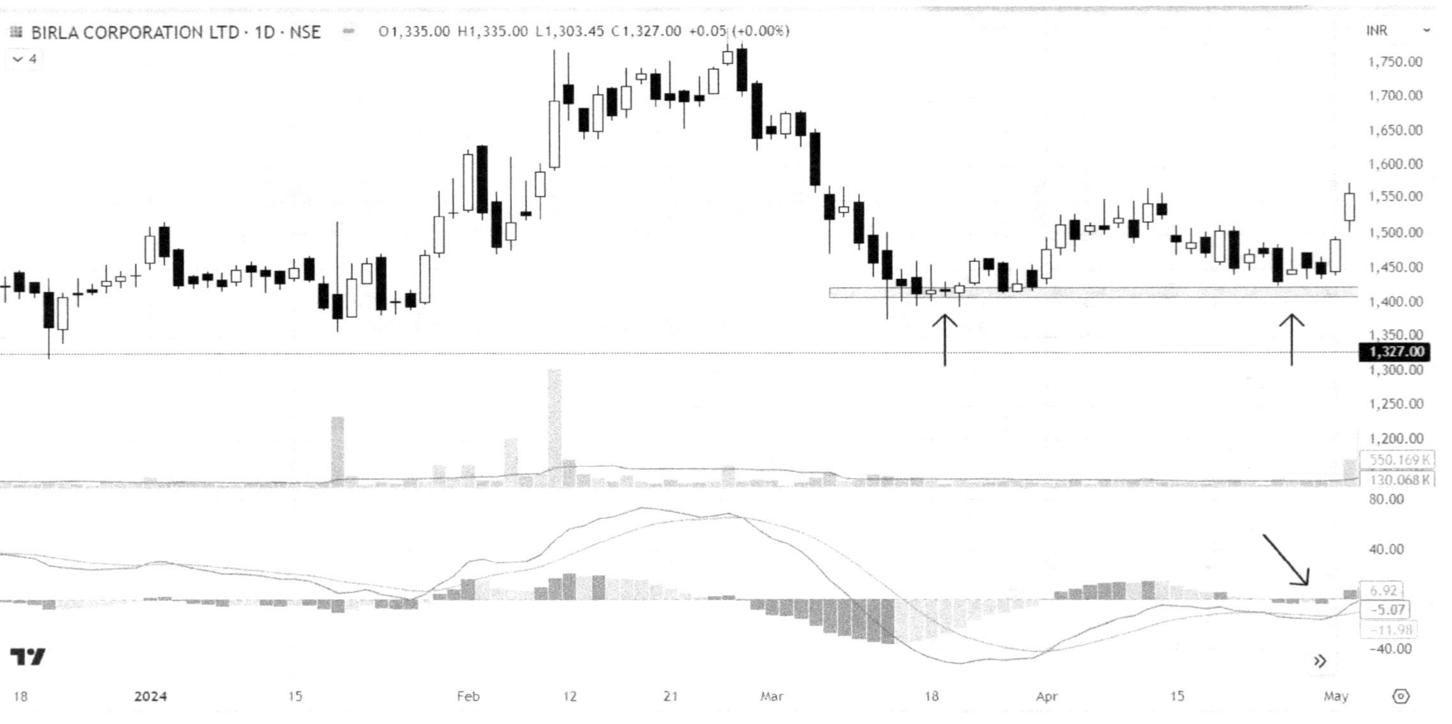

Image 8.8: Daily chart of Birla Corporation Ltd. when MACD turned bearish

Now let us check another chart where MACD complimented the price action.

Image 8.9 is the daily chart of Max Estates Ltd. We can see that it broke out of a cup and handle pattern. The MACD also gave a crossover above the signal line. When an indicator or an oscillator compliments a good price action move, it always adds conviction to the trader to execute the setup. Once a trader enters this setup, they should hold it till the time the MACD does not cross below the signal line again and the divergence or histogram turns negative again. So MACD gives us an entry signal, tells us till when to hold the stock, and exactly when to exit. It does all the analysis for us—we just have to follow it and focus on discipline and trading psychology.

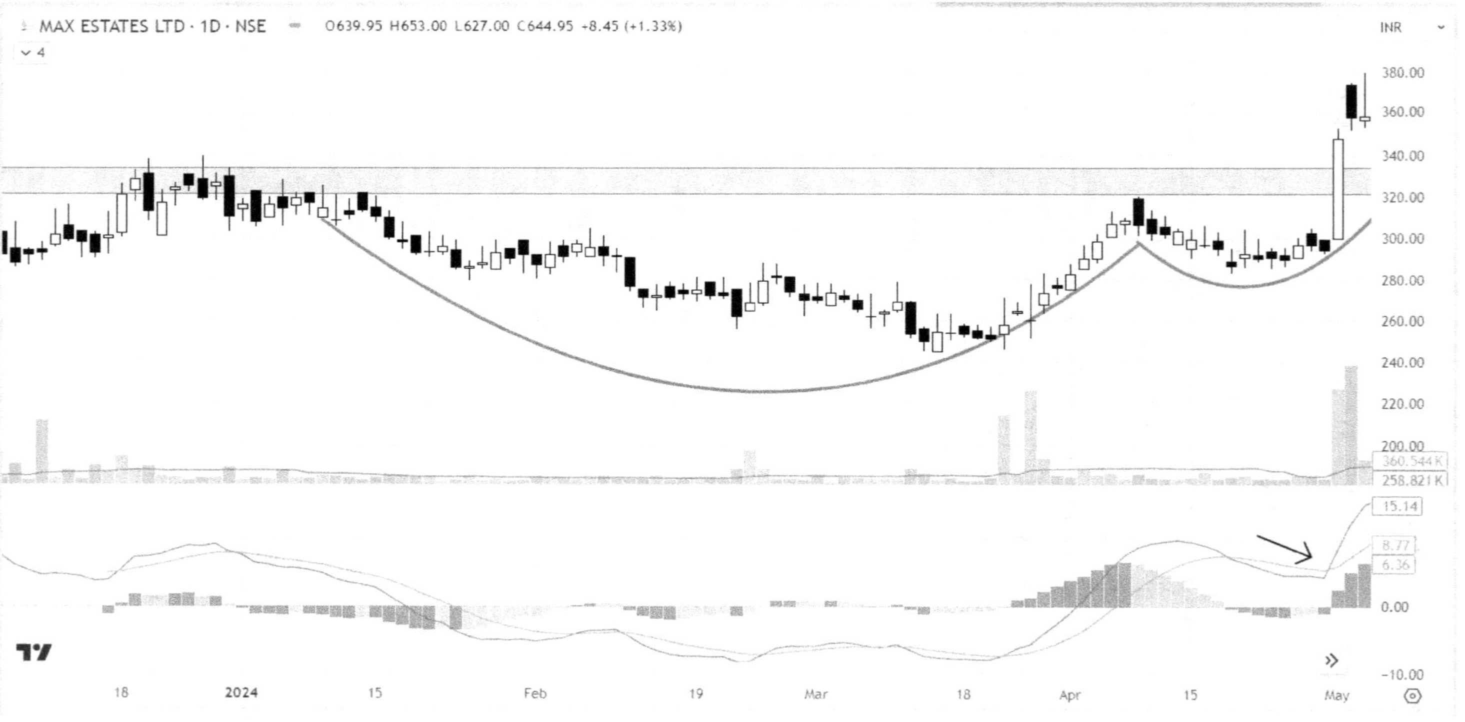

Image 8.9: Daily chart of Max Estates Ltd. showing a breakout from a cup and handle pattern

Let us check a monthly chart now and see how MACD complimented the price action.

Image 8.10 is the monthly chart of Century Enka Ltd. It gave a good upward move when the MACD had crossed over (first arrow). The price action was favourable—it broke out of a base along with huge volumes and as a result, the stock doubled from that point. It gave an exit signal when the MACD crossed below and then it saved us a lot of time as the stock again went into a sideways zone where the price remained stuck in a narrow range and started making another base after that. So not only did it give a significant entry point, it helped to ride most of the trend, made us exit at a great point and then even saved valuable time and hard-earned money during the time when it just went sideways. After that, it broke out again from the monthly base pattern and MACD also just crossed over, signalling that this could be just the start of another upward trend and that you could enter the trade and ride the trend till it lasts.

By booking stocks like this, you free up your capital to deploy into other stocks and utilise it better instead of staying stuck in a trade, waiting for things to turn out according to your desire.

MACD is a great indicator that can add a lot of value to your trading system and is really easy to use. It uses a combination of moving averages and does all the hard work. It provides direct entry and exit points. It is very beneficial for new traders and experts.

Like any other indicator, this can also be lagging as it is derived from price action itself, so sometimes you may get the signals a bit late. That is why it would be a great idea to always add basic price action along with any indicator to get the best of both the worlds.

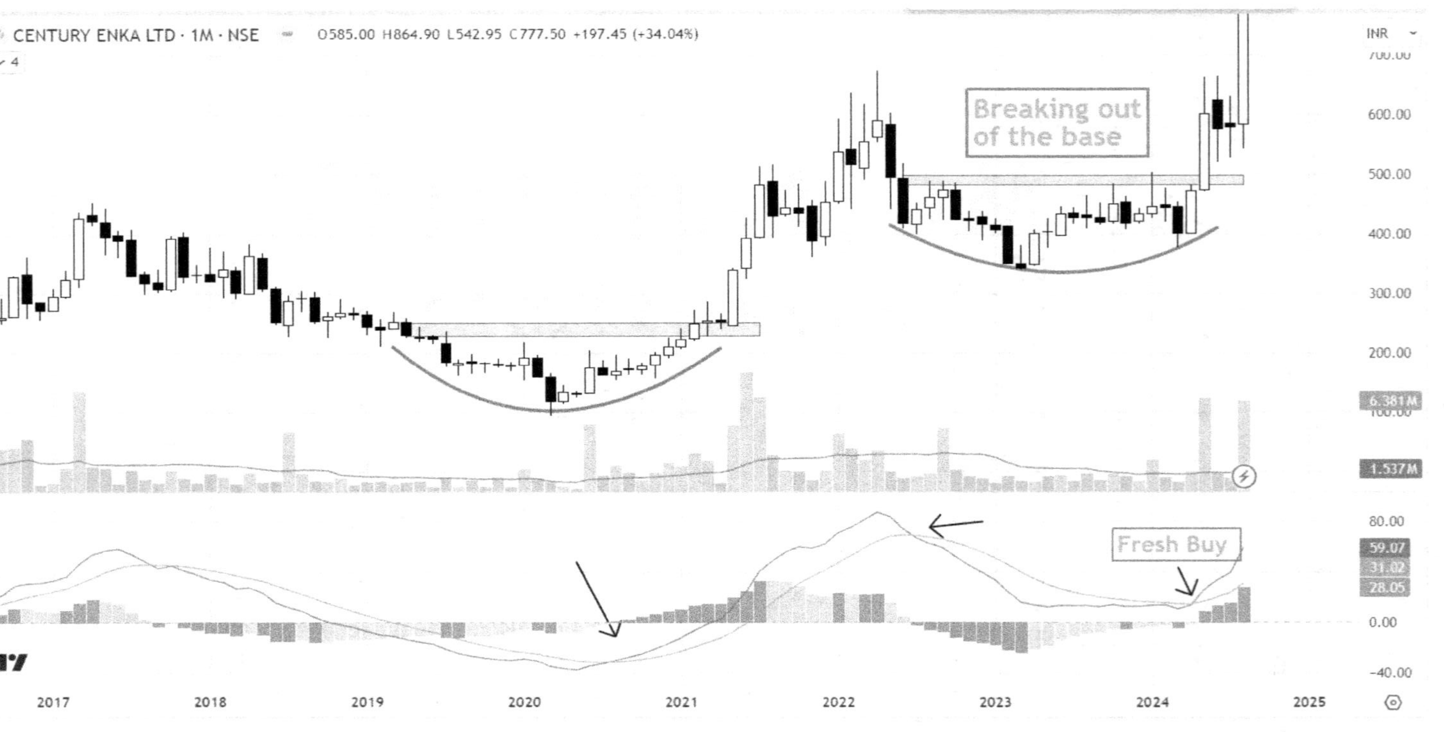

Image 8.10: Monthly chart of Century Enka Ltd.

"There is time to go long, time to go short and time to go fishing."

—Jesse Lauriston Livermore, American stock trader considered as the pioneer of day trading

9

Relative Strength Index

Relative Strength Index (RSI) was developed by J. Welles Wilder Jr. According to Investopedia, RSI is a technical indicator that is used in momentum trading to measure the speed and magnitude of a security's recent change in price. It is used to check the relative strength of a security and if the same is in the overbought or oversold zone. Besides indicating the strength, it can also be used to identify the potential change in the trend or a corrective pullback in price. Not many people use RSI for momentum, but I do it.

RSI is displayed as a line graph and has values from 0 to 100. Most people believe that a reading of 70 or more indicates that it is in overbought zone and a reading below 30 means that it is in oversold zone. When something is in overbought zone, it is fair to start looking for a reversal. Similarly, if something is in oversold zone, we should look for an entry signal because something that is already oversold has the potential to now change its trend and start moving up. They are not completely wrong, because that is how most people have been taught to use RSI. But let us look at it from a unique perspective.

According to my experience and study of thousands of charts, quite often, if a stock or index shows an RSI of more than 70, which ideally means that it is overbought, it keeps on gaining momentum for a long period of time before finally showing a reversal sign. Look out to 'buy' when RSI is in this zone instead of looking for a reversal. Similarly, if a stock or index has an RSI of 30 or below, it may indicate that it is really weak and can actually fall much more before eventually showing any signs of a bullish trend.

A stock showing an RSI of 30 means that it may be in the process of breaking its 52-week low or life lows and would probably have broken a lot of supports till then.

Let us look at a few bullish examples in various time frames and see for ourselves if RSI going above 70 really indicates an overbought zone.

In the monthly chart of Nifty in image 9.1, we can see that RSI has been plotted at the bottom and it is within its usual range of 0 to 100. On a charting platform, a red line shows the overbought zone (when RSI goes above 70) and a green line shows oversold zone (when RSI goes below 30).

In image 9.1 when the RSI was above 70 (first highlighted box, which ideally would be the overbought zone and make us look for a reversal sign), Nifty moved up to almost 300%. It went from 2200 to 6300 levels and RSI was in the 'overbought' zone almost the entire time. Later in 2014, it went up from 6600 to 9000 levels. During that time too, RSI was above the 70 zone most of the time. When Nifty went up from 12200 to 18000 levels later, again RSI showed similar action. This was a monthly chart. We will check a lot of examples which have various time frames so that you have a better idea.

Image 9.1: Monthly chart of Nifty with RSI at the bottom

Image 9.2 is the monthly chart of Central Depository Services Ltd. (CDSL). It gave a basic horizontal breakout and the RSI went above 70. Once this happened, the price moved up from 430 to 1600 level. During this entire time, RSI remained in the 'overbought' zone. I am sharing this example here to illustrate that overbought does not always mean that it is the end of the trend. In fact, many times, it is the beginning of the new trend.

After the upward move, the price dropped back to 900 levels. When the price moves up again and has given another horizontal breakout, the RSI is again above 70, which indicates that it can yet again give a good up move.

Image 9.2: Monthly chart of Central Depository Services Ltd. (CDSL) with RSI

Image 9.3 is the monthly chart of BSE Ltd. showing RSI. It gave a basic horizontal range breakout after a long time and RSI also went above 70. During this time, the price went up from 470 to 1000 level. Later, when the price retraced, it fell back to the same level from where it had broken out and bounced back up. As the bounce was taking place, the RSI also started to move up along with the price. It again went above 70 and remained above the 70 zone and the price went up from 630 to 2600 this time.

You can see through these charts that RSI above 70 does not mean a warning sign or a potential reversal sign and we should know how to use it in our favour.

Image 9.3: Monthly chart of BSE Ltd. showing RSI

Image 9.4 is the monthly chart of Elecon Engineering Company Ltd. This has been a hot topic for discussion lately as many traders felt that they missed out after looking at this chart and the way it moved up.

The stock had been trying to breakout above the range of 100 since the year 2009. It tried to break out multiple times in 2015, 2016 and even 2018, but always got rejected from the same range of 90–100 price levels. RSI also never went above 70 during this time. It finally managed to breakout above the resistance in 2021 and RSI also went above 70. The price went from 100 to 200 really quickly and then fell back to the same zone which had been acting as a resistance earlier. As you can see in the small highlighted box, RSI went below 70 for a brief span of time during this period. Then it went up again above 70 once the price bounced back up after falling back to the breakout retest zone. This time, the price shot up from 100 to almost 1000 levels in under two years. During this entire move, the RSI remained above 70 too.

You can see that RSI can remain above the overbought zone and the price can move up by 10 times! Let us take another example to prove this point.

Image 9.4: Monthly chart of Elecon Engineering Company Ltd. with RSI.

Image 9.5 is the monthly chart of Hindustan Aeronautics Ltd. (HAL). It shows an uptrend and gave a basic horizontal breakout. The RSI also went above 70 and remained there while the price went up from 760 to 2800 levels.

Image 9.6 is the monthly chart of Tanla Platforms Ltd. showing RSI. It had remained under a resistance for a long time and gave a breakout after almost 12 years. Once it did, it picked up a lot of momentum and even the RSI went above 70. The price went from 100 to 2000 in less than two years! During this entire time, the RSI remained above 70. Traders who were fearful of watching the RSI go above 70 would look for the opportunity to exit this move at every minor pullback and would have missed this enormous move.

Image 9.7 is the is the monthly chart of Trident Capital Ltd. It gave a basic horizontal breakout. RSI also went above 70 and the price moved up from 11 to 60 levels in one year.

Image 9.5: Monthly chart of Hindustan Aeronautics Ltd. (HAL) showing an uptrend and horizontal breakout

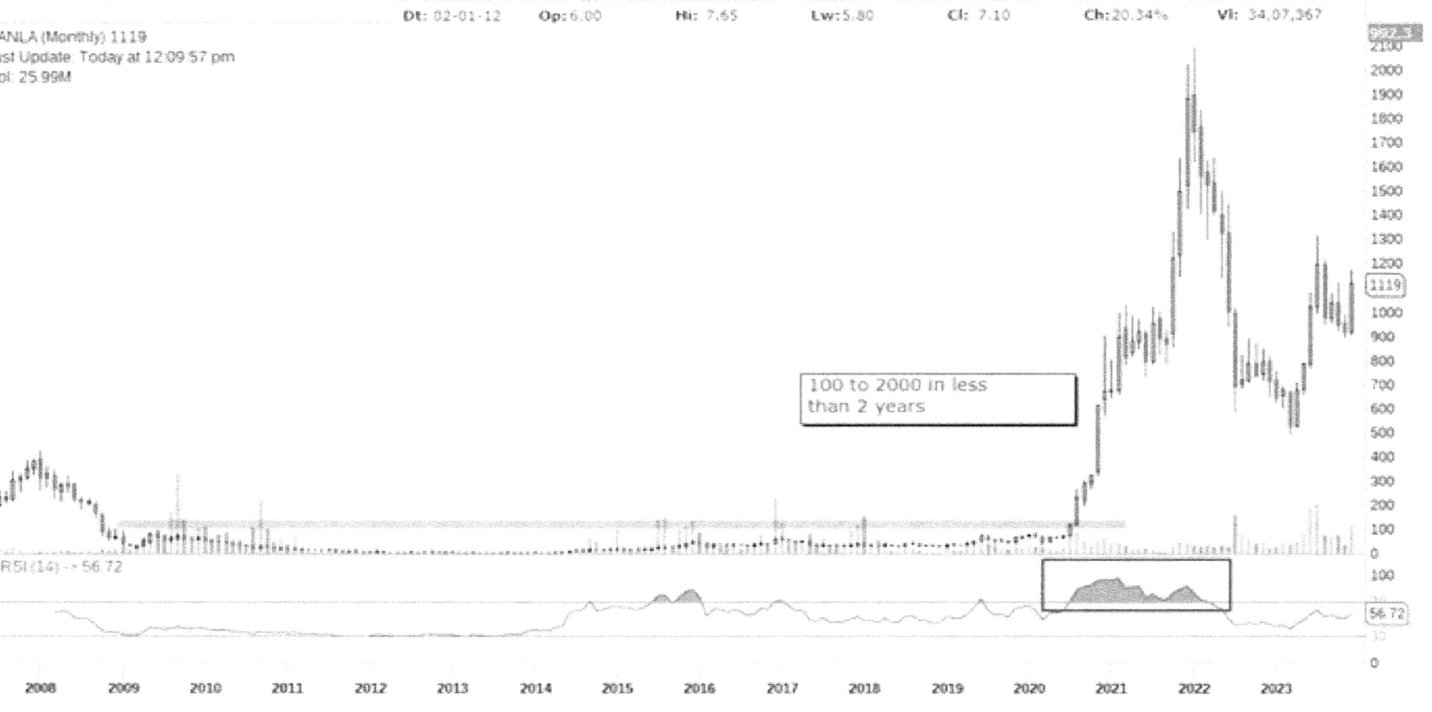

Image 9.6: Monthly chart of Tanla Platforms Ltd. showing RSI

Image 9.7: Monthly chart for Trident Capital Ltd. with RSI

In image 9.8, the monthly chart of Power Finance Corporation Ltd., we can see that it had been struggling to breakout above the level of 140 for a long time. It attempted to move past this resistance multiple times in 2014, 2017 and in 2022. When it finally did, it moved up from 140 to 400 levels and RSI also broke above 70 for the first time after all these years. This perfect combination is enough to get great moves in stocks if a trader has the patience and discipline to sit on these kinds of moves with conviction.

Image 9.8: Monthly chart of Power Finance Corporation Ltd.

In image 9.9, the monthly chart of REC Ltd., there is a similar pattern. The stock tried to breakout above 140–150 zone for a long time trying to move past it multiple times in 2014 and 2017. It finally managed a clean breakout in the year 2023. The RSI also went above 70 for the first time after almost 12 years. The result is in front of us; the price went up 300% in less than a year!

Image 9.10 is Tata Elxsi's monthly chart. It gave a basic horizontal breakout in 2021 and the RSI also went above 70. Thereafter, the price went up from 1,600 to 9,000.

I am discussing so many monthly charts to show you that these kinds of patterns can be found easily. I want you to check your favourite stocks and look for similar patterns in them. You will be surprised to see that patterns like these would have occurred in most of your favorite stocks too and you may have had positions in them too at one point of time but exited too early because of lack of conviction, or because you had an entry rule but no clear or defined exit criteria.

Image 9.9: Monthly chart of REC Ltd. with RSI

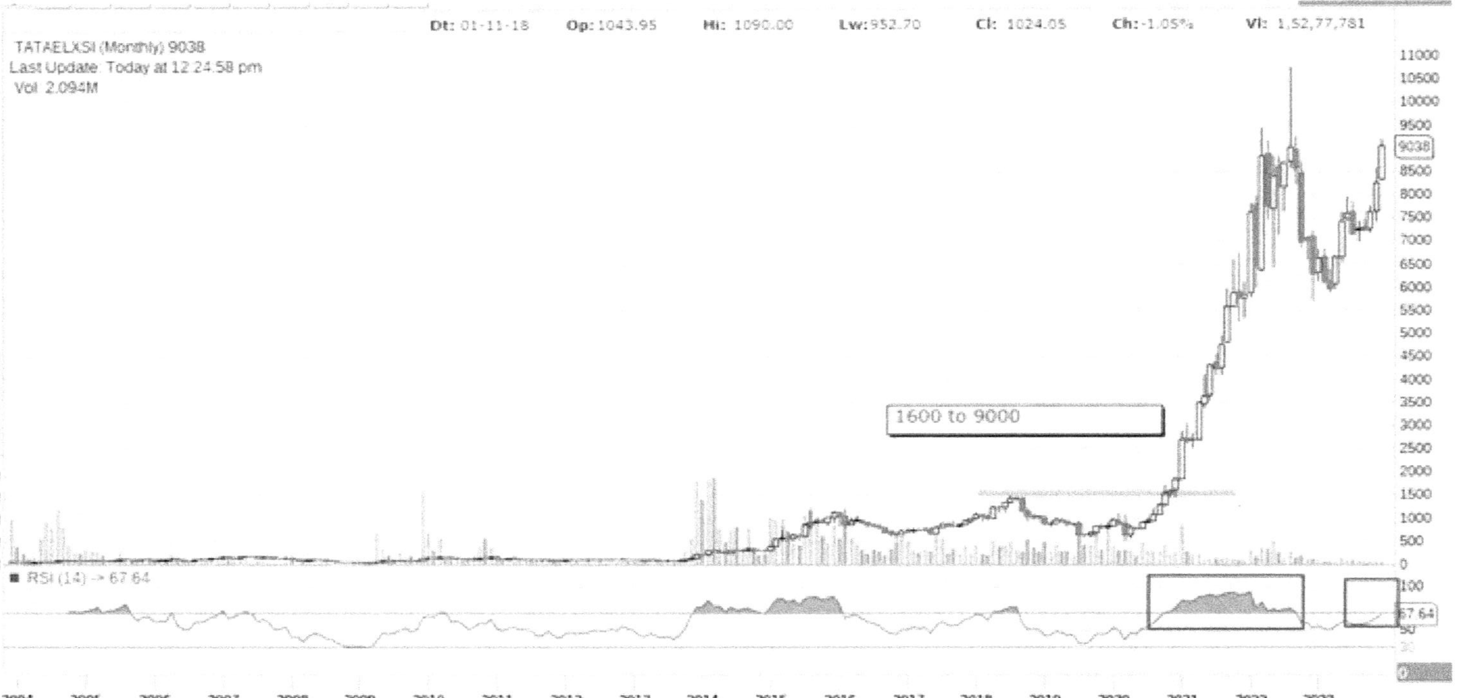

Image 9.10: Monthly chart of Tata Elxsi with RSI

The next one is a social media favourite. There were many memes made on the ITC Ltd. stock as it got stuck near the 200 level for a long period of time. In image 9.11, when the stock price broke out, the RSI also went above 70 after many years.

It took the price up from 200 to 450 levels in almost a straight line. It is uncommon for a blue-chip stock like this one.

Image 9.12 is the monthly chart for Apar Industries Ltd. It gave a horizontal breakout after five years and RSI also went above 70 for the first time since then. The price very quickly moved up from 1,000 to 5,500 and there were still no bearishness signs in this chart.

Now that we have seen a lot of bullish examples where the RSI went above 70 and the stocks gave a great upward move.

I hope these charts have motivated you to check and hunt for similar patterns in your universe of stocks.

Now let us check out a few bearish examples where the RSI went below 30 and the price kept falling to make new lows.

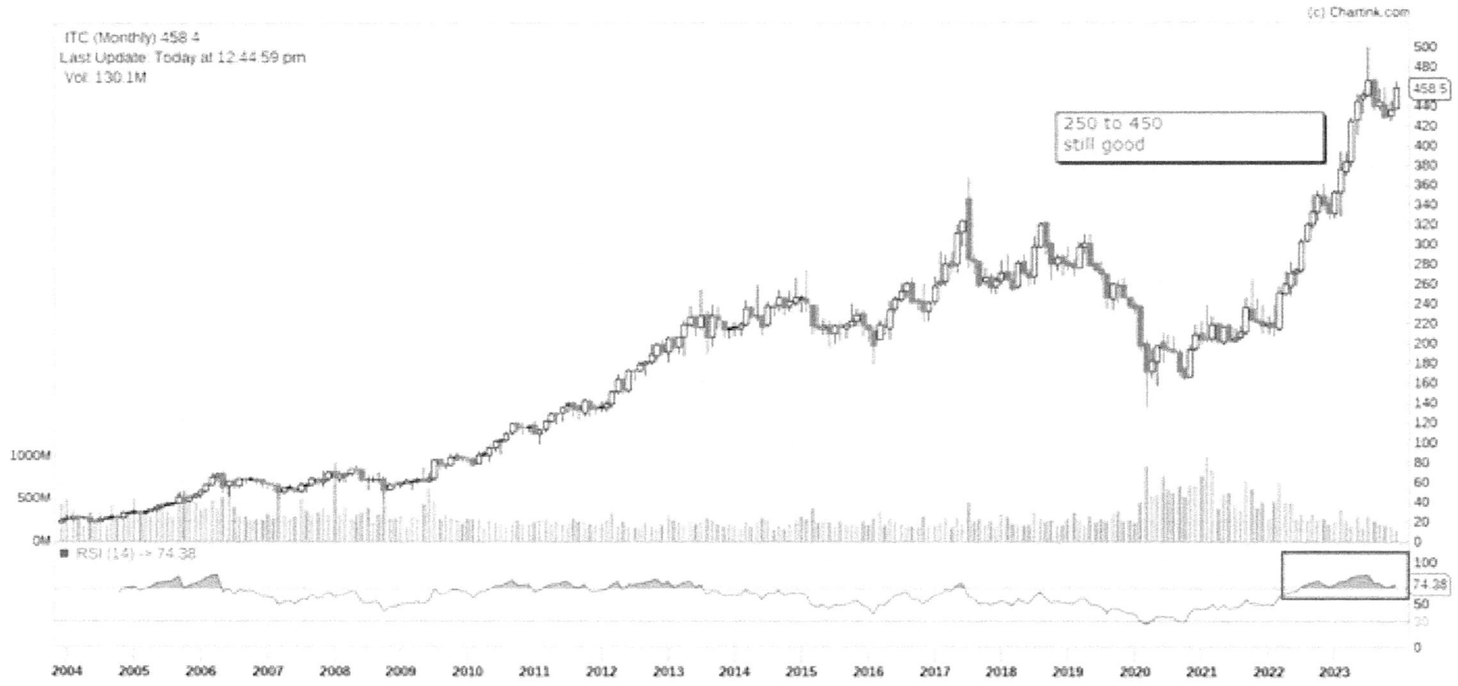

Image 9.11: Monthly chart of ITC Ltd. with RSI showing a steep rise

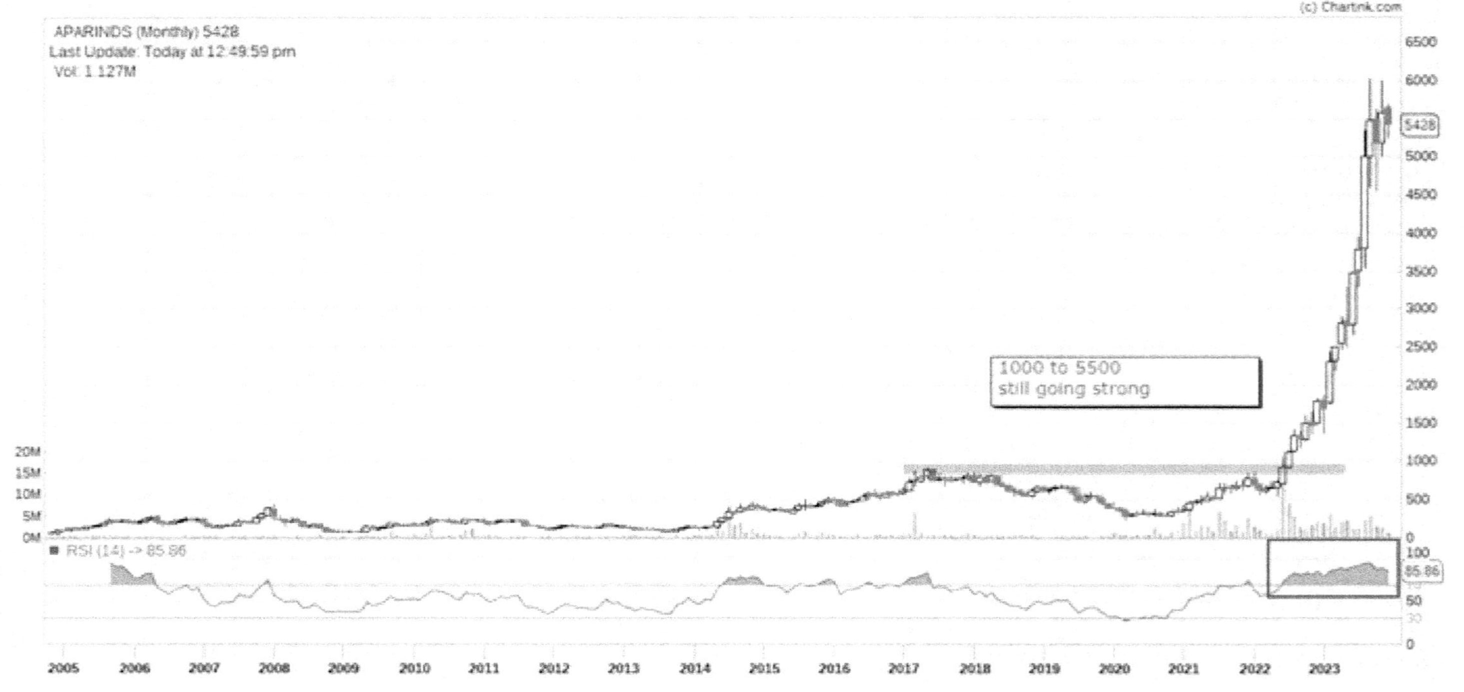

Image 9.12: Monthly chart for Apar Industries Ltd.

Image 9.13 is Reliance Capital Ltd.'s weekly chart. I am showing you extreme examples because I want you to see how low something can go even after it is in the 'oversold' zone according to the traditional way of looking at RSI.

When the RSI went below 30 and turned green (highlighted in rectangle box), the price fell from 100 to 5 in less than one year! Also notice that the overall structure was bearish (sellers were strong) as it was making lower highs, lower lows and was trading below all the important moving averages like 20, 50 and 200. So, there is no point in buying these kinds of setups. But many new traders make the mistake of buying something which is constantly falling just because they feel 'how much more can it fall now?'

Image 9.14 is the weekly chart of Dewan Housing Finance Ltd. (DHFL, now Piramal Capital and Housing Finance Ltd.). This is another extreme example. Once you start scanning stocks, you will find many stocks like these and such examples will not feel so extreme. Here we can see that it fell from 600 to 15 levels! During this entire time, the RSI was trading below 30. It came above the 30 for a short span of time during which the price was still in sideways. It did not even break above the big bearish candle's high. There was no point in buying this stock during that time as the structure was still bearish (buyers were still in control). Sometimes traders keep looking for buy signals in falls like these, but remember, when something falls so quickly and makes these kinds of big bearish candles, nine out of ten times it will not see it's life highs ever again. If someone has a stock like this in their portfolio, it is always best to exit according to the stop-loss rule and just look for some other stock instead of looking to get bargain prices of the same stock.

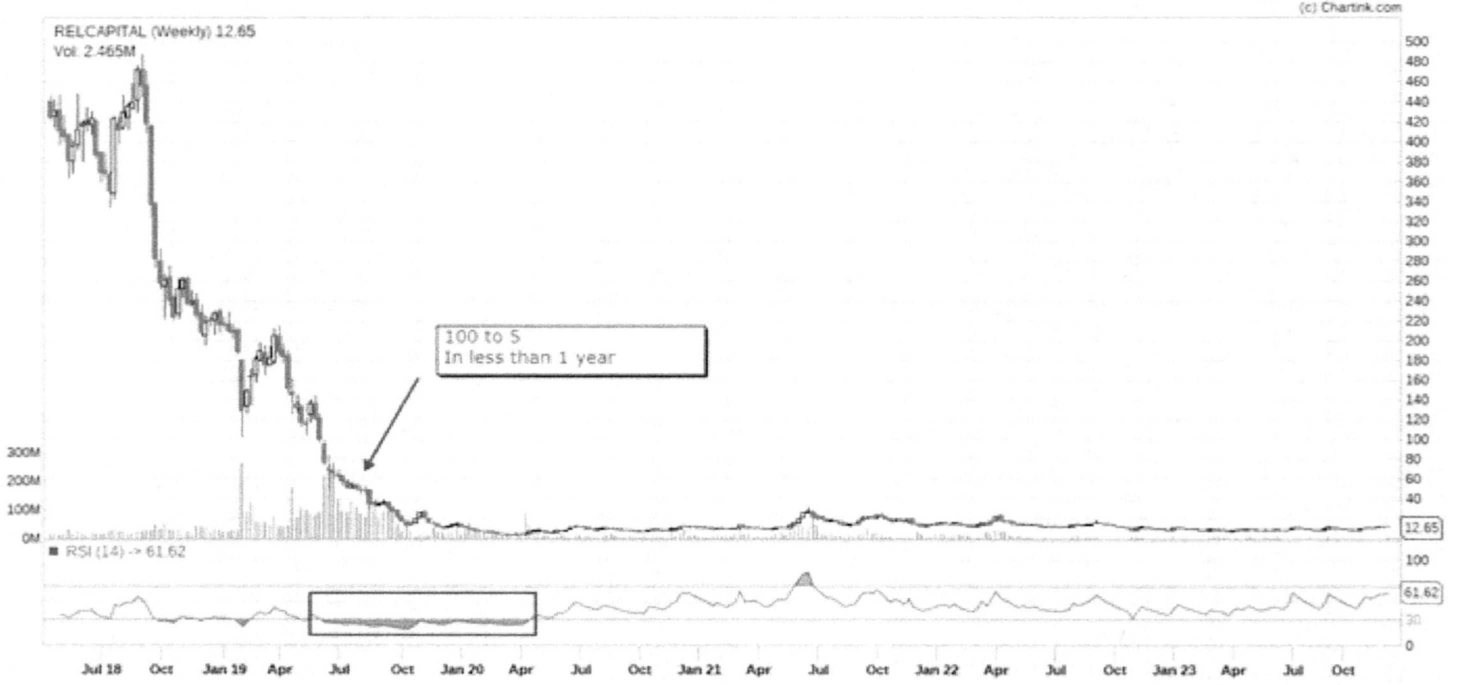

Image 9.13: Weekly chart of Reliance Capital Ltd. with RSI

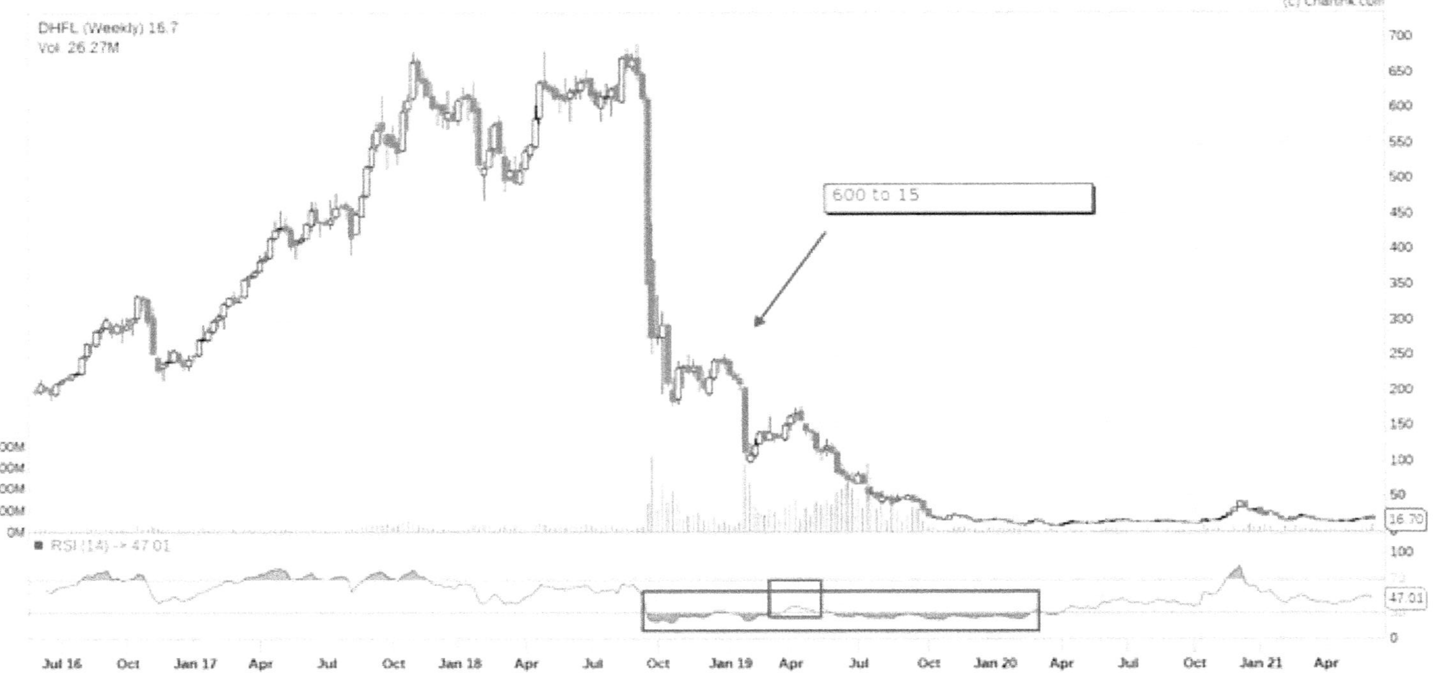

Image 9.14: Weekly chart of Dewan Housing Finance Ltd. showing RSI

Image 9.15 is the weekly chart of Cox and Kings. The stock was already in a downtrend and once the RSI went below 30, the price went down from 120 to 1 and it eventually got delisted!

Image 9.16 is the weekly chart of Adani Total Gas Ltd. (ATGL). Once the RSI went below 30, the price dropped from 3,000 to 550 levels in almost a straight line. The RSI remained below 30 for almost the entire year after this fall, only to bounce back above it at the end of the year.

Looking at the latest price action, some may feel that the stock doubled even after breaking so much from the highs. But, if they would have kept holding it for the entire year, they would have lost all patience and would be eager to just see that cost price again. Even if someone bought it later when the RSI was already below 30, it would be really difficult to keep holding the stock for the entire year in loss and they would have exited as soon as they would have seen even a 5–10% profit after bearing all the pain of watching the stock in loss every day.

Now that we have seen how RSI works from a different perspective and witnessed a lot of bullish and bearish examples, let us look at a very simple to follow but extremely effective trading strategy.

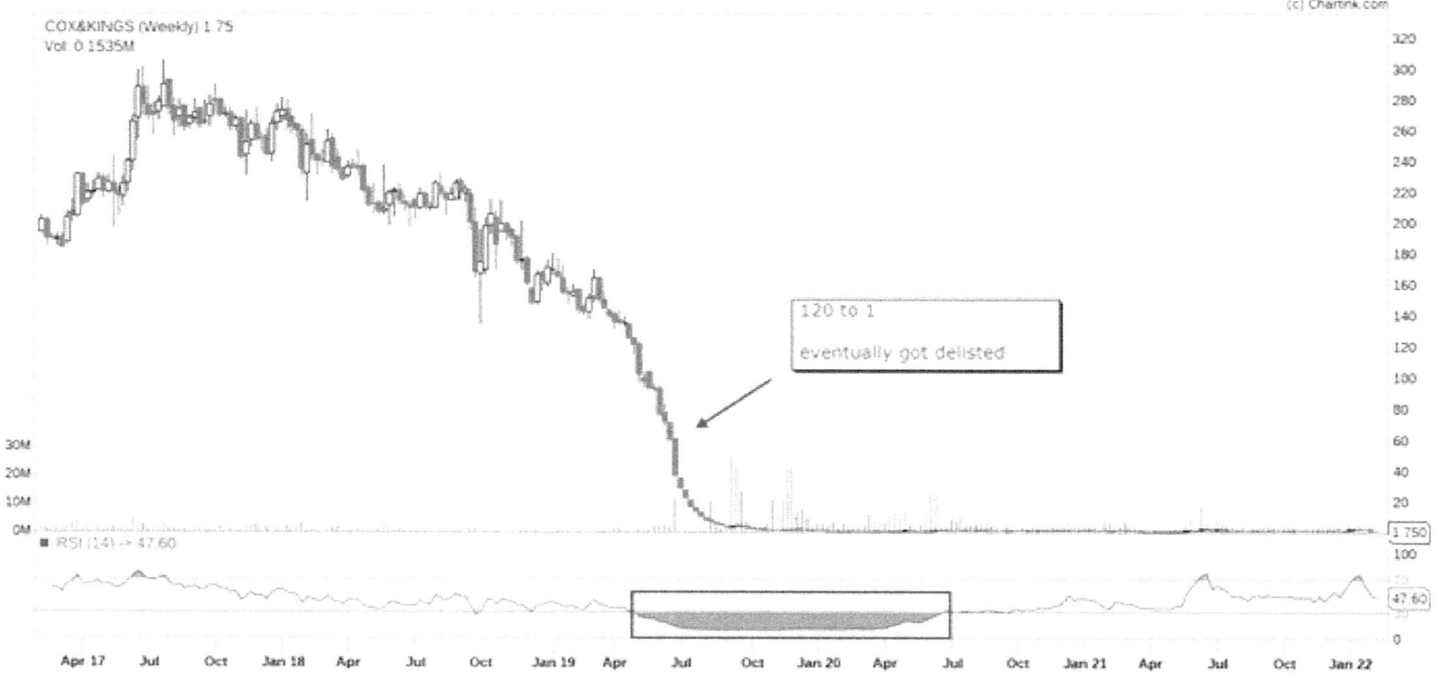

Image 9.15: Weekly chart of Cox and Kings

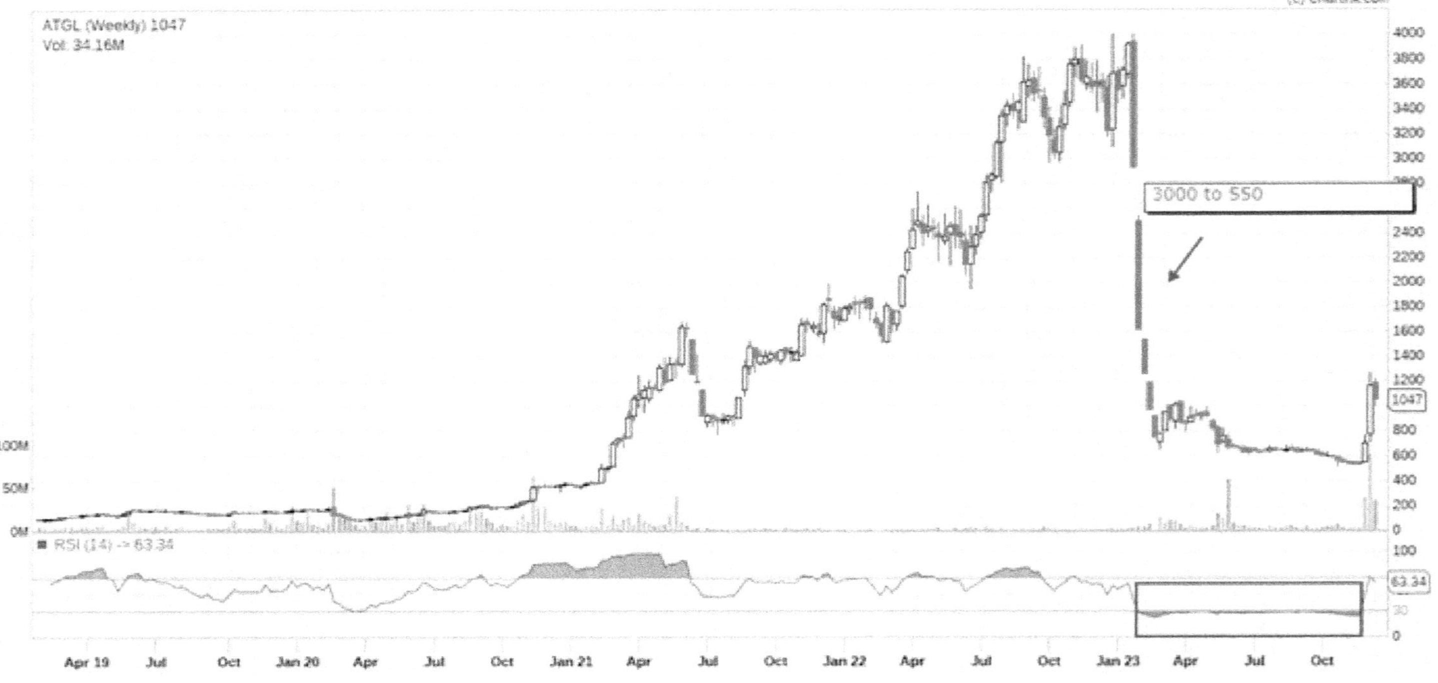

Image 9.16: Weekly chart of Adani Total Gas Ltd. (ATGL) with a steep decline in RSI

The 60-60-50 RSI Strategy

Let me explain this strategy with an example. Suppose you are driving your car on a highway. The highway is as smooth as it can get and you are really enjoying the drive. This highway which is well-constructed and smooth, is giving you a pleasurable ride and this assures you that there won't be any problem with your ride today as the road that you have chosen is really well-built and will take you to your destination with ease.

This 'highway' is your 'monthly chart'. Look at the stock in which the monthly chart's RSI is above 60. It means that the stock is in bullish momentum (buyers are still in control) as it shows an intact overall bullish structure in the higher time frame. A smooth highway, which means a stock which has a bullish monthly chart is a good sign and you can analyse it further.

Once you know that the highway that you are driving on is perfect, you need to make sure that your car is in good running condition. The servicing of the car has been done regularly and the fuel is sufficient for the ride. This will ensure that the car that you are driving is in good condition and the highway on which it is being driven also supports it.

The 'car' is your 'weekly chart' here. Along with the monthly chart, we need to make sure that the weekly chart is also such that the RSI is above 60. If the RSI in the weekly chart is also above 60 as well, it demonstrates that the bullish trend is intact as the buyers are still standing strong and everything looks great so far.

Now that we know that the monthly chart or the highway is great and smooth and the car or weekly chart also looks fine, let us try to ascertain what should be an ideal scenario on the daily chart.

The RSI on the daily chart should be just trading above 50. It may have just crossed the level of 50 or it may be retesting the 50 level from above.

With the highway example, think of it as the highway is fine, the car is also in top condition, but you stopped for some time in between. That may be because you want to take a break and get out of the car to stretch a bit. There may be some obstacle on the highway which forced you to slow down the car for some time. Or, there may be a speed bump which forced you to slow down a bit. But since the highway and car both are great, you have slowed down just for a brief period, and there is technically nothing wrong here. You will resume your journey pretty soon.

From the stock's perspective, you can assume that the overall trend of a stock was intact. That is why the monthly and weekly chart were in a bullish momentum as they were trading above the RSI 60 and there may be some kind of news in the market which made almost all the stocks correct for some time and your stock also took a dip. There is nothing wrong with your stock or its overall momentum. It just saw a corrective move because of an event which was not in anybody's control (something which will always keep happening in the stock market).

This scenario in which the RSI in the daily chart has retested the level of 50, gives you a great entry point as you can capture a stock which is in a strong uptrend (as highlighted by the monthly and weekly chart) and is at a bargain level in the daily chart because of the momentary fall it witnessed.

You could have just scanned for stocks in which the RSI in the daily time frame is retesting the 50 level. But that would have been incomplete information. By checking the higher time frames, you make sure that you are entering a stock which is already in an uptrend and has more chances of rising back up again instead of just entering any random stock. The stocks in which the higher time frames show a bullish structure have much better chances of continuing the up move as the buyers are picking it up with momentum and find value in it, that is why they are ready to buy it at higher levels too.

Let us look at a few charts to understand the 60-60-50 RSI strategy practically.

Image 9.17 is the monthly chart of Angel One Ltd. Always use a top-down approach as you need to make sure that the higher time frame's structure is bullish and you can proceed to check the lower time frames too. The stock price came out of a base a couple of months back and continues in good form. The main thing to focus on here is the RSI and if it is above the 60 level. It is trading above the 60 level which fulfills the criteria for this strategy as far as the monthly chart is concerned.

Now that the monthly chart looks fine, check the weekly chart.

Image 9.18 is the weekly chart of Angel One Ltd. Here too, the RSI is well above 60. The RSI went above 70 and was in the overbought zone. The price still went up from 1,800 to 3,200 levels and the RSI remains above the overbought zone. Hence, stocks keep going up even after coming into the overbought zone, and that is completely fine.

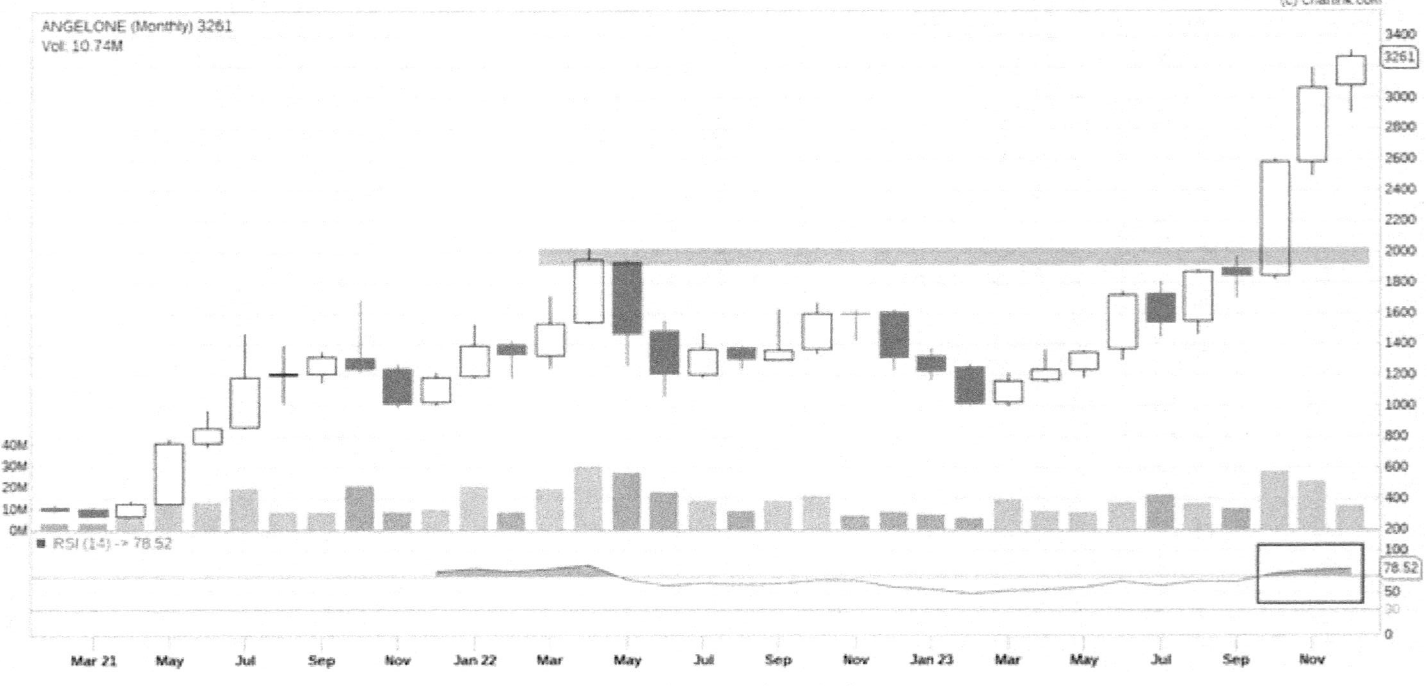

Image 9.17: Monthly chart of Angel One Ltd. with the 60-60-50 RSI Strategy

Image 9.18: Weekly chart of Angel One Ltd.

Now that we know that the 'highway' (monthly chart) and 'car' (weekly chart) are looking fine, let us check the daily chart.

Image 9.19 is the daily chart of Angel One Ltd. Whenever the RSI came and touched the 50 zone, it bounced back pretty well proving that it gave us great buying opportunity where the risk to reward ratio was also favourable. Since the highway was good and the car was well maintained too, the small breaks in between the journey should be embraced with open arms as these are the zones where the stop-loss would be at a minimum level. You can always exit the stock if the RSI falls below 50 EMA on a daily candle close level.

Whenever you buy something, you need to make sure that you enter at a level where the maximum loss is always set to a minimum point which means that you are already entering at a level where you know that even if your stop-loss hits (which may get hit many times in this or any other strategy of this world) you will exit with a minimum loss, ready for the next trade. That can be either in the same stock when the RSI trades above 50 levels once again since the RSI on weekly and monthly times frames is trading above their respective 60 levels or you can scan for other stocks which show a similar pattern. That is, RSI above 60 on monthly and weekly charts and bouncing off or breaking out of 50 RSI in the daily chart.

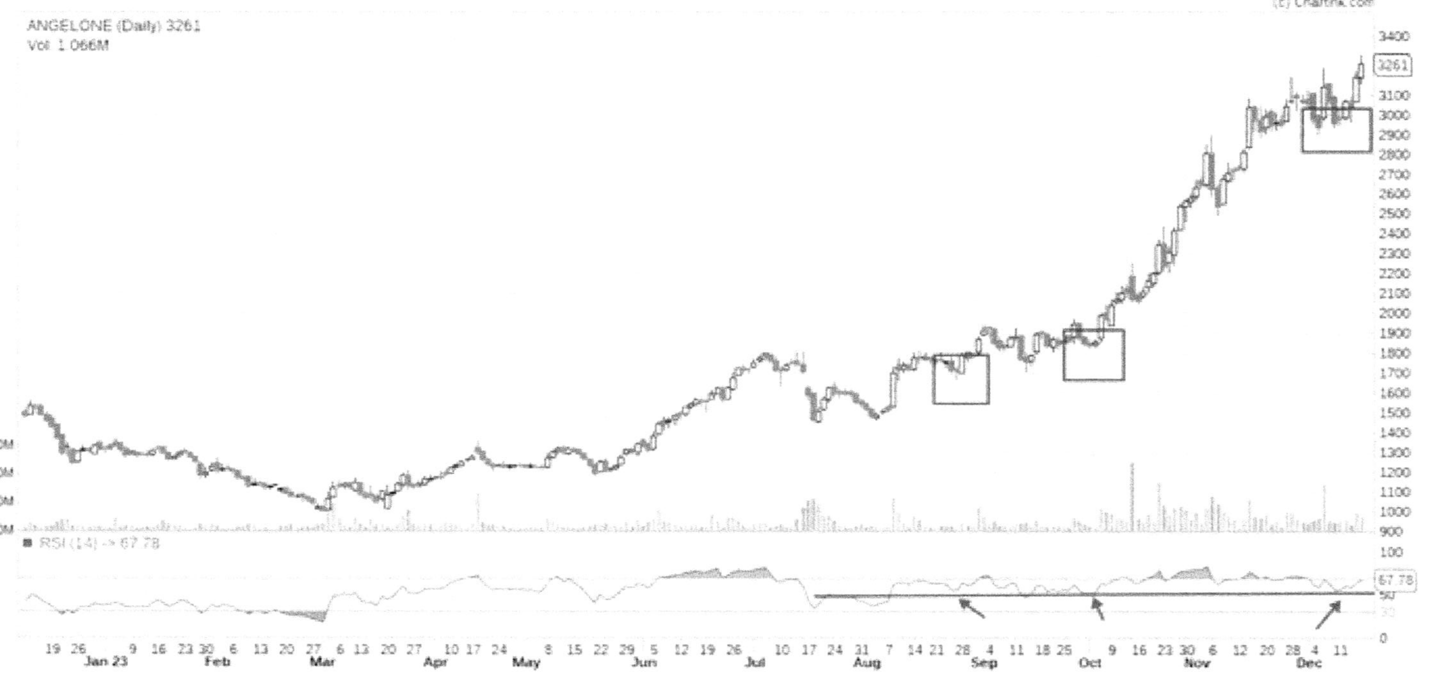

Image 9.19: Daily chart of Angel One Ltd.

Let us look at a few more examples to get a better conviction of this strategy.

Image 9.20 is Hero MotoCorp Ltd.'s monthly chart. The RSI is trading above 60 and has recently crossed above the 60 level. In the weekly chart (image 9.21) the RSI is trading above the 60 level. In the basic price action it has given a breakout from a rounding bottom pattern and is trading above its previous resistance level of 3,600.

Look at the RSI and see if it is trading above 60 level or not. But if you get a nice behaviour of the price action along with it, it is like icing on the cake!

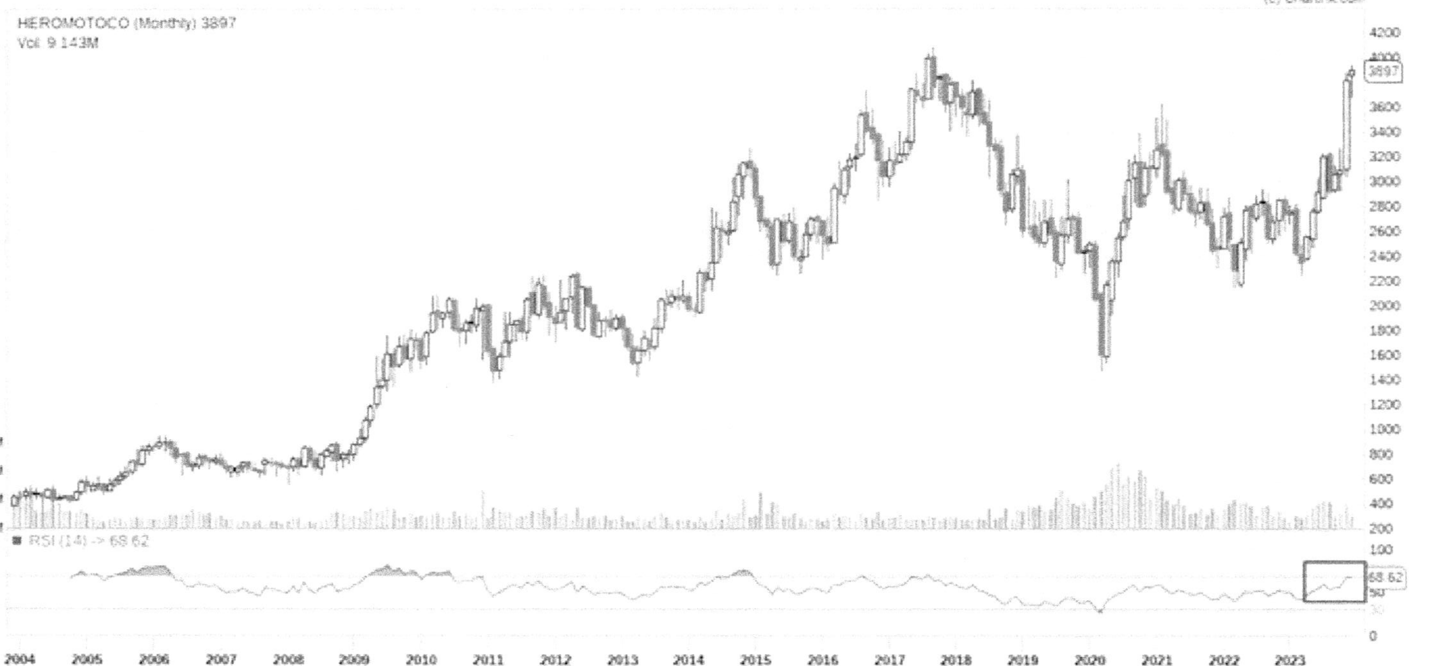

Image 9.20: Monthly chart of Hero MotoCorp Ltd. where the RSI is trading above 60

Image 9.21: Weekly chart of Hero MotoCorp Ltd. where RSI is trading above 60

On the daily chart of Hero MotoCorp Ltd. (image 9.22), whenever the RSI came and bounced off the level of 50, it gave a quick bounce and the price continued to move up further.

You could have entered in any of these instances when the RSI was bouncing off the 50 level or 'pyramided' which means that you could have added more shares to your initial position. Pyramiding is a great technique which is used by a lot of professional traders of the world as it essentially makes you ride a good stock (stocks in which the higher time frames are strong as they would be trading near all time highs and above important moving averages) with a decent position size too (more than the usual size that a trader would normally take—I personally prefer entering a position with 5–7% of the total capital in one stock and pyramid it up to 15–20% of total portfolio). Many times, you would have entered a stock at the right time and even held onto it with patience, but you did not have a good position size. You may have made a good percentage move in that stock, but that did not leave any significant impact on your portfolio as the actual profit was not that big.

You can also buy a good position size in a stock right away when you are buying it for the first time, but the thing is that you do not know beforehand if a stock would move in our favour or would hit our stop-loss. When you enter with a small position size, you can cut the position with a minor loss if your stop-loss hits. If the stock does not hit your stop-loss and starts to move in your direction, then you can add more shares to it later so that you can bet more on the stock which has already proven itself and is showing an upward trend.

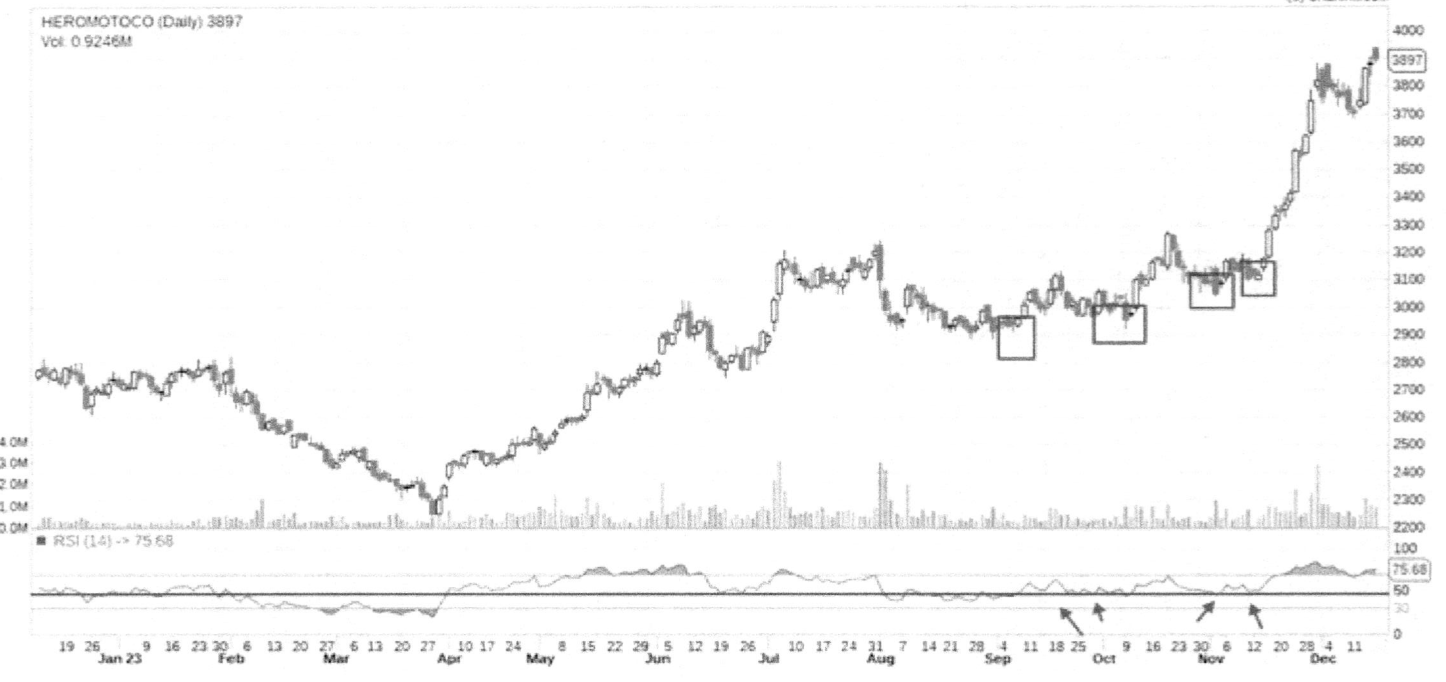

Image 9.22: Daily chart of Hero MotoCorp Ltd.

In the next example, let us first see if the criteria of this strategy get fulfilled in the monthly and weekly chart.

Image 9.23 is the monthly chart of Zensar Technologies Ltd. By now, you know the drill. Anytime you see a monthly chart, the first thing you will check is if the RSI is trading above 60 level. Here, RSI is above 60 level as required. This stock is breaking above the life highs, which is a good sign. It demonstrates that it has broken all previous resistances and is free. Some new traders may think that if a stock is at life highs, it may start falling, assuming that it has already gone up so much, how much more can it rise? But experienced traders would agree that if a stock makes new highs, it proves the fact that it has strength and people are ready to buy it at any level. That is why it is trading at this level whereas so many other stocks may be trading below their life highs or even their life lows.

Now let us check its weekly chart in image 9.24. When the RSI went above 60 and, in fact, went above the 70 (highlighted), the price went up from 300 to 550 levels. It almost doubled when the RSI went into the 'overbought' zone. After that, the price went into a slight corrective mode and retested 450 levels and RSI also came down and touched 50. Following this move, the RSI again went above 60 and continued trading above 60, which is exactly what we want in this strategy.

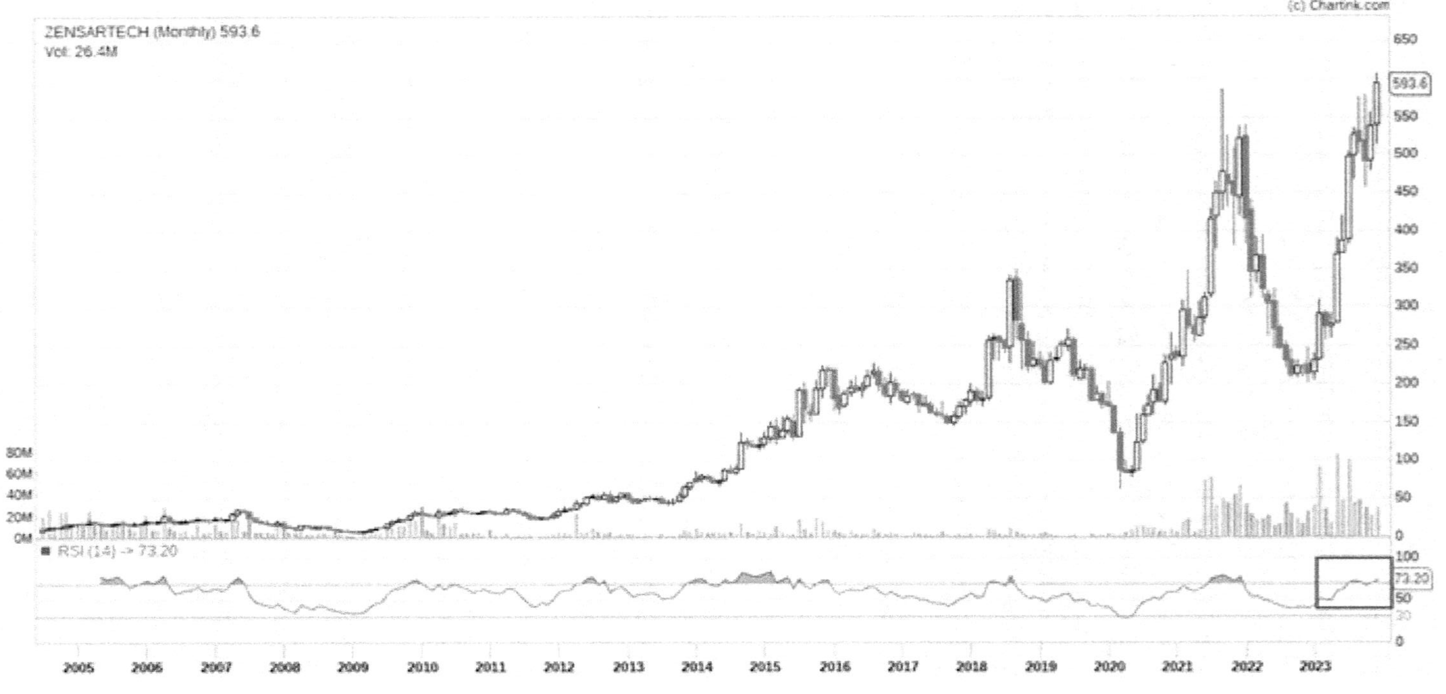

Image 9.23: Monthly chart of Zensar Technologies Ltd. with RSI trading above 60

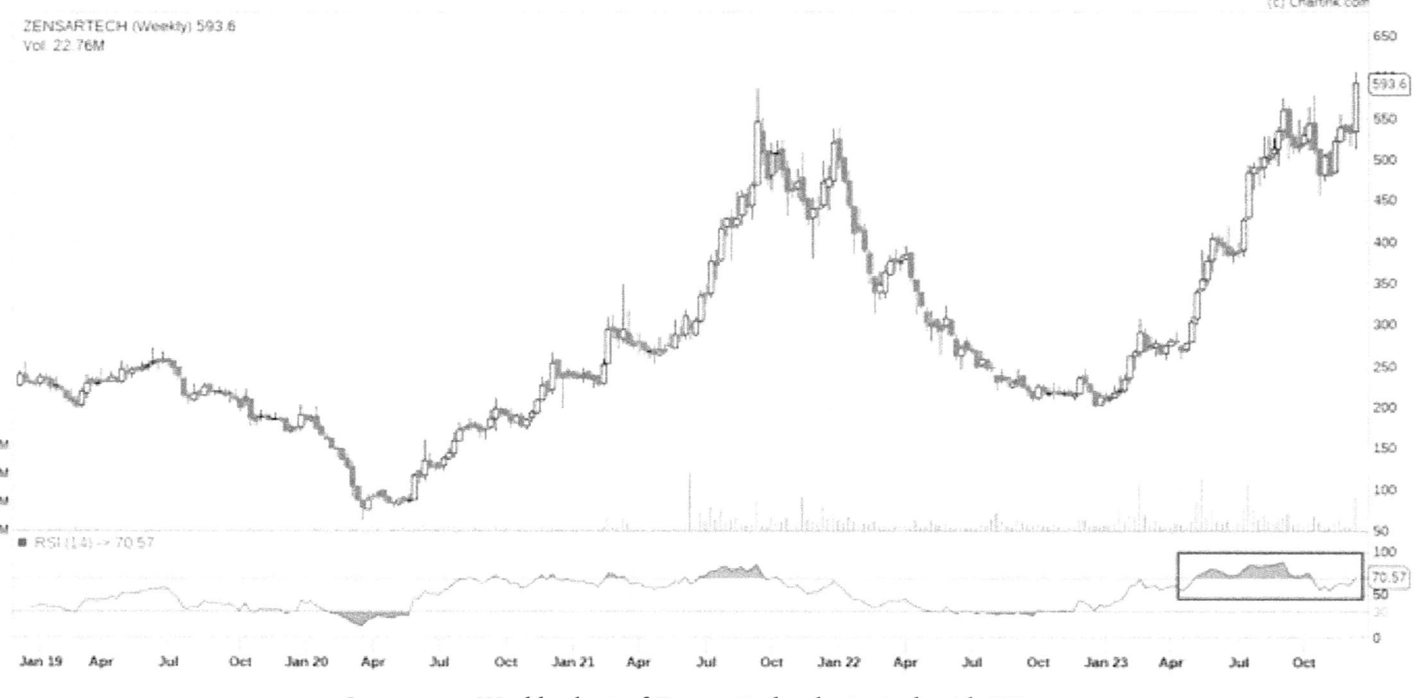

Image 9.24: Weekly chart of Zensar Technologies Ltd. with RSI

On the daily chart of Zensar Technologies Ltd. (image 9.25), the price took a support and bounced every time RSI went to 50 and bounced. Another thing to notice here is that once the RSI went below 50 around October 2023, the same zone of 50 RSI acted as a resistance in November 2023. Just like moving averages act as dynamic support and resistance, the RSI here is also acting as a dynamic support and resistance. Wait for the RSI to again move above 50 if you want a better entry, which happened soon as seen in image 9.25. Once the RSI went above 50 and the price moved from 500 to 560 levels, the price again started to drift down a bit in December 2023, the RSI again took support from the 50 levels before moving up sharply giving another entry point. Yes, you will not know in advance if the up move would be so sharp or not, but you just have to follow the process and take entry according to your setup. The result is not in your hands and that is fine.

As the saying goes, "We can't predict what the market is going to do and we don't NEED to predict to make money in the markets."

Image 9.25: Daily chart of Zensar Technologies Ltd. where RSI acts as a dynamic support and resistance

For the next example, KPIT Technologies Ltd., let us look at the monthly chart (image 9.26). The price has been moving up almost in a straight line. Many traders may not even try to trade this kind of stock and would look for other stocks which have fresh breakouts or have just started to move up from a support. But let us analyse all the time frames of this chart for a better picture. In the monthly chart, the criteria is getting fulfilled, which is, the RSI should be above 60.

Now let us check the weekly chart (image 9.27). Here too, RSI is trading comfortably above 60, hence we can go to the daily chart and study it further.

In image 9.28 the stock price gave a fresh opportunity for entry when the RSI touched 50 and bounced off it. From the price action perspective, it made a bullish candle near the 1,450 level which has been acting as a support over the past few days too. By entering at this level, you can actually get into a trade with a very small risk and that is the most important thing as we have discussed earlier. If you enter at a zone where the loss is minimum, you have won more than half of the battle as you have only the risk in control, the reward can be multifold if you sit with a winning trade with patience and self-discipline.

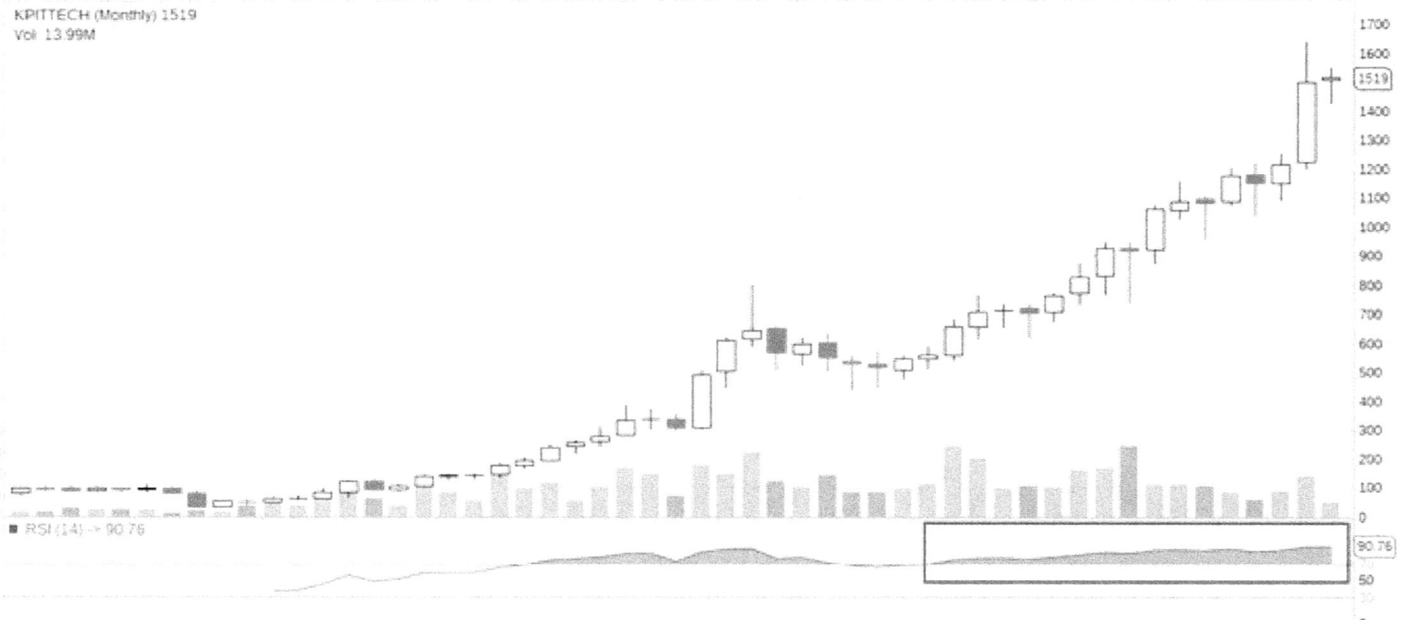

Image 9.26: Monthly chart of KPIT Technologies Ltd.

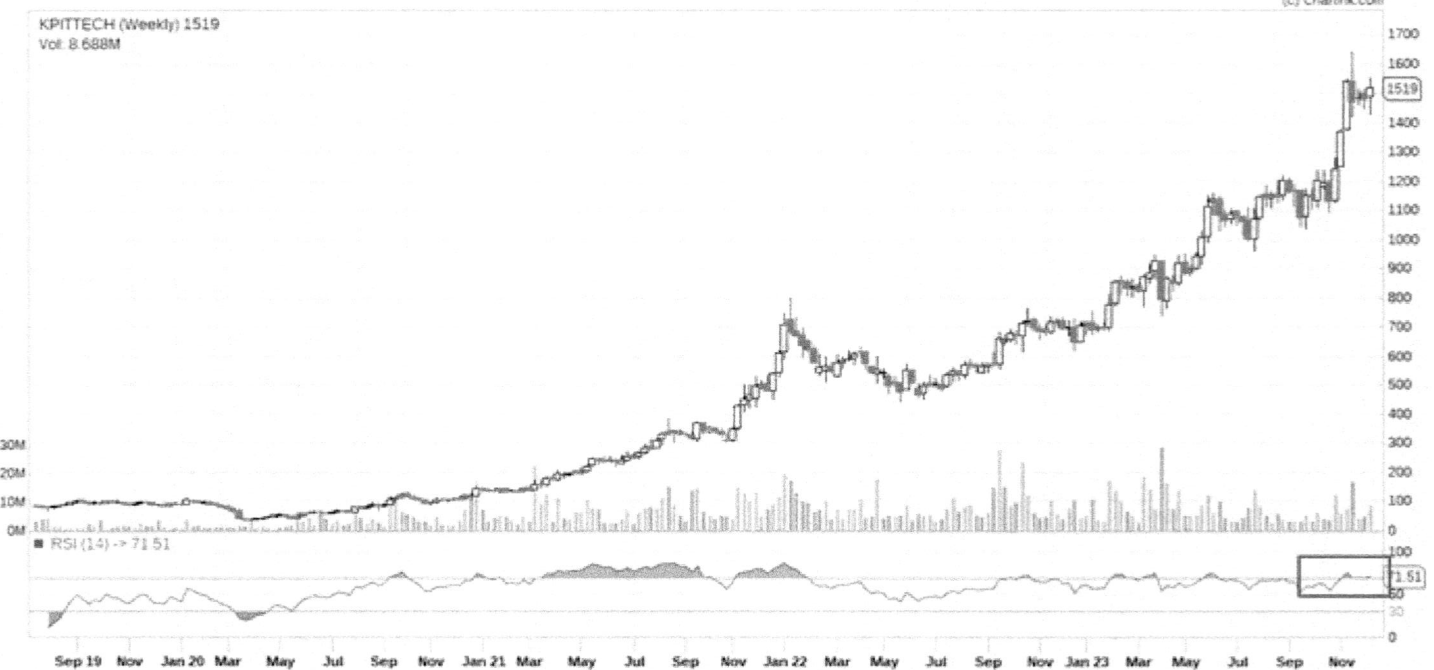

Image 9.27: Weekly chart of KPIT Technologies Ltd.

Image 9.28: Daily chart of KPIT Technologies Ltd.

On IDFC First Bank's monthly chart (image 9.29), the stock price gave a breakout from a big base and broke out above the high of 2017, which was around 84. Thereafter, it moved up to touch the level of 100. Then it retested the breakout level and tried to bounce back up. The most important thing which you look at here from the strategy's perspective is that the RSI is trading above the level of 60. Now that we know that it is, let us check the weekly chart.

In the weekly chart (image 9.30) it has just crossed above 60 on the RSI. It is even better if we find a scenario like this in which the higher time frame chart has just crossed above or bounced off the 60 level. It indicates that it can start to pick up momentum from here and you can grab the opportunity at the right time.

Now that the weekly chart is really nicely set up as the RSI has just crossed above the 60 level, let us see how the daily chart is holding up.

On the daily chart (image 9.31) the stock price just bounced off the 50 RSI a couple of days before and that was the perfect entry point. The basic price action was already in an uptrend as it was making higher highs, higher lows. It bounced off a higher low along with bouncing off the 50 RSI. Confirmation by basic price action along with 50 RSI acts as icing on the cake here.

We do not always need to get validation from the price action in this strategy. But if the price action compliments the RSI too, it adds more conviction to take the trade. This is true for any kind of strategy, though. All the indicators are derivates of the price itself, we use indicators as they simplify following the price action.

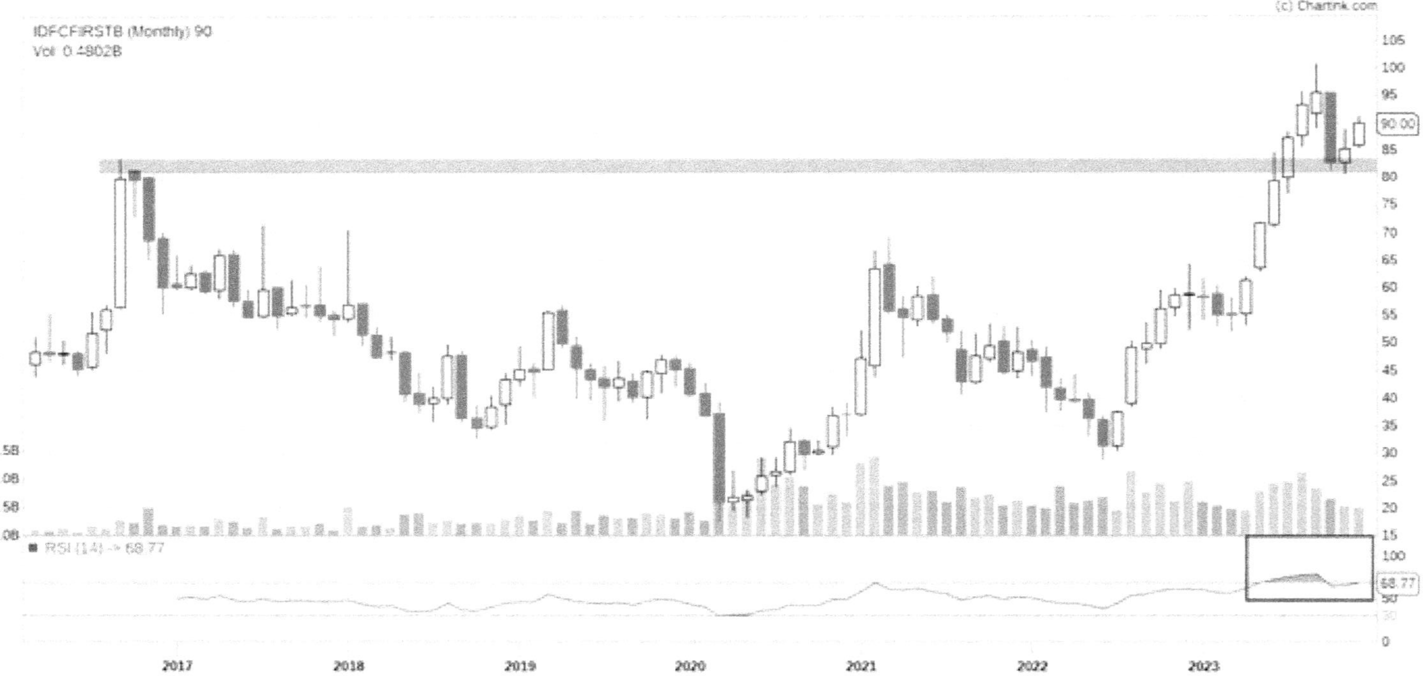

Image 9.29: Monthly chart of IDFC First Bank

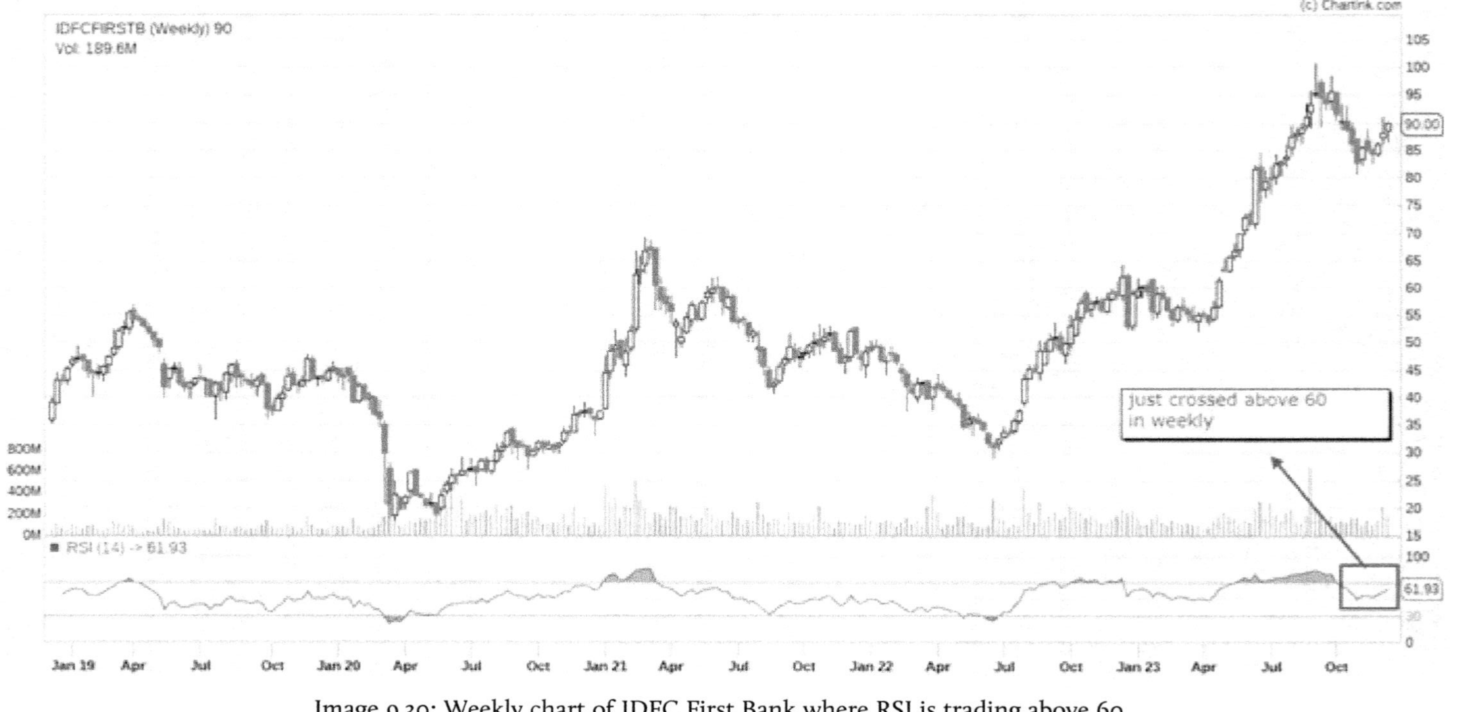

Image 9.30: Weekly chart of IDFC First Bank where RSI is trading above 60

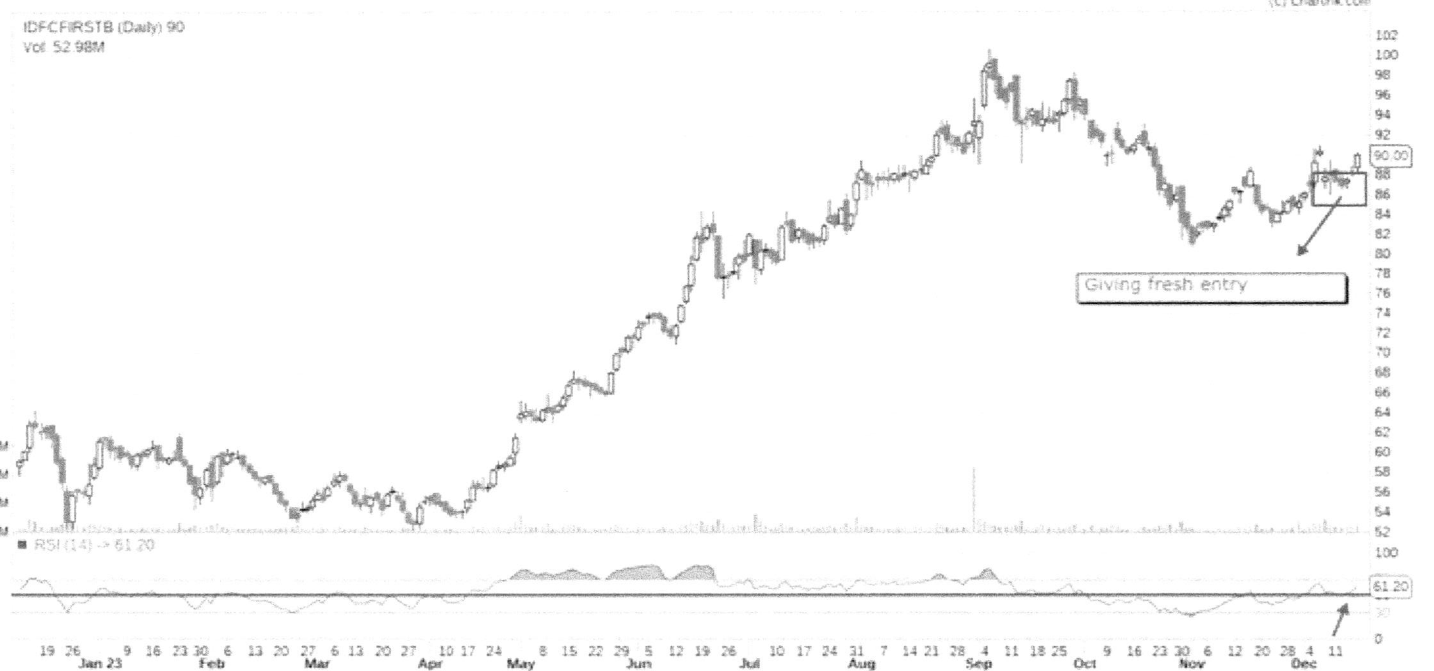

Image 9.31: Daily chart of IDFC First Bank where the basic price action was in an uptrend

The next example is Steel Authority of India Ltd (SAIL). In the monthly chart (image 9.32), there is a similar pattern as the weekly chart of the previous example (image 9.30). Here it gave a fresh move above RSI 60, which indicates that it is starting to gain momentum.

In the weekly chart (image 9.33), the RSI is comfortably trading above 60. Now let us check the daily chart.

In the daily chart (image 9.34), we can see from where it bounced from the RSI 50 mark and the way it moved up after that. Here too, earlier, when the RSI was trading below the 50 level, it acted as a resistance and price kept falling whenever that happened. It was only once that the RSI broke out above the 50 level that the RSI started behaving as a support. Whenever it bounced off the 50 level, there was a good up move in the price. In the later bounce, it gave a great up move and the price went up from 90 to 111 level in a few days itself.

Image 9.32: Monthly chart of Steel Authority of India Ltd. (SAIL)

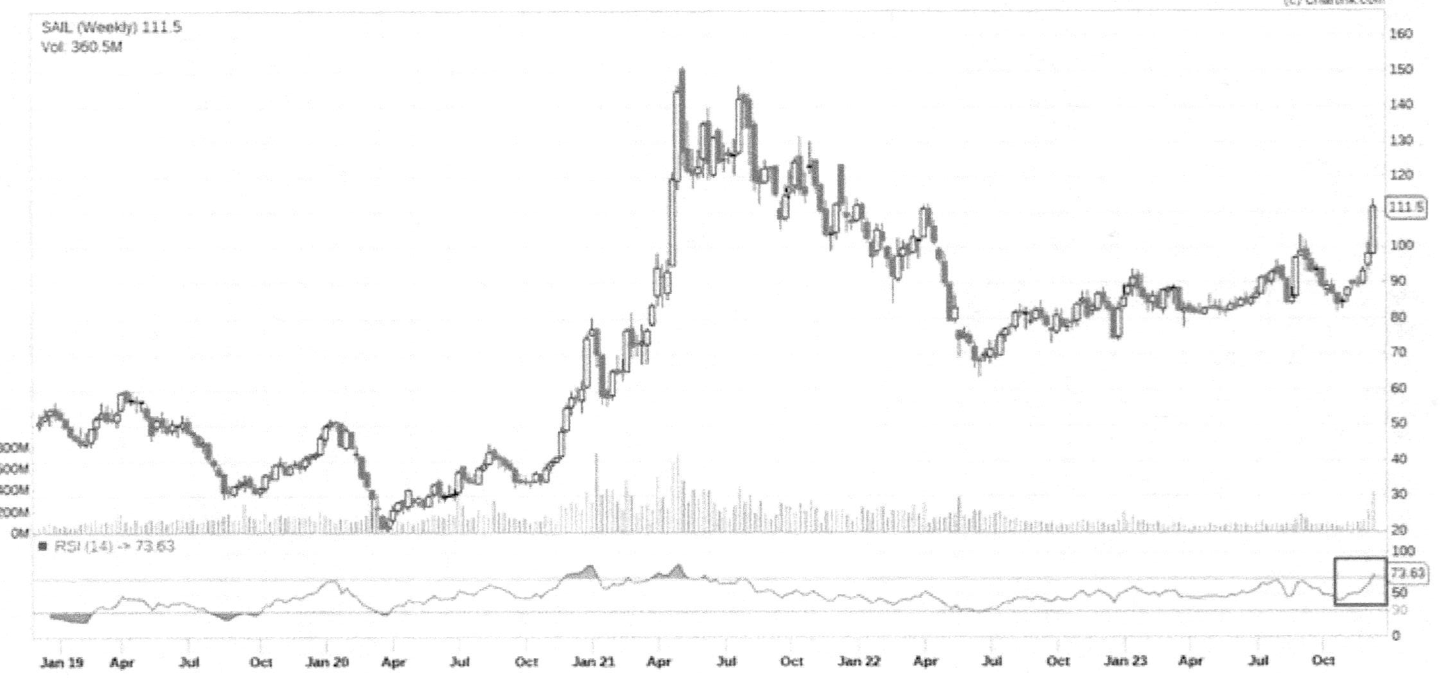

Image 9.33: Weekly chart of Steel Authority of India Ltd. where the stock is starting to gain momentum

Image 9.34: Daily chart of Steel Authority of India Ltd.

Indian Railway Finance Corporation (IRFC) was a favourite among many traders in the years 2023 and 2024. In IRFC's monthly chart (image 9.35), the RSI has been trading above the 60 level for a long time and during this period, the price went up from 40 to 100 level. The RSI remained above the 60 and in fact 70 level too. As discussed earlier, many traders would have stopped looking at this stock as they may think that it has already moved up so much in a short span of time, so how much more steam is left now? But I hope you have had a perspective shift and realise that something that has moved up can continue moving up much more, with even more momentum.

In the weekly chart of IRFC (image 9.36), the RSI has been trading above the 60 level. Recently, the stock broke out of a range and the volume also spiked up along with this move, adding more conviction to the up move. Whenever price moves up along with volume, it is always a great sign and adds conviction to the move, indicating that a lot of players (mostly big ones) are taking an interest in it.

In the daily chart (image 9.37), the RSI had been indicating that the up move would start as it broke out above the 50 level. Then the same level of 50 started acted as a support, giving multiple entry points.

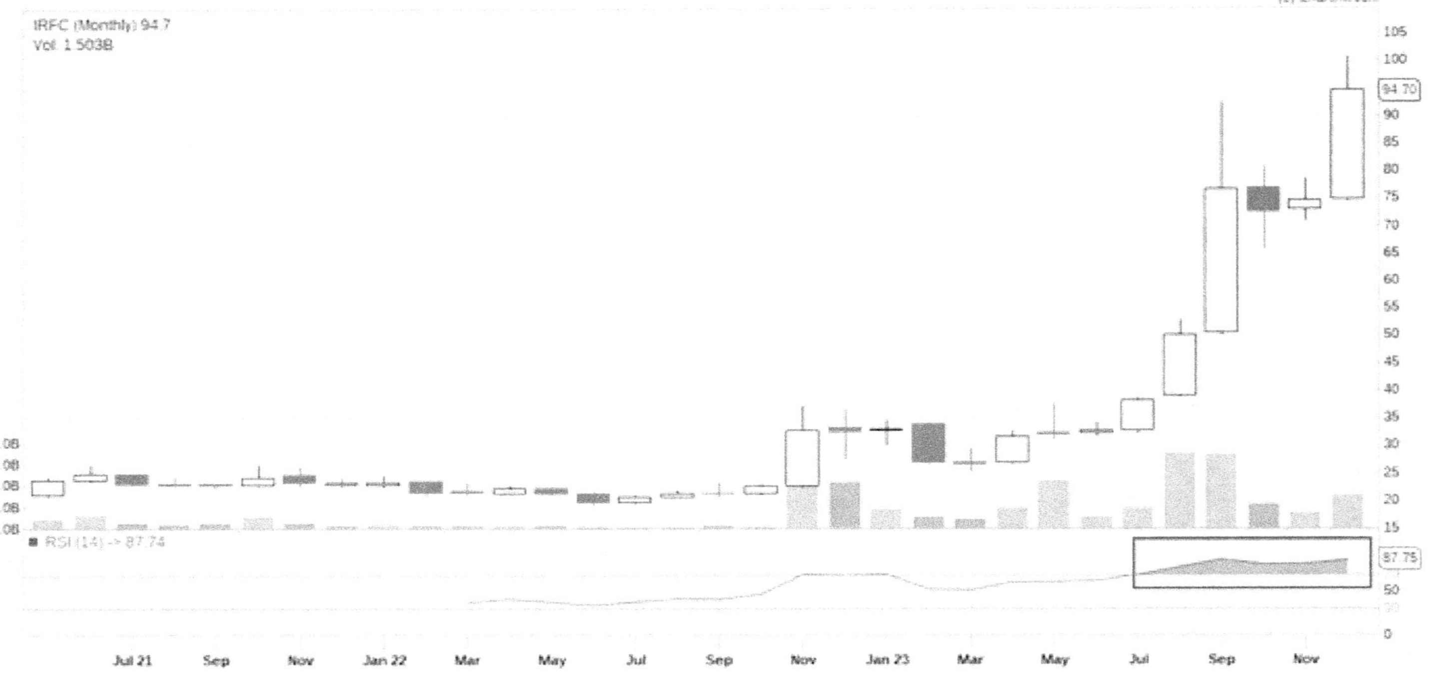

Image 9.35: Monthly chart of Indian Railway Finance Corporation (IRFC)

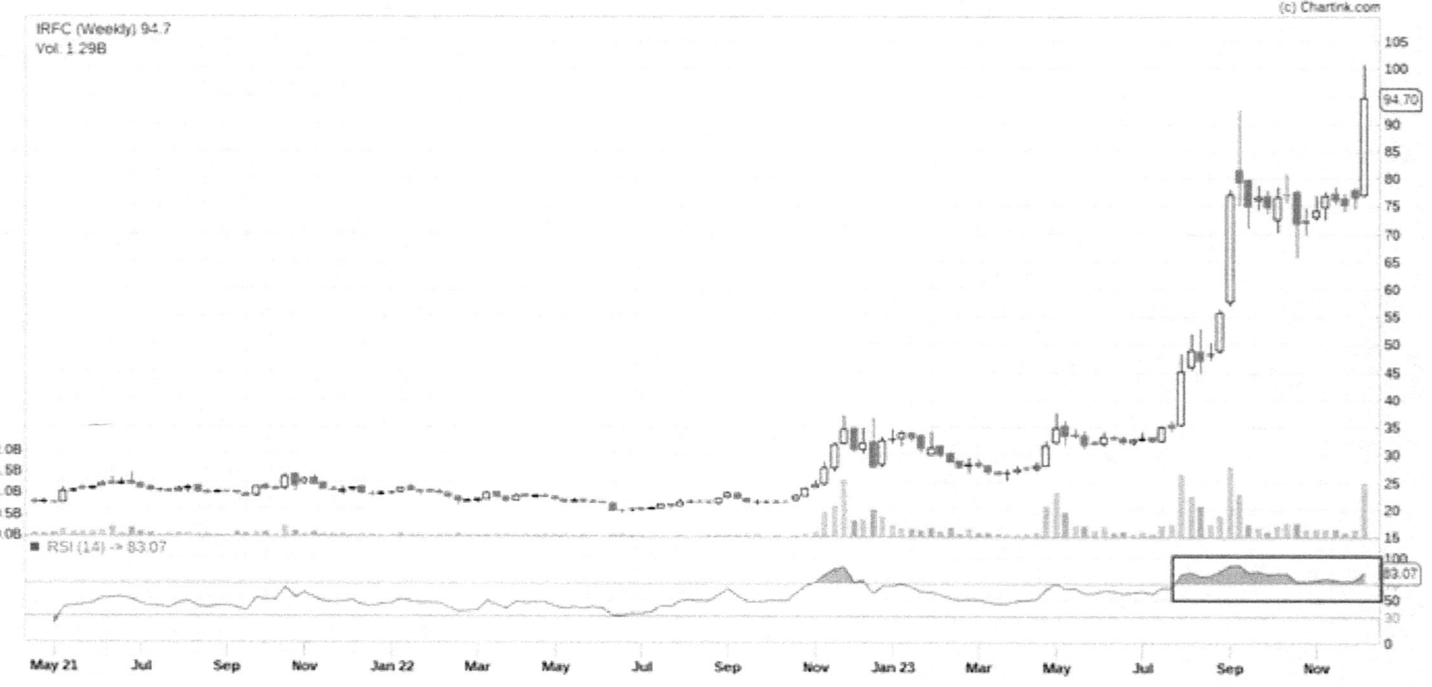

Image 9.36: Weekly chart of IRFC where the RSI has been trading above 60 level

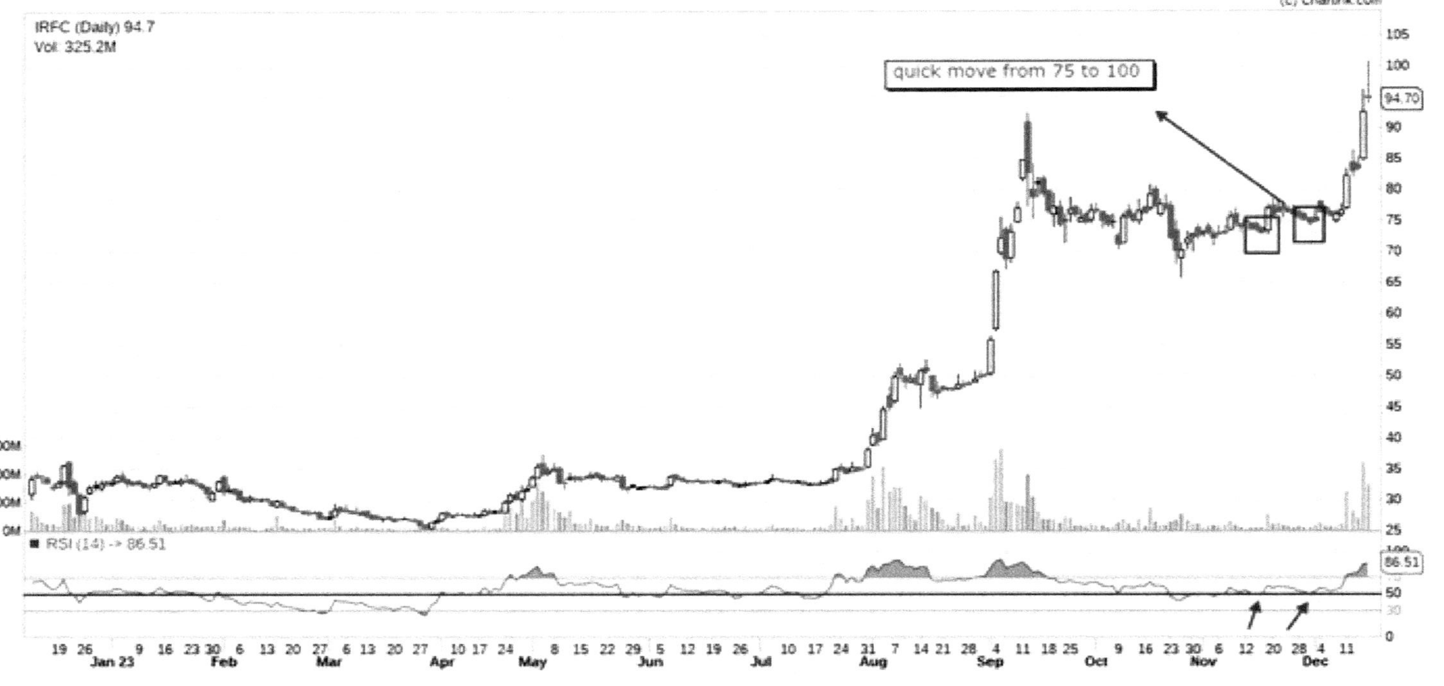

Image 9.37: Daily chart of IRFC

The last example of this strategy is Geojit Financial Services Ltd. Geojit's monthly chart is shown in image 9.38. The price made a rounding bottom and started to move up along with good volumes. The RSI is also trading above the 60 level.

In the weekly chart of Geojit Financial Services Ltd. (image 9.39) too, RSI is trading above the 60 level, which is exactly what we want for this strategy to work seamlessly.

In the daily chart (image 9.40), once the RSI came and bounced off the 50 level, it gave a perfect opportunity for entry and the price shot up in a matter of two days itself, giving us handsome profits in no time!

You must be really excited to try this out yourself on your universe of stocks. I really want you to try this out on the maximum number of stocks you can so that the point is driven home and you understand how simple and effective strategies are to make decent money in the markets. We do not really need anything complex. Complexity looks good for teaching as it may sound fancy, but you need easy-to-follow steps which you can execute without much thought as the main goal is to make money in the markets and not to write a thesis. Hence, the simpler the strategy, the better it is.

To check this strategy on the Upsurge platform in video format, please scan this QR code

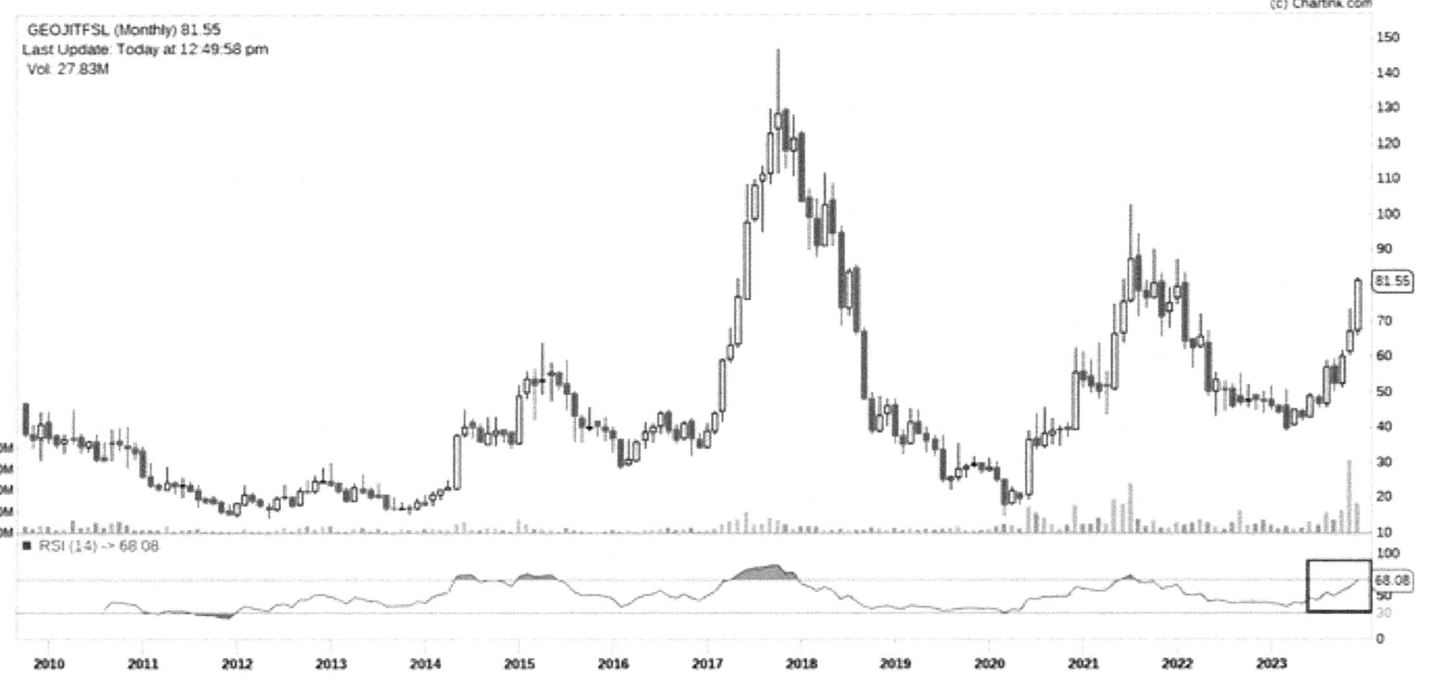

Image 9.38: Monthly chart of Geojit Financial Services Ltd. where the price made a rounding bottom

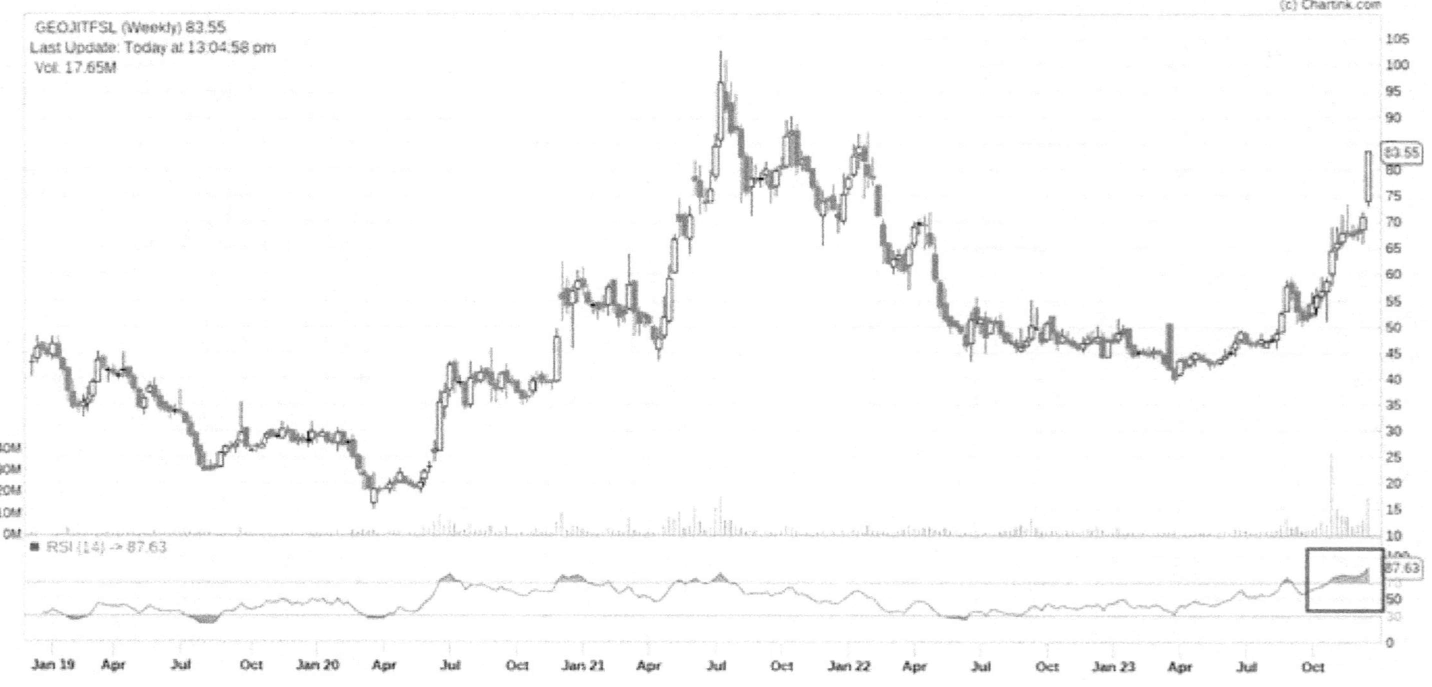

Image 9.39: Weekly chart of Geojit Financial Services Ltd. where RSI is trading above 60

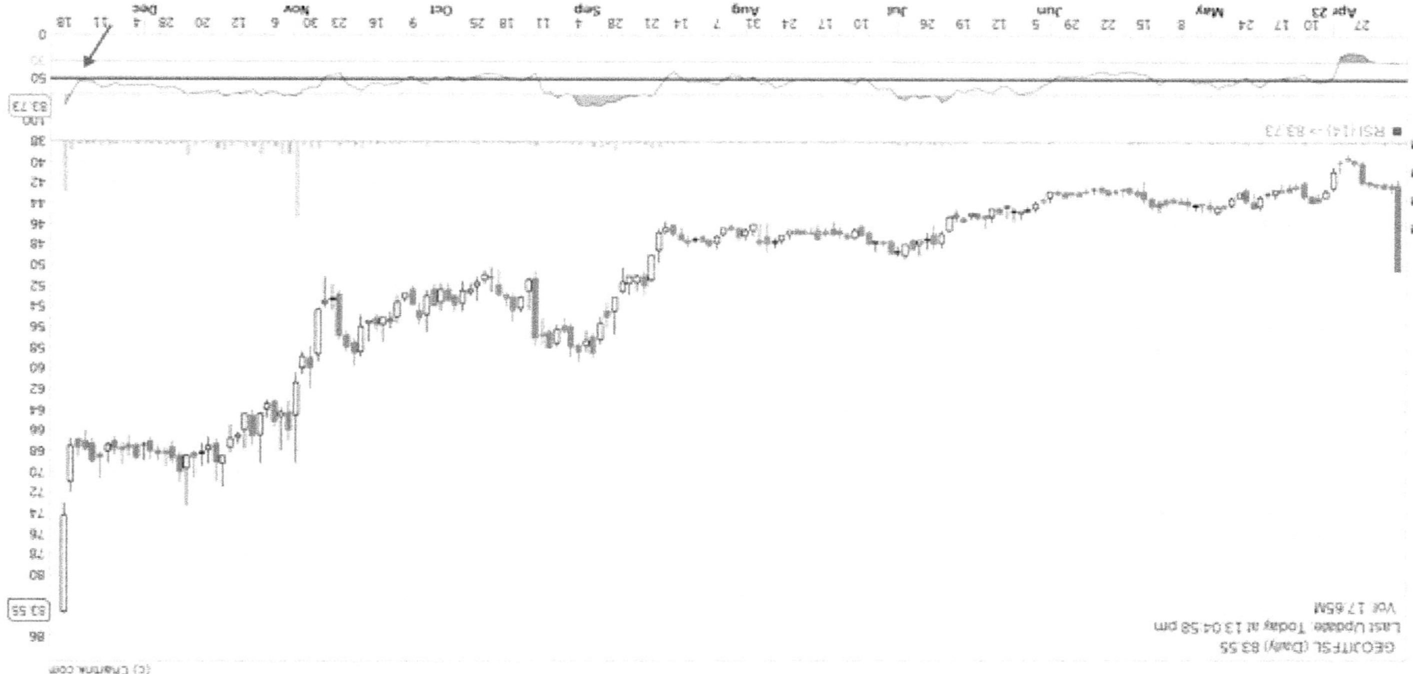

Image 9.40: Daily chart of Geojit Financial Services Ltd.

III

ESSENTIAL TOOLS FOR TRADING

"There is the plain fool, who does the wrong thing at all times everywhere, but there is the Wall Street fool, who thinks he must trade all the time."

—Jesse Livermore, American stock trader

10

Checklists: Even Pilots Use Them

According to Dictionary.com, "A checklist is a list of items, as names or tasks, for comparison, verification, or other checking purposes." A checklist is an *aid,* a helping tool for something that involves repetitive tasks. We have a limited amount of memory and attention so it helps in reducing human error.

Even if someone has a monkey mind, which keeps on jumping from one emotion to the other in the blink of an eye, it is advisable to follow a systematic approach to trading which lists down all the steps that need to be followed for effective trading. This is where checklists help.

The chances of error caused by our emotions are reduced to a large extent if we use checklists. It still cannot be zero, as we may interfere in the process at any time. Even algorithmic traders face this problem. They may have built an amazing algorithm trading process with complete back-testing, which may have given a proven no-loss outcome and *still* may mess it up by over-running the process in the case of emergencies or panic.

I find it funny when people advise new traders to trade without emotions. We *are* humans because we have emotions and we cannot block it or turn it off at will. Yes, there are systems and processes like meditation and mindfulness through which we can learn to manage our emotions and handle our reactions to some extent, but we can never get rid of our emotions. We do not even need to do that to trade effectively.

We can create a checklist and follow that religiously to trade peacefully and effectively. Defining our rules and noting them down on a checklist helps us follow them and avoid getting derailed off our set path.

Whenever someone puts a trade, they hope to make money or get out with a small loss and move on to the next trade. But the problem arises when you do not follow your own plan. You end up trading according to your emotions and usually take the wrong decisions only to regret it later.

You may have decided that you will not exit the stock at a small profit and only exit if and when you get a signal. For example, you would exit only if the price breaks down below the 50-EMA on a daily chart, otherwise we will keep on holding the stock. But, there may be a situation where all the stocks in your portfolio may be falling badly on some day due to some negative news. Your stocks may not trade below your trailing stop-loss level. In fact, it may not even be close to your trailing stop-loss, moving average, supertrend, or any other signal like the RSI or MACD, but you still may exit in panic just by looking at the loss amount in your portfolio.

Negative news usually seems more negative to our brains and we start imagining the worst-case situations. Many of my friends have exited from *all* of their stocks under one minute when they panicked while watching really bad news. Multiple times, they have regretted it immediately, as the prices would bounce back up almost on the same trading day itself or the next trading day. There were times when the news was fake and the stocks would shoot back up even much higher than the price at which they were trading before the news broke out. At that time, my friends would regret a lot as they could not re-enter those stocks because they became really expensive—making my friends wait for a pullback, which never came in most of the cases. They regretted exiting a great stock in their portfolio in panic. There was nothing they could do about it and would only end up sharing the sad stories of missing the entire move of the stocks even after identifying it at the right moment.

A checklist tells us exactly what to do in a situation and the steps we need to take if things go wrong. The best example of checklists can be seen in the aviation industry. Pilots cannot even think about operating successfully if it was not for checklists. They have detailed checklists before the flight, during the flight and just before landing.

They have to follow a number of steps to ensure that everything goes smoothly as planned.

As traders, you should also prepare and follow a checklist which is designed according to your own rules and systems. These rules are ideally created after years of trial and error with trading systems and strategies. Once you know what is suitable and works for *you* as an independent trader, include it in your checklist and make sure to follow it religiously.

Two separate traders may have totally different checklists, yet it may serve them wonderfully and it is completely fine. You need not replicate someone else's checklist. This is one mistake which a lot of new traders make—they follow the checklist and rules of legendary traders and their role models. That strategy and checklist may have worked for them according to their capital, risk appetite, experience in the market, etc. and it may not work at all for you as there is no point in following someone else's rules.

Maintain your trading journal and reflect on what is working for *you* and why. Note down those points, form a proper checklist and trade only when those pointers are fulfilled.

Checklists are really helpful especially when you buy stocks for a longer period of time for your portfolio. The more points from the checklists are getting met, the more conviction you get to buy that particular stock.

Here is an example of my checklist before buying a portfolio stock. It will help you understand the aspects to look for while creating the checklist.

1. Is it above the 200 EMA?

This is the most important point of the entire checklist. That is why I have kept it in the very first position. If this metric is not fulfilled, I may not even look at any other checklist points.

As you know, 200-EMA is like the backbone of a stock. If any stock is trading below the 200-EMA on a daily chart, it means that its overall structure is weak and you should not buy that stock. You can look to short that stock (sell first and then book a desired profit later by buying it) if needed and if the price structure looks ready. But never buy any stock which is below the 200-EMA.

2. Is the trend intact?

Now that we have a stock which is trading above 200-EMA, see if it is in trend or not. You can see this with the very basics like checking if the stock is making higher highs and higher lows or not.

3. Is the stock trading above key moving averages or not?

Since we are talking about the long term here, check if the stock is trading above 20-and 50-EMA in the weekly chart or not.

If the moving averages are sloping upwards and the price is trading above the 50-EMA, it shows that it is in uptrend. If it is trading above the 20-EMA, it shows that it is in an upward momentum too and can continue in it's upward journey.

4. Above supertrend or not?

The supertrend strategy has been discussed in one of the earlier chapters. You can always go back and check the strategy once again and note down all the important factors that we should know while using the supertrend indicator.

5. MACD crossover or not?

Check if the MACD has crossed over or is it still trading below the signal line, which means that the divergence is negative and indicates a bearish signal. Make sure that the MACD is trading above the signal line and is positive.

Since we are looking at portfolio stocks here, so MACD should be positive in the monthly time frame. If the MACD is not favourable in the higher time frames like the monthly and weekly, it can take a long time before the stock starts moving up again and it may stay in downtrend for weeks, months and even years.

6. RSI above 50 or not?

A stock catches upward momentum only once the RSI starts to trade above 50 level. Depending on your holding period, check the RSI in that time frame. If you plan to hold for the long term, you need to check if RSI is trading above 50 or not in the weekly and monthly time frames. If you are trading for a short move, check the daily chart.

7. Net profit

This is relevant only if you want to buy a stock for your portfolio and intend to hold it for a few years. Do a basic check of fundamentals like checking if the net profit and earnings per share is increasing in the last three years or not.

There are a lot of complex things to know for studying the financials of a company. Keep it really simple as you need to focus mostly on technical analysis even for your portfolio stocks (for example, avoid a stock completely if it is trading below the 200-EMA even if the fundamentals look great).

8. Promoter + Mutual Fund + FII holding is above 50%

This is another fundamental point which you need to check only for portfolio stocks and not for swing trading. You only want to hold it for a few days, till the trend is intact, in swing trading). Check this online from any business website. See if the promoter, mutual fund and FII combined hold at least 50% in a stock or not, as it shows that the big players are interested in it.

If the promoter itself does not have much stake in a stock, or if the promoter holding is constantly declining, it could be a red flag and we need to find better opportunities where the promoter holds a decent chunk of the pie.

9. Circuit stocks

Another important part of the checklist is that the stocks we are going to buy in our portfolio should not be circuit or freeze stocks, which basically means that they should not move in circuits. Once in a while, it is possible for most of the stocks to hit circuits when the market witnesses some catastrophic news. Such days are rare and we cannot do much about it. But the stocks should have a minimum volume turnover in a day so that it does not move in a circuit. Anyone would love their stocks to keep moving up in circuits as it gives a very quick move in a matter of days. But when the same happens on the way down, you feel helpless and will not be able to exit your stocks when you need to. You can only wait for the day when the circuit opens and you can finally exit.

Sometimes when you enter a small stock and it starts hitting upper circuits, you get excited looking at your profits, but when the same stock starts hitting lower circuits, we first see our profit evaporating into thin air and then see the stock going into loss. It is one of the worst feelings for a trader to see a good amount of profit first and then exiting the stock in loss. Eventually, there was nothing that the trader could do about it. So instead of going through this emotional turmoil, it is better to avoid these kinds of stocks.

10. Micro caps

Ideally, do not buy micro-cap stocks if you are new to the market. While there is no fixed definition of a micro-cap company, it is best to avoid stocks which have a market capitalisation of less than 1000 crores. As these companies are relatively smaller and their stocks have really low volumes, most of the time, it makes it easy to manipulate. Use the best of your analysis before entering a trade in these stocks and they may behave totally opposite. It is always advisable to stick to stocks which have abundant volumes—getting in and out of them should not be a problem.

The stocks which have given amazing returns in the past would have fulfilled most of the above points of the checklist.

It can happen that sometimes a few points will not get fulfilled, and that is fine. However, the more points that get checked, the better it is.

Now that you know how to make a checklist and follow it, let's cover one of the most overlooked topics—the trading journal. A trading journal is like a balance sheet of a trader—it tells us about the patterns and behavior of the trader and how they can improve themselves by reflecting on the journal and taking appropriate steps.

Technical analysis and fundamental analysis are overrated. Discipline and patience are underrated.

11

Trading Journal: Read Your Own Balance Sheet, Not of Other Businesses

Small businesses turn into mega corporations, when they are built brick by brick, with each step following a well-defined process. Some of these have been discussed in this chapter.

UNVEILING THE SECRETS OF BUSINESS GIANTS

Have you ever wondered what makes McDonald's so special? They sell burgers, just like countless other places, but somehow, they have become a giant in the world of fast food. Sure, they use a franchise model to spread their restaurants everywhere, but so do many others without getting anywhere close to McDonald's success. And think about Amazon—it started as a small website selling books and grew into a trillion-dollar company that pretty much sells everything under the sun. How did they get so big?

THE POWER OF STANDARD OPERATING PROCEDURES (SOP)

Strong foundations are blocks of tallest buildings, having a solid consistent system in place can transform business. Let us rethink our question: How do some businesses grow so large? Or how do they become giants in their fields? Take manufacturing as an example. Making a few items is one thing, but producing them on a massive scale is an entirely different challenge. The secret to achieving such growth and scale lies in having a solid system in place. It is this system, often referred to as standard operating procedures (SOPs), that transform businesses into leaders in their industry, like McDonald's or Amazon. It is not just about what they do, but how they do it consistently and efficiently on a grand scale that sets them apart.

THE CRUCIAL ROLE OF PROCESS CONSISTENCY

Like Bruce Lee said, "I fear not the man who has practised 10,000 kicks once, but I fear the man who has practised one kick 10,000 times." You may think—if having a process is the key, then why does every business not grow big? The real question is whether they apply their process thoroughly, from top to bottom. Are they using a well-defined framework to guide their decisions at every turn? While we cannot control the outcomes directly, consistently doing the right things over the long run can significantly boost your chances of success.

This principle is not just for big businesses. It also holds true in the stock market. What sets successful hedge funds apart from the average retail trader? It boils down to their disciplined adherence to a tested process and applying it rigorously to every decision they make.

REFINEMENT THROUGH ITERATIONS—THE KEY TO SUCCESS

Stock trading involves controlling more variables, than just reading technical indicators. How do you create a process that is strong enough to improve your chances of success over time? It is all about refinement through iterations. You need to meticulously record every aspect of your trading activities.

For instance:

- Why did you decide to make a specific trade?
- What was your emotional state at that moment?
- Why did you pick this sector?
- How long did you hold on to the trade, and what ultimately prompted you to sell?

Keeping track of these details helps you understand your decisions better, allowing you to fine-tune your approach for future success.

THE CHALLENGE OF RETAIL TRADING: EMOTIONS VS. STRATEGY

It is fascinating to consider that with over 3,000 technical indicators and countless strategies for technical analysis available online, each promising significant profits, the vast majority of retail traders still struggle to achieve profitability in the stock market. This raises an important question: why do 90% of retail traders fail to make money, despite the abundance of resources and the time invested in learning technical analysis? Most retail traders do not maintain a trading journal, as they find it a tedious and dull part of the job. However, constantly logging your trades is a crucial step in building trade discipline.

WHY DO PEOPLE NOT TAKE MAINTAINING TRADING JOURNALS SERIOUSLY?

Like many documentation tasks, keeping a trading journal is often seen as a tedious part of stock trading. Additionally, maintaining a journal for just a week or two rarely results in significant improvements. However, diligently updating it over a period of 6–8 months can uncover both beneficial and detrimental patterns in one's trading style.

This is similar to adopting a healthy diet: eating well for only a few days will not greatly affect your fitness, but integrating healthy eating into your lifestyle can bring substantial and enduring results. In the same way, a trading journal can offer valuable insights that enhance your trading decisions over time.

Another reason traders neglect maintaining a journal is their over-reliance on memory. Many believe they can recall all the details of their stock holdings, target prices, stop-loss levels, and effective strategies. This reliance, however, can be deceptive. A comprehensive historical record of personal trades can be crucial for refining and improving your trading approach.

IMPORTANCE OF MAINTAINING A TRADING JOURNAL

The best way to learn is to learn from your own mistakes, and journaling is the best way to document your mistakes. The primary goal of a trading journal is to cut through all the noise and give you logical insights from your past mistakes. It is like having a coach who helps you get better with every trade. Keeping a trading journal can offer numerous advantages for traders, helping them enhance their performance and refine their strategies.

BENEFITS OF JOURNALING TRADES

1. *Strategy identification:* By journaling your trades, you can effectively identify which strategies work best for you. This allows you to capitalise on successful trading strategies and refine or discard the less effective ones.

2. *Preventing overtrading:* Recording your trades enables you to recognise whether you are overtrading or not. Overtrading can result in high brokerage and transaction costs, as well as emotional exhaustion. Therefore, finding the right balance is essential for successful trading.

3. *Capital allocation assessment:* Through journaling, you can evaluate the health of your capital allocation. This includes analysing your profit margins for each profitable trade and assessing the efficiency of your capital rotation strategies.

4. *Sector analysis:* Keeping track of your trades helps you identify which sectors you excel in. This insight allows you to focus on sectors where you have a deep understanding of the business dynamics and a proven track record of picking winning stocks.

5. *Emotional cycle recognition:* Journaling your trades enables you to identify patterns in your emotional cycle. You can pinpoint times when you should avoid trading due to heightened emotional states and develop risk management strategies for maintaining discipline, especially after winning streaks.

FOUNDATION OF AN EFFECTIVE TRADING JOURNAL

Although there are myriad Microsoft Excel spreadsheet templates for trading journals floating online, have you ever wondered what makes one trading journal better than the rest? It is similar to how everyone has their shoe size—each trader has their unique way of keeping tabs on their stock trades.

While we all care about how we are doing by evaluating our performance metrics, some trading journals only focus on tangible reasons like monitoring financial performance metrics, such as profits, losses, duration of stockholdings, and transaction fees. However, we need to include intangible reasons as well.

TIPS ON CREATING A COMPREHENSIVE, FUNCTIONAL TRADING JOURNAL

A better trading journal would be a perfect mix of tracking tangible and non-tangible metrics. It should be adaptable and customizable enough to cater to your future needs and to new metrics that you would like to track and provide a well-defined framework for your risk management.

Here are a few types of most commonly used trading journals.

1. Maintaining your journal on Excel
This is the journal that I maintain on an Excel file. It has all the basic things that I need like:

Date of entry: The date on which I entered the stock.

Script: Name of the stock.

Strike: Price at which it was bought.

Quantity: The total number of shares that I bought.

SL: Price at which I will take the stop-loss and exit.

SL Points: Difference between the cost price and the stop-loss price.

SL%: The stop-loss in percentage terms.

Max Risk: This is calculated by multiplying the stop-loss points with the quantity. It tells me the maximum amount of money I am ready to lose in a trade. This is really important as I already know the amount which I am ready to lose and if I want to enter that trade or not.

Date Ex: Date on which the stock was exited.

CMP: Current market price.

Gain point: Total points that I have gained in a trade.

Gain %: Total gain in percentage terms.

Amount: Total amount which we get by multiplying the cost price with the total quantity.

Exit Amount: Amount after exiting the stock, whether in profit or in loss.

P/L: Net Profit or loss that I made in a particular trade.

Open/Close: This is to note if the stock is currently running (open) or has been already booked (close). I have used a basic filter in this column where I can select the option to see the trades which are already closed or open, to know how many trades are currently running so that I can track only those.

Entry and exit reasons: This is probably the most important part of the journal. You need to write the exact reason for entry and the exact reason for exit. Once you start maintaining this part, you get to know that you exit your positions without any reason, most of the time. Once you note down the same thing a number of times, it will help you change this habit. Whenever you wish to exit a stock without reason the next time, your subconscious mind will stop you from doing so.

Traders can add another column to their trading journals—Emotions/feelings while entering and exiting.

2. Basic physical journal

These are just like notebooks and are best suited for people who prefer writing down things on paper with a pen, rather than using digital media. There are a lot of journals available online. I have tried using this one which my friend Jaskirat Singh has developed:

Existing solutions, such as basic ledgers from traditional brokers or Microsoft Excel sheets do not reward maintaining a trading journal. They offer limited customisation and lack the advanced analytics needed for a nuanced understanding of one's trading patterns. Moreover, while there are web applications for maintaining a trading journal, many are tailored to the U.S. market. These solutions often come with a pricing model not suited for Indian retail traders and lack integration with Indian brokerage firms, creating a significant gap in accessibility and functionality.

ADDRESSING THE GAPS—INTRODUCING TRADINGJOURNAL.AI

With the advancement of modern technology, trading journals need to become more intelligent and adaptable. Considering these gaps, I felt a strong urge to come up with something that would fix these issues. Even though the tools available have some good features, their shortcomings can hold traders back from getting a deep understanding of their trading habits. The shortage of tailored insights and the absence of built-in risk management tools further compound the challenge of achieving consistent trading success. This is where my journey with TradingJournal.ai begins. My conviction in this platform stems from a clear recognition of the needs of Indian retail traders—a segment that has been underserved until now. TradingJournal.ai is a thoughtfully designed solution, leveraging artificial intelligence to offer personalised insights. Its affordability and compatibility with Indian brokers mark a significant value addition over the limitations of other platforms.

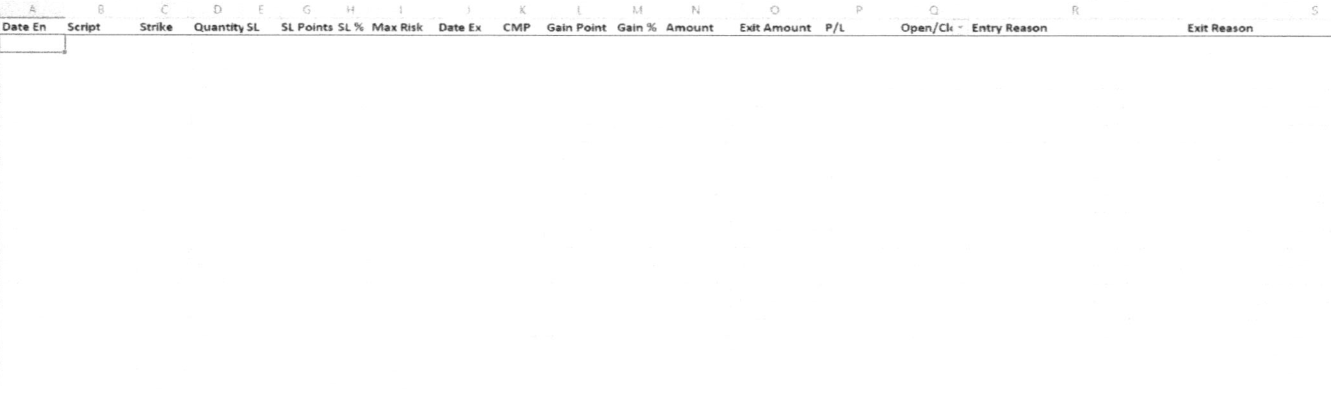

Image 11.1: Trading journal spreadsheet

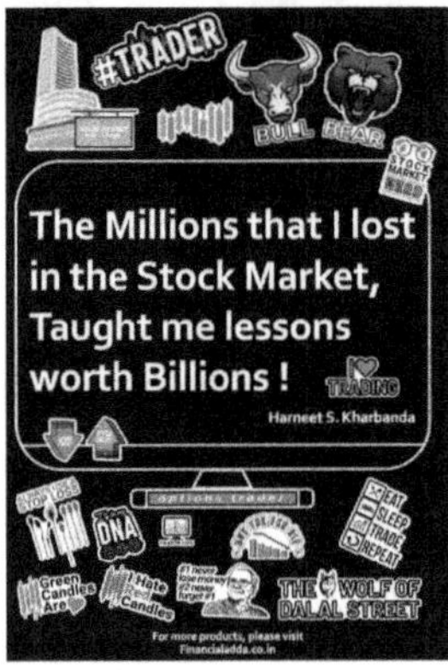

Image 11.2: Trading journal front cover (top) and back cover (bottom)

ENHANCING TRADING DISCIPLINE WITH TECHNOLOGY

The uniqueness of TradingJournal.ai does not just lie in its technical capabilities. It is also about the ethos behind it—a tool created by traders, for traders. It is designed to incentivise discipline and strategic planning through features like customisable performance tracking and integrated risk management algorithms. These elements are not just bonuses, but are central to the platform's purpose of enhancing the trading journey. While I am closely

Date _______________________

Day _______________________

Net balance _______________________

Symbol

Entry

Exit

Qty

SL

Target

P&L

Notes

Financialadda.co.in

Imagee 11.3: Journal pages to note down the details of our trades along with notes/lessons from the trades.

associated with TradingJournal.ai and believe in its potential, my motivation is to address the unmet needs of Indian retail traders. It is about offering a tool that not only fits their trading landscape but also elevates their trading discipline and strategic insight.

Here are a few screenshots from TradingJournal.ai.

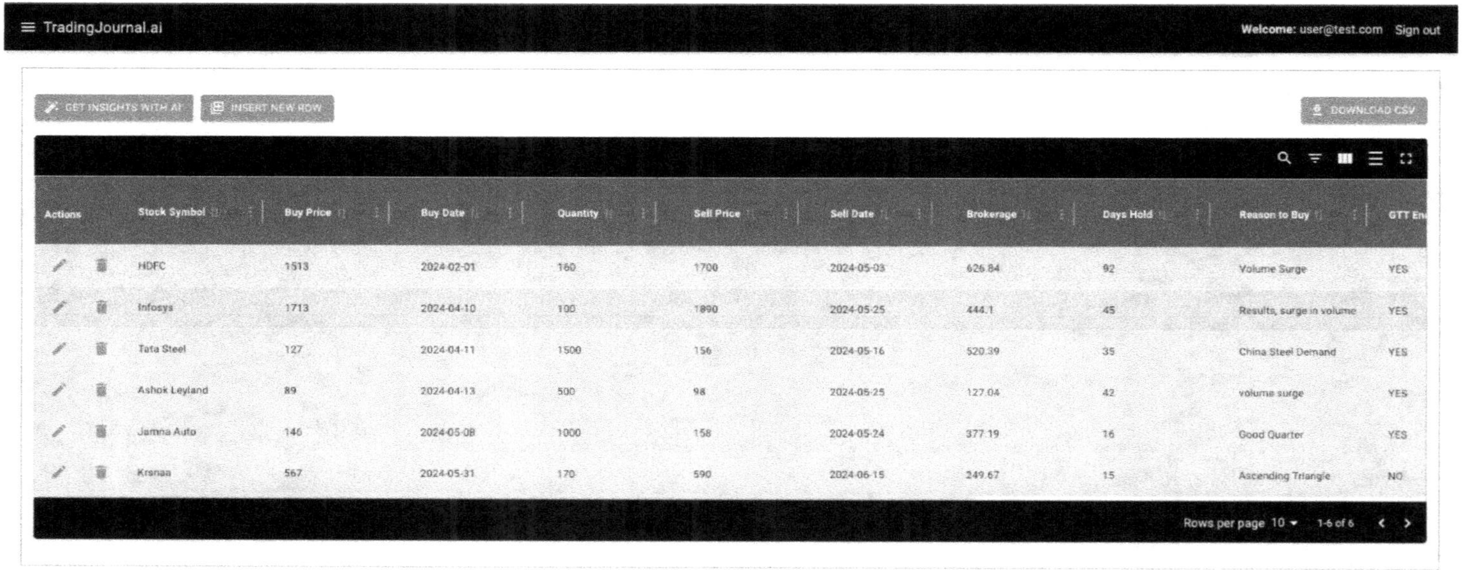

TradingJournal.ai   Welcome: user@test.com   Sign out

GET INSIGHTS WITH AI   INSERT NEW ROW   DOWNLOAD CSV

Actions	Stock Symbol	Buy Price	Buy Date	Quantity	Sell Price	Sell Date	Brokerage	Days Hold	Reason to Buy	GTT En...
	HDFC	1513	2024-02-01	160	1700	2024-05-03	626.84	92	Volume Surge	YES
	Infosys	1713	2024-04-10	100	1890	2024-05-25	444.1	45	Results, surge in volume	YES
	Tata Steel	127	2024-04-11	1500	156	2024-05-16	520.39	35	China Steel Demand	YES
	Ashok Leyland	89	2024-04-13	500	98	2024-05-25	127.04	42	volume surge	YES
	Jamna Auto	146	2024-05-08	1000	158	2024-05-24	377.19	16	Good Quarter	YES
	Krsnaa	567	2024-05-31	170	590	2024-06-15	249.67	15	Ascending Triangle	NO

Rows per page 10 ▾   1-6 of 6

Image 11.4: Screenshot from TradingJournal.ai

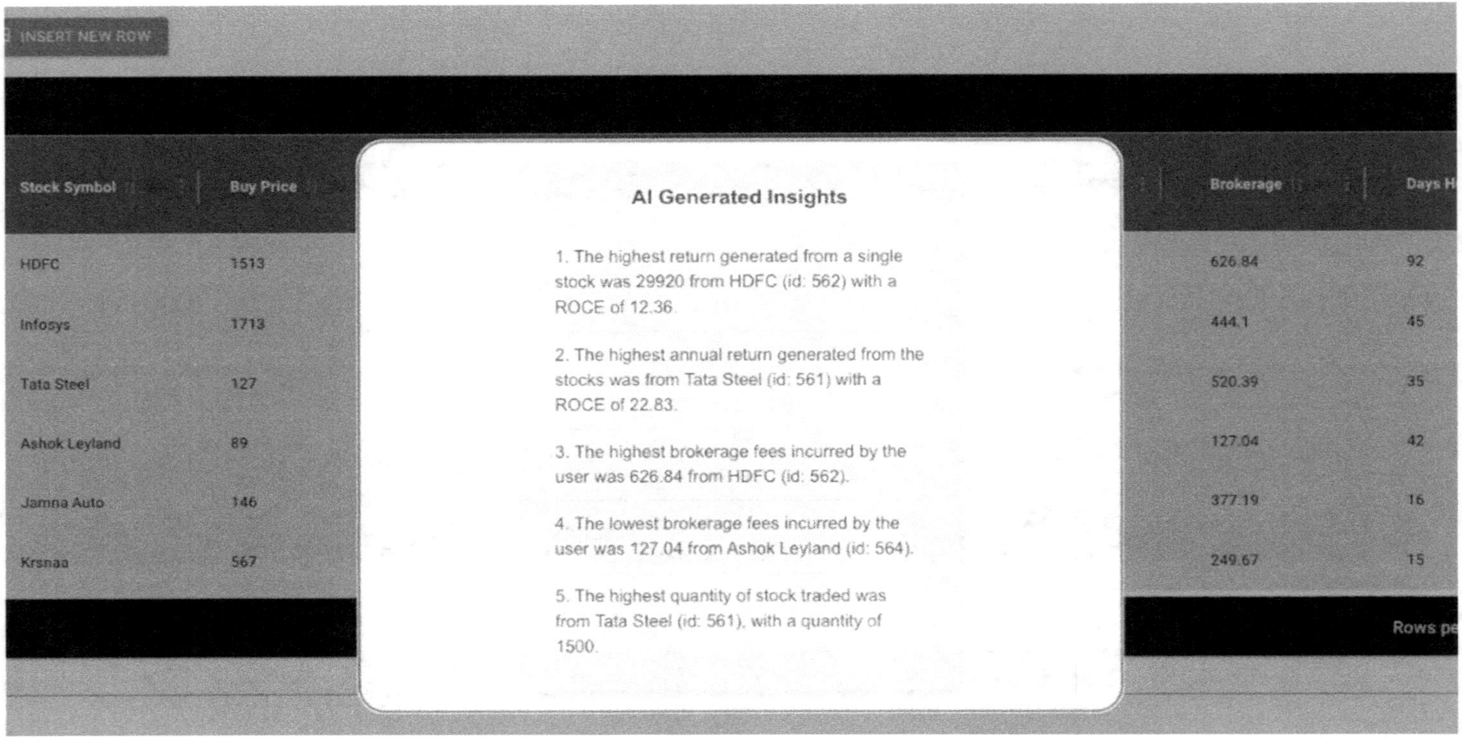

Image 11.5: Screenshot from TradingJournal.ai offering insights

IV

TRADING PSYCHOLOGY

*"The key to trading success is emotional discipline.
If intelligence were the key, there would be a lot more
people making money trading... I know this will sound
like a cliche, but the single most important reason that
people lose money in the financial markets is that they don't
cut their losses short."*

—Victor Sperandeo, American financial trader, index
developer and financial commentator

12

Humans are Designed to Make Trading Errors—Learn How to Think Differently

Trading is a stressful job. Do not be fooled by the influencers who post about trading off the beaches while they are on vacation. Trading psychology is the study of how traders behave and react towards their trading and markets. It is the study of noticing the patterns which all the traders show and how to understand the types of biases you are stuck in and how to overcome them.

Many traders do not even realise that they are following a pattern and that pattern may be giving them constant losses. And yet, they may still not see that clearly and would eventually repeat those patterns and keep losing money.

Patterns are hard to break once they are formed, but until we acknowledge that we are stuck in some pattern or biases, we can never come out of it and improve our overall trading and, in fact, life. Initially, most traders are not even aware of the biases they are stuck with. Once they understand the patterns and realise how it affects their decisions, only then do they start to think about some solutions. Trading requires full focus and is best done in a relaxed state of mind. If you cannot focus and keep yourself calm, you get carried away easily and take irrational decisions while trading, which can often result in huge blunders.

Many traders who cannot control their emotions, stress about their trades, get into overtrading and end up taking huge position sizes on a single day and blow away their entire capital in a matter of days. Traders can get stuck in a lot of biases and patterns. Let us discuss how to overcome those to become a profitable trader.

There are times when traders are not ready to take a loss even though it seems like the sanest decision to take one at the moment. They avoid it for days, weeks and even months and end up staying stuck in a losing position—losing their hard-earned money and even their peace of mind. The reason in their mind could be different, but the real reason is always the same, that is, avoiding the pain of taking a loss.

Here are a few examples of how traders fool themselves and avoid taking a loss when they clearly should.

1.   When the trader says that they have made enough profits in the trade so they should exit it, they may actually be afraid of having to return this profit to the markets. The real reason is that they want to avoid the pain of losing a part of this profit.

If traders exit according to pre-decided criteria, then it is fine. But most often, there is no reason for exiting a trade and traders just exit looking at the profit amount.

Exiting according to the numbers in the profit-and-loss screen is not a strategy. Ruled by fear, traders end up taking a small profit. In most cases, the price continues to climb higher and traders regret and curse themselves for missing a great move. They end up calculating that they could have made so much money if they had just held on to the stock a little longer, regretting selling it too soon.

So exit only when the strategy indicates it and not by looking at the profit or loss amount.

2.   As I am losing, so I may as well increase my stake to get a good average price.

Traders try to convince themselves that they are bringing the average price down by adding more positions in a losing stock. That may work in some cases when they are very sure about the fundamentals of the company and have real conviction in their study. But, most of the time, that is not the case, and traders just add to the falling stock because they refuse to hurt their ego and want to justify their initial reason of entering that stock.

3.   When a stock gives us a profit, keep booking partial profits and reduce the stake.

Traders may want to take it easy at this stage. But once again, they want to avoid the pain of giving the profits back to the markets. When a stock is in uptrend and there is no reason to exit, keep holding on to it. In fact, "add" more positions to it. Pyramiding up has a lot of benefits. Once you enter a stock, you cannot enter with a huge position size as you are not sure yet if the stock will start moving in the desired direction or not. So, initially you may just test the waters and start out with a basic position size.

Once the stock proves that it is in an uptrend, increase the position size according to the pre-decided technical levels. For instance, adding more positions when the stock retraces back and bounces off the 20-EMA on the daily chart. By adding more positions to the winning stock, make sure that once you are making money, you maximize it. There is no point in making a 100% in a stock if you just take 0.5% of your total portfolio position in it. It will not affect the portfolio much. Whereas, a 50% move with a 10% position size would move the portfolio up significantly.

Remember, you want to win big when you are in a winning trade and you want to lose the least amount of money when you are losing.

Now let's talk about the problem of instant gratification and how it affects our trading. It means the immediate fulfillment of our desires or needs. The word "immediate" is most important here. We even get ready to accept a less rewarding benefit immediately rather than a much bigger or better reward in the future.

If you ask a kid if they want one chocolate immediately or two chocolates the following day, it is most likely that they will go with the first option. Traders do the same thing on many occasions. They prefer to book a much smaller profit, even though they know subconsciously that there is no reason to exit and it would be better to keep holding the stock for much bigger rewards in the future. Still, they end up selling it too soon only to regret later and keep repeating this pattern.

Due to our fast-paced lives, the problem of instant gratification has multiplied manifold. We have forgotten how to wait for things. We want everything immediately.

The same holds true for expectations from the market. Traders want their profits to come as quickly as possible. That is why they do not want to ride their investments and feel like booking profits as soon as they appear on the screen.

For the same reason, every new trader wants to start with intraday trading. They have zero knowledge about the markets but they are clear that they want to start with intraday only.

As mentioned earlier in this book, there is nothing wrong with intraday trading. It is the most difficult type of trading so traders should not start trading with it. They have to take multiple decisions in a day within a short span of time and manage their emotions along the way. A study was conducted by Fidelity Investments on their flagship mutual fund (Magellan fund), when Peter Lynch managed it (1977–1990). During this time, the Standard and Poor's 500 (S&P500) gave an annual return of 14.47%, whereas his mutual fund gave an annual return of 29%. Despite this, the average investor lost money during this period!

How was this possible? When the fund performed so well, it made Peter Lynch one of the best investors of all time, and the fund became the biggest fund, how did the average investor lose money? The reason is simple: markets do not go up in a straight line, there are a lot of ups and downswings and phases of sideways or no returns. Investors entered the fund with high expectations mostly when the fund was performing really well. When they entered and saw no returns for just the next few months, or if the fund and markets declined, they exited as they had wanted quicker returns, thanks to instant gratification. This is why when you see the historical data and notice how well the markets have performed, you start thinking that it is really easy to make money in the markets and anyone can do it.

But the psychological hurdles of your mind make you realise that it is not that easy when you are in a position; when you have the stakes on the line; when your hard-earned real money is involved.

That is why trading psychology is of utmost importance and trades and investors should study about it much more than they currently do. The problem with trading is that there are no entry barriers. You do not need any qualification to become a trader. You just need to open an online demat account and you can start trading on the same day.

When a new trader takes their first trade, two things can happen—either the stock will go up, or it will go down. Thanks to beginner's luck, it mostly goes in their favour.

They start believing that trading is indeed really easy and they start daydreaming of all the profit that they can make and how this field is so much better than any other field out there. They curse themselves for not thinking about trading full time earlier in their career under the assumption that they could have made a fortune already and would be trading from the beaches just like they see on social media.

I am not saying that all of this is not possible. I am not discouraging anyone from trading full time. But, I just want to make you understand that it is not as easy as it looks or is portrayed by some guys who have some vested interest in showing off that lifestyle. Moreover, trading would yield the best results when you do not have to depend on it for your monthly bills and expenses. Trading should be done part time and the full focus should always be on a person's primary source of income, doing the work that they are already pursuing.

The thing is, markets are not always trending. There are a few months in a year where the markets give easy moves and show momentum. It is easy to make a good amount of money during this time. Then there are times when markets keep falling. Short sellers may make quick money during this time, but cash traders just need to wait it out till the markets make a base and start rising again so that they can hop on the bus.

And, there are times when the markets do nothing. Markets just go into sideways mode, there is a lot of choppiness in a small range and stop-losses get hit on both the sides. Breakouts would fizz out and whatever you do, you end up losing money. You realise that it would be better to sit out and wait for better and easy trending phase.

But your monthly bills and fixed expenses will not stop. In fact, they will increase every year thanks to inflation.

If you trade full time and it is your only source of income, you would try and trade throughout the year, even when your favourite trading setups are not present. You may try to trade forcefully, and if you end up losing money in a few trades, you would try to recover quickly to make sure that you can pay your bills which could eventually make you lose more money.

Trading is done well with extra money, which we do not need in the near future. Your emotional attachment to your capital matters a lot because if you cannot afford to lose money, you will end up losing it. This could happen due to trading out of fear and not taking rational decisions.

It is important to focus on your health so that you may be able to take decisions and think clearly when the situation requires it. People who follow healthy practices for their mental well-being, usually benefit a lot from the following practices.

MEDITATION

Meditation is a practice in which you use mental and physical techniques to clear the mind and focus, which helps to reduce stress and anxiety.

There are many forms of meditations like walking meditation where you focus on your breathing and walk consciously in nature. It is very helpful in bringing the stress levels down.

Then there is a body scan meditation where you focus on each part of the body one by one and enhance your mindfulness.

Mantra meditation, which I personally practise, involves repeating a sacred sound or word which you chant out loud or whisper silently to yourself.

MINDFULNESS

Mindfulness also helps in reducing stress as it is the art of doing everything with focus. You think about doing everything and therefore, our decisions are more sorted and calculated.

In trading, sometimes you take a position which you never intended or planned to do, but just took out of fear of missing out, or just because another big trader or investor was taking a position in it. You regret it later when the stock does not give the desired result and end up losing money on it most of the time. It happens because you rarely trade mindfully—you just trade out of greed and fear.

YOGA

Yoga is much more than just bending or stretching the body. It also helps to reduce the stress a lot.

As traders, we end up sitting in front of the computer the entire day, analysing stocks, checking charts, finding new stocks, watching informational content or while reading books. If you are not physically active, your health will take a toll—what use is any skill or any worldly wealth if you do not have the health to enjoy it?

BREATHWORK

Breathwork is the simple technique of controlling your breath intentionally to improve your mental, spiritual and even physical well-being. Most of us do not breath properly now due to stress. We take shallow breaths and do not practise diaphragmatic breathing. Breathwork can help to reduce stress, anxiety, anger, and trauma. You know how much these factors affect a person's trading as everything is connected to your emotions. If you get stressed or frustrated, you will never trade properly as you will not be able to think rationally.

SPENDING TIME IN NATURE

Spending time in nature has many benefits like improving your physical health, mental health and overall emotional well-being. As a generation, we are constantly on our phones, sitting in front of our computers most of the time and it drains energy.

The benefit of swing and long-term trading is that you can actually spend time away from the screen. you do not have to constantly stare at the screens and watch the market tick-by-tick. You can scan the stocks on the weekend and just check the markets for 10–15 minutes during market hours to see if you need to execute a trade or not. You can use alerts on a charting website to take care of that too and spend that extra time in nature, read a book at a local park or just go for a walk.

Most of the time, during the market hours I often sit in my neighborhood park, reading a book. It feels so rejuvenating and relaxing!

BEING COMFORTABLE ALONE

Being a trader is a lonely job. You rarely need a team to be a trader, nor do you need to work under a boss. A trader usually spends most of their time alone, sitting in front of the computer, analysing stocks and watching charts for a significant amount of time. Yes, you do not need to sit in front of the computer once you have understood the process and taken position in your selected stocks, but you need to spend a lot of time during the learning phase.

Trading, unfortunately, is still not seen as a legitimate business in our society and most traders hide their profession from others. The times are changing and now trading is getting the recognition that it deserves. Despite that, there are a lot of traders who do not even let their dear ones or family members know that they are trading. If they win, they celebrate alone, if they lose, they try to hide their feelings.

A trader needs to learn how to manage their emotions alone and be stable and calm in all conditions. This is where spirituality helps a lot.

ACCEPTANCE OF THE UNCONTROLLABLE

Trading helps us to realise the eternal truth—*'what we do is in our control, the outcome is not.'* If you understand this simple thing early in life, you would be in a much better position. We usually end up complaining about all the things that are not in our control.

You need feedback in anything you do and trading gives the quickest feedback. If you traded well, followed your plan and did not let emotions overwhelm you, you get rewarded. If you get carried away by your emotions and end up breaking your own trading rules, you get punished by the markets almost immediately. Over time, you will understand the importance of just focusing on the action which is your dharma or duty of executing the trades without the end result in mind. As traders, we just need to execute one trade after the other and not let the uncontrollable future outcome affect our next decision. If you took a trade and followed your plan, irrespective of whether it gave you profit or loss, just execute the next trade. It is that simple, but difficult to follow and sometimes takes years to realise that you do not need to think about the outcome and just focus on the action.

HABITS OF A SUCCESSFUL TRADER

Habits are repetitive behaviours which we indulge in subconsciously and it helps in taking us closer towards our goals. We lead our lives according to our habits most of the time.

While habits shape us and result in accomplishing our goals, they can even distract us from our goals if they are not supporting enough and are not constructive. Therefore, always be aware of your habits and follow a set of habits which helps you achieve your desired result with no or minimum deviations.

Here are some habits of a successful trader:

1.   *Successful traders do not rely on an individual trade*: Successful traders know that the trade they are going to take is just one out of thousand trades and they do not lay emphasis on each and every trade's outcome—they just move on to the next one. New traders give too much importance to each and every trade and sometimes get too emotional when the trade goes in the opposite direction.

2.   *Successful traders plan their trade **before** entering*: Successful traders know that they may get emotional once the market is live.

So, they plan their trade before entering. That way, they can easily plan out their entry and exit according to their trading strategy and trade without the biases and emotions which usually arise once the market is open.

3.   *Successful traders know how much they can lose*: Successful traders know beforehand how much money they are ready to lose in a trade before entering a trade. They usually mark their stop-loss levels before entering the trade. Once the price goes below that pre-decided level, they exit and save their money. They use that capital to look for the next trade. New traders, on the flip side, usually decide where to exit once they are already in a trade, as they do not have a fixed level in place where they wish to exit the stock. They usually exit the stock when they can no longer handle the amount of loss that they see on the screen.

4.   *Successful traders keep learning*: Learning never stops for successful traders as the market never stops teaching. You get to learn so much about the market and about yourself once you stay in the game long enough. Apart from learning from experience by trading, you also need to keep upgrading our knowledge by reading books, watching podcasts, attending conferences where you can socialise with like-minded people—watching courses and attending live workshops, basically anything which can help you gather useful knowledge about the markets.

5.   *Successful traders have realistic expectations*: Successful traders know that trading is a business and not a casino where you can turn a few hundreds into a few crores very easily. You should treat it like a business where you need to learn about this field, start with a small capital and increase the capital gradually once you get hold of the process and have a profitable strategy in place which you can apply comfortably.

6. *Balanced lifestyle*: Successful traders know that trading is a part of their life and not all of it. While they may have spent a lot of time learning all about trading and would have spent most of their day looking at charts, they do not continue that habit once they start making progress. They know the importance of leading a balanced lifestyle where they give importance to their health and social life as well.

There is no point in trading well and making money if you do not have the health to enjoy it.

These were the few habits of successful traders. Now let us look at how trading shapes who you are. You enter the markets to earn money, but markets give you much more than that. Markets change you as a person, for the good.

You end up improving so many aspects of your life in the process of becoming successful traders. You remove so many mental blocks as you start focusing on psychology which reveals a lot about your own mindset and why you do the things you do. You question a lot of things, which leads to changes in your belief system and opens up new realms of thinking.

The importance of focusing on the process and not worrying about the results is actually practised in the stock market, where we focus on putting one trade after the other without getting emotionally involved with the outcome.

You also start managing your emotions better. Mastering fear and greed, which you may never have even thought of confronting, are actually most applicable in day-to-day operations of trading. Soon enough you realise that to manage these emotions, you need a well-structured plan and follow that instead of trying to fight these emotions.

Focus on the things you can control and let go of the things you cannot. Spirituality also talks about focusing only on the controllable aspects of life and leaving the rest to the higher powers of the universe.

Markets also teach you to stay humble. Whenever you start making big profits in the markets, you tend to show off and end up taking even bigger position sizes to magnify the profits. You may end up giving back the profits and even a part of your capital to the markets as you cannot handle your mindset while trading with bigger position sizes. That big loss after a series of profits is like the markets slapping you on your face! You get back to your senses and realise the mistake that you were committing by listening to your egoistic mind.

The loss teaches you to be humble and get back to following the process irrespective of the outcome.

To excel in any field, you need to be consistent and the markets teach you how to do that. Let me explain this with the example of weight loss. You can lose a lot of weight in a very short span of time by using shortcuts. But you would fail very soon and gain back most of the weight and, in fact, put on even more weight than before. To lose weight and keep it off, you need to change your lifestyle and then be consistent in maintaining it.

Likewise, you can earn a big amount of money in markets by using shortcuts, but markets will reward only those who follow a process and stick to it consistently without looking for shortcuts.

www.ingramcontent.com/pod-product-compliance
Lightning Source LLC
LaVergne TN
LVHW020025160726

843469LV00044B/1651